Perspectives on the Older Scottish Tongue

To all associated with the making of *DOST* (1931–2002) and to all who use it.

Perspectives on the Older Scottish Tongue

A Celebration of DOST

Edited by
Christian J. Kay and Margaret A. Mackay

Edinburgh University Press

© in this edition Edinburgh University Press, 2005
© in the individual contributions is retained by the authors

Edinburgh University Press Ltd
22 George Square, Edinburgh

Typeset in 11 on 13pt Ehrhardt
by Hewer Text Ltd, Edinburgh, and
printed and bound in Great Britain by
MPG Books Ltd, Bodmin

A CIP record for this book is available from the British Library

ISBN 0 7486 2281 0 (hardback)

The right of the contributors
to be identified as authors of this work
has been asserted in accordance with
the Copyright, Designs and Patents Act 1988.

Recipient of a University of Edinburgh
Award for Distinguished Scottish Scholarship

Contents

Editors' Preface

The editing of this volume in honour of the *Dictionary of the Older Scottish Tongue*, its makers and its contents, was a task we embraced without hesitation. Both of us have had a strong association with *DOST*, Dr Mackay as a student of its second editor, A. J. Aitken, and later as Director of the School of Scottish Studies, alongside which *DOST* was compiled for fifty years, Professor Kay as the first Convener of SLD (Scottish Language Dictionaries, which takes forward the joint interests of *DOST* and the *Scottish National Dictionary*) and as director of parallel research projects at Glasgow University. Friendship, collegiality and respect for the tremendous achievement represented by the completion of *DOST* fired our enthusiasm for a book which would give scholars an opportunity to show how they had used *DOST* and how its contents and methods might be exploited, interpreted and developed in the future, and students an opportunity to sample the riches in its twelve volumes. It is thus a celebration, a guide and a challenge in one.

The disciplines and topics represented by past, present and potential users of *DOST* are many, varying through applied arts and crafts, architecture, dialectology, domestic life, history, linguistics, literature, onomastics, science, social organisation, transport, and institutions such as education, law and religion. Some whom we approached for a contribution were unable to accept the invitation owing to other commitments but we include them in our thanks for we know that they declined with regret. To all who were able to furnish chapters we extend our gratitude. It has been a pleasure for us to be party to their insights, and we are delighted at the echoes which appear between and among the chapters, a mark of the support which *DOST* gives to truly interdisciplinary scholarship.

We are also grateful to past staff of *DOST* and present staff of SLD, and to staff at Edinburgh University Press, Sarah Edwards and James Dale in particular, for help throughout.

For the exhibition held in 1967 at the National Library of Scotland to mark the centenary of the birth of Sir William Craigie, founder and first editor of *DOST*,

A. J. Aitken wrote of Craigie's qualities of 'kindliness, co-operation and wit' and of his 'almost superhuman achievement as lexicographer, editor and teacher'. The story of *DOST* is one of dedication and service to the highest ideals of scholarship by all engaged in its creation and support. We too have experienced 'kindliness, co-operation and wit' as we worked on this volume, nor could *DOST* itself have been completed without them.

Christian J. Kay, University of Glasgow
Margaret A. Mackay, University of Edinburgh

CHAPTER I

Introduction

Alasdair A. MacDonald, University of Groningen

This book is conceived not only as a companion to, but also as a celebration of, the *Dictionary of the Older Scottish Tongue* (in the familiar abbreviated title, *DOST*) – that wonderful, imposing, comprehensive, challenging, meticulous, authoritative, occasionally frustrating, multi-volume, heavyweight (!), lexicographical monument, which deservedly occupies its secure place in the reference sections of all university libraries where philology is taken seriously. In the following pages, the contributions of more than a dozen experts are testimony to the enormous resource that *DOST* represents for anyone investigating the language, history, literature, religion, law, society, economy, agriculture, physical geography, architecture, and material culture of Scotland in the period up to the early eighteenth century. Although this list of potential areas of interest is long, it is not guaranteed to be exhaustive, and, in view of the cornucopia of information contained in the pages of this great dictionary, it is entirely fitting that one of the contributors should round off her chapter with the quotation, 'Here is God's plenty!' For the present writer it is a great honour and a real pleasure to be invited to provide a preface to such a collection of essays.

DOST is concerned with the Older Scots language, the ancestor of modern Lowland Scots, which – alongside Gaelic and English – is one of the three long-established languages currently in use in Scotland. All of them, however, are imports. Around probably the middle of the fifth century, Q-Celtic speakers from Ireland arrived in the West of what is nowadays Scotland, just as Germanic speakers were invading and settling the South, East and North of what is now England. From these two bases, Gaelic and English gradually spread further and further in the direction of what counts today as central Scotland. In the case of both, this was at the expense of the P-Celtic language, various forms of which were in use by the Picts, Strathclyde Britons, Cumbrians and Welsh. Yet neither is P-Celtic native to the British Isles, and it must be admitted that we know nothing of the languages of the neolithic inhabitants, such as the peoples who built the houses at Skara Brae or erected the stone circle of Callanish. 'In the beginning was the word', but in what is now Scotland the first word was most certainly not spoken in Scots.

In its origins, Scots is a development from Northumbrian Anglo-Saxon, and is therefore just as old as modern standard English, which stems, in a complicated way, from other types of Anglo-Saxon. Scots, however, is not well attested in its early centuries, and the first surviving work of literature is John Barbour's historical romance *The Brus*, of c. 1375. As Scots developed, it enriched its native vocabulary by borrowing from the languages with which it came in contact (Latin, Norse, French, Gaelic, English, Dutch). By the later Middle Ages it had become the vehicle of a vigorous and subtle literary culture, with a range of stylistic registers adequate to their respective genres. Because of the common origin in Anglo-Saxon, influence from English upon Scots was always possible. In the works of the great Renaissance *makaris* (for example William Dunbar, Gavin Douglas) anglicisms are by no means unknown; at that stage in the history of Scots such forms may have been fashionable, and intended to demonstrate these writers' acquaintance with the works of the most prestigious poet of medieval England, Geoffrey Chaucer. In the mid-sixteenth century, however, with all the cultural upheaval associated with the Reformation, English linguistic norms come increasingly to be tolerated; this is reflected, for example, in the innovative spelling conventions gradually introduced by Scottish printers. By the seventeenth century, the elite among Scottish poets (e.g. William Drummond of Hawthornden) had for their formal compositions in effect opted to write in English. This caused Scots to undergo a certain diminution in status, whereby it would henceforth tend to become the characteristic expression of informal, spoken, personal, and demotic language-use. The consequence of this was that, as far as the Scots vernacular literary tradition is concerned, there had virtually to be a new beginning in the eighteenth century.

The Older Scots language cannot be said to have enjoyed a period of 'classical' purity – whatever that might mean – since it is normal for languages to be in a state of flux. Such change is morally and politically neutral, and does not lend itself to being captured in loaded or provocative terms such as 'domination' and 'decline'; rather, what the linguist sees is transformation through variation. *DOST* offers in principle an analytical account, one that is as complete and thorough as possible, of the lexis of all manifestations of pre-1700 Scots. In such a work of historical semantics, comparative etymology has an important role to play, but the true foundation of the analysis is ever the examination of usage. Indeed, it is the wealth of illustrative quotations that gives *DOST* its encyclopaedic identity, making it a corpus in its own right. By a two-way process, moreover, just as the quotations are sorted out and arranged to structure the semantic analysis, so the latter inevitably leads the reader back out towards the real, everyday world of pre-1700 Scotland. Far, therefore, from supposedly being a series of desiccated and academic tomes, the volumes of *DOST* actually hold up a mirror to all the intellectual, emotional, social and physical experience of early

Scotland. The irreverent undergraduate jibe – '*DOST* to *DOST* . . .' – could hardly be further from the truth, and the cultural value of this dictionary cannot be too highly praised.

In the year 2002 the final part of *DOST* was published, and this happy event has led directly to the present volume of essays. However, there is a sense in which the work of lexicography is never done, since after publication there is always a wish to take account of new insights and supplementary information. In addition, there are now for *DOST* the challenges of digitisation and electronic searchability, to say nothing of the prospect of integration with the sister work, the *Scottish National Dictionary*, in order to attain a coverage of all phases of the Scots language. The present moment is the right one for a stocktaking of just what has been achieved through the completion of *DOST*, and it is here that the essays in this volume enter the picture.

In her contribution, Marace Dareau tells the story of the history of the work – how it began as the brainchild of Sir William Craigie (of the *Oxford English Dictionary*), and was prosecuted by a series of editors, among whom pride of place indubitably goes to the late A. J. (Jack) Aitken, whose outstanding work on *DOST*, and on the study of the Scots language in general, was fittingly celebrated in a tributary volume of essays, *The Nuttis Schell* (Macafee and Macleod 1987). Interestingly, the model provided by the *OED* was most powerful in the opening, and again at the closing, stages of *DOST*; in between, Aitken was to carry the practice of historical semantic analysis to still higher levels of refinement. Two contributors (Paul Schaffner, Keith Williamson) discuss the methodology of *DOST* in the light of comparable projects: *MED* (the recently completed *Middle English Dictionary*), and LAOS (the ongoing Linguistic Atlas of Older Scots). Donald Meek reviews the various usages of a pair of related words (Gaelic *sgaoil* and Scots *scail*), indicating the degree of semantic overlap, or lack thereof; in the process he confirms *DOST*'s assumption of a borrowing from Celtic, rather than *OED*'s of a borrowing from Germanic. From such a discussion it is clear that the example of *DOST* will be of great benefit to the compilers of the new historical dictionary of Scottish Gaelic, the Faclair na Gàidhlig. Bill Nicolaisen shows how the data normally available to the lexicographer can usefully be eked out from the neighbouring disciplines of toponymy and onomastics, since not a few independent words recorded in *DOST* are first attested, often centuries earlier, as elements in place names.

Several of the contributors investigate what *DOST* reveals concerning social life in early Scotland. Angelo Forte and David Sellar focus on different aspects of the law; Sandy Fenton's topic is Scottish awareness of wine, while Iseabail Macleod reports on what *DOST* has to tell us about cereal terms; Allen Simpson examines the older Scottish terms for the tricky subject of weights and measures, and Bruce Walker discusses the terminology appropriate to traditional house construction. Here too belongs Jane Dawson's paper on kinship words, from which *inter alia* we learn that in medieval Scotland (but not England) the gossip was characteristically a male figure. For her part, Priscilla Bawcutt shows that all students of literature in Older Scots are enormously indebted to the precision, range and subtlety of *DOST*. In the course of his long career the lexicographer Jack Aitken wrote memorably on various topics pertinent to Older Scots literature; reciprocally, the critic Bawcutt shows how literary interpretation must at all times be grounded in a profound familiarity with the language employed by the medieval poets and writers.

We see, therefore, that *DOST* offers much more than 'merely' explanations of old, obscure or obsolete words. As the essays in this volume collectively show, *DOST* is both a triumph of lexicographical science and an inexhaustible repository of cultural information; it is a work of which all Scots may be proud, and for which Scots and non-Scots may be equally grateful; it is, moreover, a scholarly achievement of the first rank, which has established Older Scots as one of the best documented languages of pre-modern Europe.

CHAPTER 2

DOST and the Literary Scholar

Priscilla Bawcutt, University of Liverpool

There have been many dictionaries in my life, ranging from the humble to the monumental. The first, encountered as a child, was the family copy of Chambers', chiefly useful, as I recall, for completing crosswords. In later schooldays there were various bilingual dictionaries, the most notable of which was a French–English dictionary (published by Gasc in 1945), which brought home to me very vividly the reality of language change in the modern world. It contained three different supplements, the last of which (from *abri-caverne* to *viseur de bombardement*) recorded some of the enormous, though often ephemeral, effects of the Second World War upon the vocabularies of French and English. At university, in highly philological undergraduate courses, I was introduced to *OED*, and began to learn some of the many ways in which a great historical dictionary can assist literary scholars.

The *Dictionary of the Older Scottish Tongue*, however, has long had a special place in my heart. It was the first dictionary which made me aware of the complicated process of modern dictionary-making: the first dictionary where I corresponded with the editors, who not only gave me precious advice concerning intractable words but became personal friends; and the first where I visited the office, and was privileged to investigate some of the precious files and archives. In later years it was an honour (though, in a sense, no more than a statement of the obvious) to become one of *DOST*'s 'Friends'. In my own work, most of it concerned with the editing and criticism of older Scottish poetry, *DOST* has been of enormous value. What follows will illustrate a few of the ways in which it has assisted one scholar, and may, in turn, help others.

DOST is obviously valuable to all readers who encounter obsolete or archaic words in older Scottish texts. This is a primary service which should never be forgotten or disdained. But for readers with literary interests *DOST* provides far more than the elucidation of unusual spellings or the explanation of 'hard' words. It supplies a wealth of information about the connotations of Scots words and phrases, and also about the registers to which they belong. It achieves this in two ways: first, by providing explicit guidance as to usage with terse comments such as 'fig.', 'proverb.', 'only in verse' or 'chiefly allit.'; and secondly, by providing copious illustrations of such usage in the form of quotations. In these practices *DOST*, of course, follows the precedent established by *OED*. But it is worth noting that many of *DOST*'s editors seem to have had a great interest in older Scottish literature, and displayed in their publications a corresponding sensitivity to the stylistic aspects of language. The dictionary's first editor, Sir William Craigie, remarked in the preface to volume I (p. ix): 'I have had the advantage of a familiar knowledge of the Scottish tongue from my earliest years, and an interest in its older literature from the age of twelve'. Craigie not only published many reviews and articles concerning Scottish poetry, including his British Academy lecture on Scottish alliterative poetry (Craigie 1893; Craigie 1898; Craigie 1942), but also edited some of the most important sixteenth-century Scottish literary miscellanies, such as the Asloan Manuscript, the Maitland Folio and the Maitland Quarto. More recently A. J. Aitken's numerous publications included a seminal article on 'The language of Older Scots poetry' (Aitken 1983).

Sixteenth-century Scottish poets were self-conscious about the language they used. Gavin Douglas, in particular, held strong views about 'the langage of Scottis natioun', its relations with other languages, and his own desire for 'fowth' (abundance):

> Nor ȝit sa cleyn all sudron I refus,
> Bot sum word I pronunce as nyghtbouris doys:
> Lyke as in Latyn beyn Grew termys sum,
> So me behufyt quhilum or than be dum
> Sum bastard Latyn, French or Inglys oys,
> Quhar scant was Scottis – I had nane other choys.
> Nocht for our tong is in the selwyn skant
> Bot for that I the fowth of langage want . . .
> (*Eneados*, Prologue I, 113–20)[1]

Both Douglas and Dunbar were linguistic experimenters and innovators. As R. J. Lyall has recently stressed, they jointly contributed to a stylistic revolution in early sixteenth-century poetry (Lyall 2001). Our understanding of their style and the extent to which their language resembles or differs from that of their contemporaries is assisted by *DOST*. Sometimes the information to be found there confirms initial guesses and hunches, but sometimes it surprises and disconcerts.

Douglas's taste for learned Latin neologisms, whether in the *Eneados* or in the aureate passages of *The Palice of Honour*,[2] is substantiated by numerous entries in *DOST*. There are no citations, other than Douglas's, for such words as *precordialis* (*Eneados*, VII. vi. 14), or *umbrate*, *vegetant* and *virgultis* (*Palice of Honour*, 40, 48, 107) – clearly they never took root in the language. Another word, *vivificative* (*Palice of Honour*, 42), has only one later citation, from John Rolland, a poet who imitated Douglas's style somewhat slavishly. *DOST* also confirms and illustrates the 'sudron' aspects of Douglas's diction. These are not confined to spellings and pronunciation – 'sum word I pronunce as nyghtbouris doys' – but include anglicised and often archaic morphology, such as infinitives ending in -*in*, and various lexical items, such as 'morrow', besides 'morn', and 'myche', besides 'mekyll'. (For further discussion, see Bawcutt 1976: 64–5; 143–8.)

One small but interesting aspect of Douglas's style, his fondness for the verbal prefix *to-*[2], is well documented by *DOST*. On this prefix it comments: 'chiefly in early verse and DOUG[LAS]'. Two main uses are distinguished: (a) with verbs expressing violent movement, breaking, smashing, etc. – 'asunder, apart, in pieces'; and (b) as an intensive – 'utterly, completely'. Not surprisingly it is common in Douglas's powerful descriptions of battle and storms:

> The craggis all about this rolk war worn,
> With wedderis blast to holkyt and to torn.
> (*Eneados*, VIII. iv. 115–16)

Douglas characteristically uses these verbs in the form of past participles: *to-holkyt*, 'eroded', *to-torn*, 'torn apart, lacerated', *tofruschit*, 'crushed to bits', *to-smyte*, 'utterly smitten', *toschyde*, 'split asunder', and *to-sparpillit*, 'scattered utterly'. The sense of *to-* is frequently further intensified by the use of *all-* or *al-*, as in a simile referring to the destruction of a tree's branches:

> Quhen thai beyn catchit and alltoschakyn fast
> With the fell thud of the north wyndis blast.
> (*Eneados*, XIII. i. 15–16)

These verbal forms are a distinctive feature of Douglas's diction. No other contemporary poet used them to the same extent, and for many his is the only use recorded by *DOST*. It is possible that Douglas found the extra syllable a metrical convenience, but more important, I suspect, was their aura of antiquity, which would seem appropriate to the translation of an ancient poem. Their use is characteristic of the *Eneados*; by contrast, only one instance occurs in *The Palice of Honour* (see line 1368 and note).

Dunbar is a very different poet from Douglas, and what *DOST* illuminates is the sheer diversity of his vocabulary:

his words come from a wide variety of registers – legal or liturgical, formal or vulgar, Latinate or Scots, poetic or everyday, archaic or newly coined. Among the poets of this time he is unrivalled, not merely for the width of his vocabulary but for his sensitivity to the connotations of

words and phrases. His poems abound in ironies, puns and various
kinds of wordplay.

(Bawcutt 1992: 348)

If one recognises the varied origins of his vocabulary, one appreciates more
fully these ironies and other aspects of Dunbar's meaning. One small example is
hukebanis, 'huckbones, hucklebones', in a passage from *The Flyting* which
ridicules the skeletal appearance of Walter Kennedy:

> Thy rigbane rattillis and thy ribbis on raw,
> Thy hanchis hirklis with hukebanis harth and haw,
> Thy laithly lymis ar lene as ony treis.
>
> (no. 65. 180–2)[3]

DOST's only other record of the word derives from household accounts – 'For a
heuck bone of beif'. Dunbar here speaks of Kennedy rather as if he were a corpse
or piece of dead meat, and the effect is painfully reductive. Another word whose
derisive sense is strengthened when more is known of its other uses is *sowklar*.

> My sowklar, sweit as ony vnȝoun.
>
> (no. 25. 53)

'In secreit place', the poem in which this occurs, is a dialogue between two lovers.
It is characterised by burlesque of the language of endearment, and abounds in
animal imagery, pet-names, diminutives and sexual innuendo. *Sowklar*, literally
'suckler', was a term for a young, unweaned animal, and it fits well with similar
images applied to the young man – 'calfe', 'kid' and 'stirk' – and terms which refer
to weaning, such as 'new spanit' and 'vnspaynit'. *DOST* not only confirms that
sowklar was very much a farmyard term – Dunbar's is the only poetic use
recorded – but also indicates that in later Scots (and probably in Dunbar's time) it
was an insult; thus a 'Toun-clerk' was clearly much offended to be called 'ane
suckler, and other injurious words'.

A phrase with very different connotations occurs in *The Thrissill and the Rois*,
where the Eagle, king of birds, is commanded by the goddess Nature to rule
justly:

> And mak a law for wycht fowlis and for wrennis,
> And lat no fowll of ravyne do efferay,
> Nor devoir birdis bot his awin pray.
>
> (no. 52. 124–6)

It seems unlikely that, in context, a modern reader will have difficulty in
understanding *fowll of ravyne* as bird of prey. Yet, apart from Dunbar's, *DOST*

records no other use of this phrase, or indeed of *ravyne*. The term *ravenous foulis* is occasionally found, occurring in Douglas's *Palice of Honour*, in a passage with a sense rather similar to Dunbar's:

> To noy the small the greit beistis had na will,
> Nor Rauenous foulis the lytill Volatill.
>
> (1421–2)

The usual Scots term for a bird of prey, however, was *fowll of reif*, which was used both by the poet Richard Holland in *The Buke of the Howlat*, and also in prose, such as the Acts of Parliament (see *reff(e*, n[1]). Consultation of *DOST* establishes that *fowll of ravyne* was uncommon, and strengthens the likelihood that in this highly Chaucerian poem Dunbar echoed Chaucer's *The Parliament of Fowls*, where the phrase occurs twice (323 and 527).

Proverbs and similar brief, formulaic sayings were much used by older Scottish poets – often, though not exclusively, in didactic verse, such as *King Hart* or Dunbar's moral poems. Many of these sayings, however, have become obsolete and nowadays are likely to pass unnoticed by readers. Here too *DOST* is often informative, making it clear that some usage was not peculiar to a single poet, but once formed part of a shared stock of popular wisdom. Dunbar's 'Schir, for ȝour grace, bayth nicht and day' (no. 63) has the refrain:

> God gif ȝe war Iohne Thomsounis man.

DOST's collection of citations for *John Thomson's man* is fuller and more helpful than the entries for this term provided by the distinguished proverb-collector B. J. Whiting (Whiting 1949–51; Whiting 1968). It makes one aware of the phrase's implications and Dunbar's audacity – he prays, in effect, that the king should be a henpecked husband – and also that it remained current in Scots for two centuries until at least the end of the seventeenth century. *DOST*'s entry for the word *lous*, 'louse', adds a further dimension to a line in *The Flyting*, ridiculing Kennedy and his wife:

> Thair is bot lys and lang nailis ȝow amang.
>
> (no. 65. 148)

This is clearly contemptuous, but *DOST* records a Danish saying that parallels the phrase *lys and lang nailis*: '*have intet andet* (= to have nothing but), or *vaere rig paa* (= to be rich in) *lus og lange negle*, to be destitute'. This, together with the alliteration, suggests that Dunbar's comment might have been equally proverbial in Scots. *DOST* recently assisted me not only to understand the sense of a scrap of Scots verse, but to recognise its origins as an expanded proverb. A rare early edition of Ovid's *Metamorphoses* in Edinburgh University Library (Ovid, Incunabulum 111) contains several Scottish inscriptions, including the following: 'thocht the wynd blaw neuer so loude It will loyne at the last / The man is ane sempill schrew that may nocht byde ane blast'. *DOST*'s entry for *lown(e*, v. provides the appropriate sense for *loyne*: 'become calm, die down'. More interestingly, however, one of the illustrative citations derives from Fergusson's *Proverbs*: 'Blaw the wynd neuer so fast it will lowne at the last' (Beveridge 1924: 20).

Alliterative poetry, both English and Scottish, was characterised by a distinctive, usually archaic, poetic diction. *DOST* provides much information about the origins, survival, and restricted circulation of many components of this diction, such as the ancient poetic synonyms for a hero or warrior: *freke, grome, her(e, lede*, or *wy*. Its citations also document the popularity of alliterative doublets and other set phrases and formulae. A few instances from Dunbar's *Twa Mariit Wemen and the Wedo* are 'leyd vpone lyf', 'leuch apon loft', 'swerf and swoun'. The use of alliteration, however, was not confined to technically alliterative poems, such as *The Howlat*, *Rauf Coilyear* and *Golagros and Gawane*, but was widespread in early Scottish poetry. It is as evident in the battle scenes of Douglas's *Eneados* as in his Prologue to book VIII, and forms a striking feature of Dunbar's *Flyting* (no. 65) and the *Ballat of the Abbot of Tungland* (no. 4). Dunbar's 'In secreit place this hyndir nicht' contains the line:

That as ane gaist I glour and grane.

(no. 25. 19)

Neither *glour*, 'stare with wide open eyes', nor *grane*, 'groan', were restricted to poetic usage, but *DOST*'s citations for these words suggest that Dunbar's alliterative coupling of them derives from poetic tradition. In early Scottish poetry hares (and sometimes *hurcheouns*, 'hedgehogs') regularly *hirpil*, 'walk, run, as if limping'. This is a tradition which seems to have originated with Henryson's 'hirpland hair' (*Fables*, 895; Fox 1981) and Dunbar's 'hard hurcheoun hirpland' (*Flyting*, 179); it continues at least as late as Burns, with line 7 of *The Holy Fair*: 'The hares were hirplan down the furrs [furrows]'. *DOST* provides other instances from sixteenth- and seventeenth-century poets, including Montgomerie and Mure of Rowallan.

One alliterative doublet has a particularly interesting history. *Wandreth*, 'distress, hardship', was often coupled with *wa, wo*, 'woe', in Middle English texts, as various in date and genre as *The Ormulum*, *Cursor Mundi*, *The Destruction of Troy* and *The Towneley Plays*. *DOST*, under *wandreth*, records a number of poetic uses from the sixteenth century, and one surprisingly late prose use, dated 1680: 'That . . . reproacht party . . . which can hardly get leave to live on earth for a pack of ministers and professers, mickle wo and wandreth com on them'. *DOST* also records sixteenth-century uses of *wander*, a variant of *wandreth*. (The relationship between the two words seems analogous to that between *hunder* and *hundreth*, and *brander* and *brandreth*, 'gridiron'.) This reduced form *wander* is employed by William Stewart in his metrical translation of Hector Boece (1531–5): 'scho wes put to sic wander and wo' (Turnbull 1858: III, 334; see also III, 306). It also occurs twice in Lindsay's *Satyre of the Thrie Estaitis* – or more precisely, it occurs in the Bannatyne text of that work:

> Now wander and wa be to thame all thair lyvis,
> The quhilk ar maryit with sic vnhappy wyvis.
> (*Proclamation*, 95–6)

and

> Wander be to thame that it [i.e. the New Testament] wrocht
> (*Satyre*, 1132 = 2068 in Charteris print)

The edition of the *Satyre* printed by Robert Charteris in 1602 does not contain the *Proclamation*, and the second of the instances quoted above reads differently:

> Duill fell the braine that hes it wrocht.
> (2068)

Modern editors of Lindsay have failed to recognise the significance of *wander*. Douglas Hamer's edition of his works for the Scottish Text Society has a copious Glossary, but does not include the word, nor does he provide a note at either of its occurrences (Hamer 1931–6). Other editors have glossed it, variously, as 'weariness' or 'wonder' (Laing 1871; Lyall 1989). *DOST*, supplemented by *OED*, not only explains the word's significance, but leads one to think that it was preserved by Bannatyne (c. 1568) when it was on the point of becoming obsolete. Whoever was responsible for the Charteris text replaced the word by the less specialised and probably more intelligible *duill*, 'dole, grief'. (For other linguistic differences between the Bannatyne and Charteris texts, see McClure 1986.) In each of the citations from Lindsay *wander* forms part of a curse or imprecation – a linguistic structure which tends to preserve fossilised usage – and this, interestingly, may account for the word's survival in the last recorded citation of 1680.

Verbal similarities in alliterative phrases such as these indicate little more than that the users were heirs to a shared poetic tradition. Other similarities of usage in *DOST*'s citations, however, may possibly be signs of one poet's influence upon another. This is particularly likely when the words or phrases are uncommon. An example is *matutine*, 'of the morning, matutinal'. Here *DOST* cites not only Dunbar's striking metaphor for the sun, 'the goldyn candyll matutyne', but follows it immediately with a brief citation from the romance *Clariodus*: 'the lustie candill matutine'. If one reads the latter phrase in context

> Richt as the lustie candill matutine
> Begouth with cristall visage for to schyne
>
>> (Irving 1830: II. 1395–6)

it is evident that the unknown poet of *Clariodus* was influenced by the first four lines of *The Goldyn Targe*. What is more, if one investigates further, it appears that this poet's imitation of Dunbar's style and diction was extensive, and not confined to dawn descriptions (Purdie 2002).

In this case *DOST* offered no comment on the parallels of diction. But another word, also employed by Dunbar, provoked an interestingly explicit venture into literary criticism: 'J. STEWART seems to be imitating DUNB[AR]'. The headword here is *slop*, n.2 'An outer garment, a cloak, tunic or the like'. Under the figurative and conjectural sense c: '? trailing clouds', are listed two citations, the first from Dunbar's *Goldyn Targe*, 26–7:

> The purpur hevyn ourscailit in silvir sloppis
> Ourgilt the treis;

and the second a shortened version of two lines from 'To his awin Maistres', a love poem by John Stewart of Baldynneis:

> The christall skyis vith color cleir celest
> Maist cleinlie glistrit sched in siluer slops.
>
>> (Crockett 1913: 137)

It is uncertain whether Stewart understood precisely what Dunbar meant by *sloppis*, a word whose significance has been much discussed by Dunbar's editors. But there seems no doubt that he liked the phrase as a whole, and imitated it and other features of the poem from which it came, including the rhyme on *sloppis, croppis, droppis*. If the rest of Stewart's poem is read attentively, one perceives other echoes of Dunbar. The most striking of these is the conceit of the thirsty sun drinking up drops of dew:

> Quhill birnand Tytan vith his vult deuyne
> Drank vp for drouthe that recent liquor sueit.

This is a reworking of

> Depart fra Phebus did Aurora grete –
> Hir cristall teris I saw hyng on the flouris,
> Quhilk he for lufe all drank vp wyth his hete.
>
>> (*Goldyn Targe*, 16–18)

Stewart belonged to a later generation of poets, who flourished in the reign of James VI, and the most obvious influences upon his poetry were not native, but French and Italian. Nonetheless, although he never mentions Dunbar, the tradition of jewelled, aureate dawn descriptions associated not only with Dunbar but with Douglas and Lindsay was clearly still powerful.

Historical dictionaries obviously depend for their raw materials upon modern editions of early texts, whether manuscript or printed. But not all the data in these editions are wholly reliable. A. J. Aitken, who discussed the problems facing Scottish lexicographers in a number of articles, explained 'the dilemmas arising from the innumerable ambiguities of Older Scottish handwriting, and, at a higher level, of its orthographic system' (Aitken 1977: 13). These included such factors as the close similarity of long *s* and *f*, the frequent indistinguishability of the letters *c* and *t*, and above all the confusion arising from sequences of minims in the letters *i*, *u*, *m* and *n*. One of Aitken's favourite examples was *invention*, or *invintioun*: 'an occasional editorial or scribal misreading of *munitioun* or . . . *monitioun*' (*DOST*, *Additions and Corrections*). Elsewhere he writes of 'cases of egregious but frequent editorial mistranscription, such [as] the several cases of editorial *linit-stane* for *lunt-staue*, a staff for holding a *lunt* or match for a gun' (Aitken 1981: 41). The alertness of *DOST*'s editors to such problems has resulted in many discreet corrections of editorial blunders, signalled chiefly by such notes as *pr.* or *erron.* Such notes often provide food for thought. The mysterious word *swar*, *swair*, 'snare', is found only in *The Wallace*, and may well be, as *DOST* suggests, an error for *snar(e*. It is but one of many cases in the poem, which suggests that the textual relations between the manuscript and the early prints of *The Wallace* require further investigation.

Sir William Craigie, early in his scholarly career, fulminated against the many misreadings of the text in the Scottish Text Society edition of John Rolland's *The Court of Venus* (Craigie 1898; Gregor 1884). Most of these seem, unsurprisingly, to have been excluded from *DOST*: two striking examples are *feindill* (Prologue, 31), an error for *seindill*, 'seldom', and *philistiane* (I. 176), an error for *phisiciane*. Others are recorded in the dictionary, but corrected. Under the headword *lamenry*, n. 'illicit or profane love', for example, the citation from *The Court of Venus*, I. 397 reads: 'Scho feidis me with fude of lamenrie [*pr.* lameurie]'. A number of misreadings in this edition, however, were not spotted by Craigie. One instance which reached *DOST* is the ghost word *forleir*, for which the only citation is Rolland, *Court of Venus*, III. 274: 'Becaus Diomeid wald forleir / the fers Troians'. The correct reading of this word, however, in the 1575 print is simply *forbeir*. It is unfortunate that a mistranscription in a different poetic text also failed to arouse the suspicions of *DOST*'s editors, and thus created another ghost word. This is *trell*, n. which is conjecturally explained as a metathetic variant of *tirl*, n. and glossed as 'a turn, an occasion'. The sole citation for this form is 'Wirgile that was wis in a trell / Was hanging as ys kende fule weile / Be ane woman throw his fals trane' (see Shire and Fenton 1955: 50). *Trell*, however, illustrates the common confusion of *c* and *t*, and is correctly transcribed as *crell*, 'creel, basket'. The poem from which the lines come has been identified as a Scottish translation of Guillaume Alexis's *Le Debat de l'Omme et de la Femme* (Bawcutt 1996); and *crell* corresponds to French *corbeille*. The reference is to the legendary story of Virgil's infatuation with a woman who humiliated him by hanging him in a basket from a tower. A. J. Aitken readily acknowledged that a few such deceptive quotations or erroneous readings had – as he put it – 'penetrated all our defences', but he nonetheless estimated that they did not 'form more than a tiny proportion of the total or falsify our results to any noticeable extent' (Aitken 1977: 15).

One of *DOST*'s textual interventions is of great value: the correction of a single word acts as a springboard for making better sense of the rather obscure yet highly interesting passage in which it is embedded. The word in question occurs in an allegorical passage of Sir Gilbert Hay's *Buik of King Alexander the Conquerour*, where the soul is described as a King, advised by various counsellors, including Wit, Reason, Memory and Will:

> Giff he [i.e. Will] demys vrang, tha[n] cummys Sinceris,
> Quhilk Haly Spouk of Conscience callit is,
> And schawis the hart that he hes done erroure,
> And biddis him haue mynd vpone his Creatoure,
> And bringis Dis[cre]tioun in his witnessing,
> Off his erroure for to reprufe the king.
>
> (Cartwright 1986–90: 9749–54)

What does *Spouk* mean? (It should be noted that volume III of this edition, containing explanatory material, such as glossary and notes, has not yet appeared.) Any thought that the word might perhaps be related to modern *spook*, and therefore mean 'spirit, ghost', should be dismissed. *Spook* (from Dutch *spook*), entered English and Scots only in the nineteenth century, and, according to *OED*, it appeared 'first in American usage'. *DOST* records *spouk*, but then advises the reader to 'see SPONK(E, n.'; under this headword, one finds that the very first citation is this line from Hay: '. . .Quhilk haly sponk (*pr.* spouk) of conscience callit is'. *Sponk*, more familiar today in the spelling *spunk*, literally meant a spark of fire, but its early uses in Scots were largely figurative. *DOST* defines it as: 'a spark, a minute particle, a trace . . . viewed as the initiator of regeneration or the final remnant of something'.

The phrase *sponk of Conscience*, however, and its association with the mysterious *Sinceris* in the preceding line remain unexplained, and require further investigation. *Sinceris* has nothing to do with the adjective *sincere*. Line 9750 is metrically deficient, and I consider it likely that this form represents a scribal corruption of Hay's original reading: *Sin[t]er[es]is*. This learned theological word derives from medieval Latin *synteresis*, and ultimately from Greek *synteresis*, meaning 'careful guarding or watching'. The word does not appear in *DOST*, but *OED*, under *synderesis*, and *MED*, under *sinderesis*, record several Middle English uses; these spellings apparently represent the medieval pronunciation of the Greek word. A personified 'Synderesys' accompanies Conscience in *The Assembly of Gods*, an allegorical poem sometimes attributed to Lydgate (Chance 1999: 56); and in lines 496–8 of Lydgate's *Pilgrimage of the Life of Man*, a translation from Guillaume de Deguileville, *Synderesis* is defined as 'the hiher party of Resoun, Wherby A man shal best discerne Hys conscience to governe' (Furnivall 1899–1904).

Hay's phrase *sponk of Conscience* is a direct translation of the Latin *scintilla conscientiae*, and no less theological than *synderesis*. Both terms have been traced to St Jerome's Commentary on the four living creatures in the vision of Ezekiel (1:10), where the Eagle was interpreted as synderesis, and described as *scintilla conscientiae* (Migne 1884: 22): this spark was not extinguished by original sin, but constitutes the source of moral judgments. St Jerome's exegesis was highly influential in the later Middle Ages, and the concept of synderesis was much discussed by scholastic theologians. A striking divergence existed between the teachings of St Bonaventura, who placed the habit of synderesis in the will, and those of St Thomas Aquinas, who taught that synderesis belonged to the intellect (Rohmer 1903–50; Hollenbach 2003). This is not the place to pursue Hay's source, but the manner in which he uses these terms and places them within a complex psychological moral allegory suggests that he was well informed about such theological debates.

The word *synderesis* occurs elsewhere in Scots, appropriately enough in one of the 'ballatis of theoligie' in the Bannatyne Manuscript: 'Walking allone amang thir levis grene' (Ritchie 1928–34: II, 132–6). The poem's narrator hears an admonitory bird whose message is summed up in the refrain: 'Man, mend thy lyfe and restoir wrangus geir [ill-gotten goods]'. Similarly didactic birds occur in Dunbar's 'Off lentren in the first mornyng' (no. 49), and other Scottish moral poems of this period, but they rarely receive a name. In this case, however, the poet asks: 'Quhat kynd of bird art thow?' (92), and receives a reply:

> Scho answerit sone and said I tell the now
> Synderisis my name is but ony faill
> Quhilk the sall dryve to the fyre Infernaill
> Bot gif thow wirk as I do requeir
> To mend thy lyfe and restoir wrangus geir
> (94–8)

It is tempting to associate this bird with St Jerome's Eagle, but the concept of synderesis in this poem seems theologically vaguer than Hay's: elsewhere it is said that the bird's 'sermoun bait my conscience' (86), which is closer to the concept of the 'prick of conscience'; and she proffers stock moral advice, counselling the listener to rule himself 'with ressone and prudence' (89).

DOST's correction of *spouk* to *sponk* prompts a brief reconsideration of the transcription of another word in Hay's *King Alexander the Conquerour*, which has a very similar shape. Diogenes, the 'witty clerk', or philosopher, renowned for the austerity and simplicity of his life, is described thus:

> He satt vpone ane souk in-till ane tvn.
> (17658)

It is difficult to find any plausible gloss for *souk* in this context, but to read it as *sonk* gives excellent sense. According to *DOST*, a *sonk(e)* is something upon which one sits, a seat of a fairly simple and rudimentary nature, such as Diogenes would find fitting. For Douglas it was a seat of turf: 'On grene herbis and sonkis of soft gers' (*Eneados*, VII. ii. 14). In later Scots prose texts it seems to have signified a cushion stuffed with straw, especially one used as a substitute for a saddle. In this case *DOST* was not responsible for making the textual correction, but its citations are invaluable in showing why such a reading is appropriate.

It is always a mistake not to consult *DOST*. Pitfalls lurk beneath apparently simple words, even for readers long familiar with Older Scots texts. I know this from experience, since in my edition of Dunbar more attention should have been paid to the combination of *ʒung* and *lord* in Kennedy's section of *The Flyting*:

> Archebauld Dumbar betrasd the hous of Hailis,
> Becaus the ʒung lord had Dumbar to keip.
> (no. 65. 299–300)

No previous editor of Dunbar seems to have explained *ʒung lord*, or placed it in a glossary. Yet, as the final volume of *DOST* now indicates, this use of the term is one of the earliest recorded in the special sense 'heir-apparent of a landowner'. Homonyms can often mislead readers. Some historians, for instance, have assumed that *aucht*, in the legal phrase *best aucht*, means 'eighth' (MacQueen 1991: 136; Wormald 1985: 101) rather than 'property, that which is owned' (*DOST*, *aucht*, n.1; and *best aucht*). Guesswork sometimes leads to comical misunderstandings. One such is the curious interpretation as an 'avian spectacle' of a prosaic record in *The Treasurer's Accounts*: 'xix draucht of buirdis and sparris quhilk wer put up in the abbay kirk at the Quenis graces coronatioun' (Cameron 1998: 264). Consultation of *DOST* would have shown that *buirdis* signified boards, planks – not birds – and that *sparris* signified pieces of timber – not sparrows.

No dictionary, of course, is wholly perfect. It is not always easy to find one's way around *DOST*. Indeed searching for a word in its different shapes and manifestations sometimes recalls an obstacle race. (In the course of the journey, however, one learns much about the extraordinary range of spelling variants in older Scots.) But this is a minor flaw, not a major deficiency. Overall my response to *DOST*'s wealth of words resembles that of Dryden to *The Canterbury Tales*: 'Here is God's plenty!'

NOTES

1. *Eneados* references, by Prologue, or book, chapter and line, are to Coldwell 1957–64.
2. Line references are to the edition of *The Palice of Honour* in Bawcutt 2003.
3. References, by poem-number and line, are to Bawcutt 1998.

CHAPTER 3

The History and Development of *DOST*

M. G. Dareau, Scottish Language Dictionaries
Former Editorial Director of *DOST*

The *Dictionary of the Older Scottish Tongue* is a great store of treasures for the researcher or the merely curious. Its twelve volumes, as well as offering a unique point of entry to Scottish medieval and renaissance society, form a substantial monument to many years of scholarship throughout the twentieth century and, in the development of the ideas that underpin it, a bridge to the twenty-first. Yet its history has its share of precarious moments. This account of that history[1] seeks to record these moments along with the powerful sense of purpose and endeavour that informed the production of the dictionary and was expressed in the dedication chosen for volume XII: 'To Scots everywhere, lovers and students of the Scots language and all those who have given freely of their time and knowledge to help achieve the completion of this work'.

DOST was compiled between 1925 and 2001 according to the historical principles laid down in the *Oxford English Dictionary (OED)*. During the first phase, a methodology based on that of the *OED* was established. This chapter is divided into four main sections identified as those periods which saw substantial innovations affecting the text of the published dictionary. It includes an outline of the external history as well as those aspects of editorial policy which most closely impinge on the external history.[2] The final phase deals with the years 1994–2001, outlining the accelerated completion of *DOST* in July of the latter year.

This survey is based on evidence of three sorts: materials in print, chiefly in the Prefaces of the volumes of the dictionary and the writings of Sir William Craigie and Professor A. J. Aitken; official papers, principally the minutes of the Joint Council for the Scottish Dictionaries (subsequently, the Joint Council for the Dictionary of the Older Scottish Tongue); and private writings, especially correspondence held in the *DOST* Archive, now in the archives of the University of Edinburgh. In the last two categories, we are extremely fortunate to have a file of correspondence and official papers from the period 1949–58 contributed to the Archive by Professor Angus McIntosh.

1919–1948

On 4 April 1919 Dr (later Sir) William A. Craigie, co-editor of *OED*, read a paper entitled 'New Dictionary Schemes' to the Philological Society in London. In this paper he suggested that, following the completion of *OED*, a number of supplementary dictionary projects should be undertaken. These he referred to as 'period dictionaries', each being concerned with a discrete chronological period in the history of English. His last suggested scheme did not conform to the description of a period of English, but was, perhaps, the dictionary that lay closest to his heart, a dictionary of the 'older Scottish'. This proposal bore fruit as the *Dictionary of the Older Scottish Tongue*.

There seems never to have been any doubt in Craigie's mind that this dictionary of Scots should restrict itself to the earlier period – up to 1700. He saw the project as lying within his plans for English, and the major sweep of English had been encompassed in *OED*. He conceded that, in the earlier period, Scots was a language, but had no notion that such nomenclature might continue to have any truth or even advantage after 1700. He saw the language as dividing naturally into the two periods now defined by *DOST* and the *Scottish National Dictionary (SND)*.

> The older Scottish tongue . . . Considered by itself it is a very definite thing, beginning with the fourteenth century, flourishing as a literary medium from about 1375 to 1600, and maintaining a precarious existence in writing till towards the close of the seventeenth century, when a new period definitely sets in and continues unbroken down to the present day. (Craigie 1931: 9)

In a letter to Dr William Grant, the first Editor of *SND*, in January 1916, Craigie had already set out his thoughts for the future of Scottish lexicography:

> It is certainly well to be looking ahead with regard to the Scottish dictionary. I have been doing so too, and have made up my mind that when the Oxford Dictionary is finished, I shall undertake the Old Scottish one myself . . . Some time ago I asked Watson[3] whether, in the event of funds being provided for the Modern Scottish dictionary, he would be prepared to take a hand in the compiling of it . . . It would be excellent if the two Dictionaries could be produced concurrently, so that the one could link up with the other and the continuity (or otherwise) of the words be clearly shown. In that case Watson might be a kind of connecting medium for both. (*DOST* Archive)

It is thus evident that Craigie had the dictionary of older Scots in mind well before his paper of 1919 and had also begun planning the collection of the materials he would need at this time. In the same letter to Grant he outlines his thoughts on that crucial aspect of successful lexicography:

> In the collections made for the Oxford Dictionary there is an enormous amount of material which could be used for the purpose, and I shall arrange to have the use of this. Some further collecting may be wanted, but nothing to what would be necessary if the whole work had to be done from the beginning.

This collection of Scottish material consisted of some hundreds of thousands of citation slips, both used and unused, excerpted for *OED*.

Craigie set to work seriously on what was to become *DOST* in 1921, when, with the help of a number of volunteer readers, he began to expand the collection of quotations inherited from *OED*. In the winter of 1925–6, with the assistance of George Watson and Otto Schmidt, he began editing from the collections thus far available to him. By this time he had become Professor of English in the University of Chicago. In 1929 a Memorandum of Agreement was drawn up between Craigie and the University of Chicago for the publication of 'A Dictionary of the Older Scottish Tongue', which would be printed in Oxford by Oxford University Press (OUP). The first fascicle of the dictionary was published in 1931. Volume I (A–C), in six fascicles, was completed in 1937 and Volume II (D–G) in 1951. At this time the preparation and production of the published work seems to have consisted largely of excerpting and editing without the systematic press-preparation that became part of the production process at a later date. The Agreement of 1929 stated that the dictionary would be completed in twenty-five parts of 120 pages each.

1948–1981

The work of editing continued very largely under the editorship of Craigie alone until the appointment of Adam J. Aitken in 1948. Craigie had retired in 1936, returning from Chicago to Watlington, near Oxford, where he continued to edit material for *DOST*. Aitken, as Craigie's assistant, was based in Edinburgh and funded from year to year as a Research Fellow by the Universities of Edinburgh, Glasgow and Aberdeen. With the appointment of Aitken the second major period in the history of the project had begun.

Aitken was a young man of twenty-seven when he took up the post in which he was to spend the rest of his career, not that this seemed inevitable or even particularly likely in the beginning. For a number of years he was employed on temporary contracts, renewed annually, a fact that disturbed Angus McIntosh, Forbes Professor of English Language and General Linguistics in the University of Edinburgh, who was concerned for both the welfare of Aitken and the long-term interests of the dictionary. However the delicacy of relations with Chicago University Press was such that no plans for the longer-term security of either Aitken or the dictionary were feasible at this time. If relations with Chicago were to break down it would lead almost inevitably to the abandonment of the dictionary project.

Early financial problems

Although *DOST* continued to be published by Chicago University Press until 1981, there were during that period a number of crises, the first of which occurred in 1950. In 1949 Craigie had written to Mr Hemens, Assistant Director of the Press, to inform him that it had become clear that the dictionary could not be completed in twenty-five parts but was likely to run to ten or twelve more. Hemens replied that the Press was prepared to face the extra cost that this would entail with the assurance 'the intention of the University is to complete the publication of this work'.

In 1950, however, the situation worsened. In February Craigie alerted McIntosh to a change of attitude in Chicago due to rising costs and the failure to attract outside funding. The problem of the increase in scale of the dictionary and consequent rise in costs had led to Chicago's unwillingness to continue under the previous agreement with Craigie alone. However, in October a new contract was signed with Chicago to which the University of Edinburgh became a party. To help meet the increase in costs Edinburgh agreed to forego royalties, which would stop with the death of Craigie.

While this may have gone some way to securing the dictionary's future, the production itself was by no means secure. Over the next year Hemens continued to press for a reduction in scale. Craigie could not see this as a solution. He wrote to McIntosh in February 1951:

This could not be done by a simple reduction in the scale; it would
involve a real change of method which would greatly reduce the value
of the dictionary as a record of the language, while it would not
materially lessen the work of preparation. (*DOST* Archive)

In November Hemens reiterated his anxiety at the slow rate of production. Though he conceded the importance of the work, he could not deny that Chicago was finding publication a heavy financial burden. In a letter to Aitken of 20 November 1951 Craigie outlined his view of the requirements for an efficient, productive enterprise:

I enclose a letter which I have this morning received from Hemens. It
is unfortunate that the lack of assistance, even if temporary, will reduce
the amount that can be turned out this year.

To make really satisfactory progress a staff of at least four, in addition to yourself, is required, to consist of:

Two for elementary work, getting into order of date all the material for each word, making additions from the reference slips not yet copied, abbreviating long quotations, and making a complete list of spellings.

Two sub-editors to distinguish and define the senses and either draft the etymologies or supply the material for these. They should always bear in mind the importance of keeping the scale as low as possible.

The sending on of slips for the later letters might be done by one or other of these according to the time they can spare for it. (*DOST* Archive)

However the ideal staff was not available and Craigie and Aitken had to struggle on as best they might. The true grimness of the situation[4] is revealed in a letter from Hemens to Craigie the following March:

There are two areas in this financial problem where you could help. I have written about them before. In writing again I do not wish to imply that you may not be trying. However, the results are so imperceptible that I must ask you to review the matter and make a strenuous effort to do better.

We need from you a commitment and performance in line with that commitment as to the maximum total number of parts to encompass this work. When publication was undertaken it was with the expectation there would be a maximum of twenty parts. After it had been under way and a number of parts published, it was perfectly obvious that you were not keeping within that limit. Based on completion of the first approximately ten parts, it then looked as though the total would not be twenty parts, but twice that number, or more. That completely upset the financial arrangements which we had made.

The cost of alterations is the second problem . . .

At times it becomes discouraging and somewhat disheartening to fight for the funds necessary to keep this production and publishing program for the dictionary going. At one time, only a few years ago, I was instructed to have production stopped and cancel the order with Oxford. I wilfully disregarded those instructions. I believe we should do all that we can to complete publication of the dictionary. I still believe that. I had hopes, but that was all I could have, that something would happen to change the financial picture. Unfortunately that something has not happened and, if anything, the finances are worse.

I continue to hope that by working together, each of us possibly a little more carefully, the production of your Scottish Dictionary can continue without interruption. (*DOST* Archive)

However supportive Hemens might be of the project, he and Craigie differed as to the nature of an appropriate scale for such a work. It is ironic to note that our perception now is that Craigie's part of the dictionary is woefully inadequate in scale.

Solutions

The need for a resolution to Craigie's proposal for securing *DOST*'s future after his own lifetime and for the management of the project within the environs of the Scottish universities was evident to McIntosh. His perception of the value of the project both to Scotland and to Edinburgh is clear. He worked tirelessly, using all his skills of persuasion and his contacts within the academic world to bring his vision about. Craigie had laid out his thoughts on the future of his dictionary in 1949. The situation was summarised in a letter dated 6 September 1949 from McIntosh to Charles Stewart, the Secretary of the University of Edinburgh:

1. Sir William Craigie who is now 82 has completed about 2/5ths of the great *Dictionary of the Older Scottish Tongue.*
2. Having found that A. J. Aitken (of this University) is proving an excellent Assistant, he seems to be inclined to hand on the task to him. He believes that two or three others will be needed to help him.
3. He thinks strongly that Edinburgh (where Aitken is at present working) is the ideal place to operate the project. To encourage this, he has bequeathed all his books connected with it to the University if they will make them available to the dictionary staff (otherwise to Aberdeen, Glasgow, St Andrews in that order of preference).
   I should like to make the following comments:
1. There are probably numerous technical problems, housing of material, financing, etc. which will need to be solved, but I believe that this is a magnificent opportunity for us to build still further on the linguistic side, and that Craigie is right in thinking Edinburgh is the proper place.
2. In view of Craigie's age and the advisability of having his advice in any reorganisation, I think we should go into the matter as soon as possible. (*DOST* Archive)

In November 1951 the matter was brought before the Scottish Universities' Conference by Edinburgh University. The timing of this was provoked not only by the situation with *DOST* but also that of the *Scottish National Dictionary* (*SND*) which was undergoing a financial crisis of its own in Aberdeen. The outcome of this meeting is contained in a communication from the Principal of the University of Edinburgh to Hemens:

The conference made certain recommendations:

1. That editorial work on both Dictionaries should be carried on in one University, namely, Edinburgh . . .

2. That a new Joint Council should be set up, representative of the four Scottish Universities and the two Dictionaries.

3. That, following this, the four Scottish Universities should together ask for adequate financial support for both ventures; and that for this purpose they should in the first place approach the Ford Foundation and subsequently, if necessary, any other potential sources of financial assistance.

The force of these proposals . . . is that, in making an appeal for funds, it is desirable to present the two Dictionaries as together forming a major project covering the whole field of Scottish lexicography, carried on in a properly co-ordinated manner in one place; and that an appeal by the four Scottish Universities on behalf of this work of national importance would be a more powerful means of obtaining financial assistance than an appeal by (say) the University of Edinburgh on behalf of only one of the Dictionaries.

Certain points, however, must be made clear in explanation of these proposals. Firstly, they do not imply any control of the editorial policies of the Dictionaries, or any interference by one Dictionary in the affairs of the other. It is fully appreciated that their editorial methods differ in several respects, and it is agreed that all such matters of policy should remain under the present system of separate control . . .

In terms of the 1950 Agreement, what we have to lay before you is this: that the Compiler (Sir William Craigie) and the Institute (the University of Edinburgh) propose now to enter into a separate Agreement with a Joint Council which will represent the four Scottish Universities, the S.N.D. Association, and the Compiler and editorial staff of the D.O.S.T. Our object in doing so is to raise funds to establish an adequate editorial staff for the D.O.S.T. and so to improve the rate of work on the dictionary; and we are confident that if this can be achieved it will help materially to lighten the task of the University of Chicago with regard to the publication of the dictionary. (*DOST* Archive)

So Edinburgh set out its proposal. The Scottish universities would give what help they could with accommodation and a modicum of financial support, hoping (as it turned out, vainly) to raise most of the new funding required to create a viable project from wealthy American foundations. They would take responsibility for the production side if Chicago continued with publication, which, if all went well with the Scottish universities' fund-raising, would no longer be a financial burden. Above all the Scottish universities wanted to keep Chicago on board, and phrased the proposal for a Joint Council in terms they thought least likely to cause it to pull out.

It is interesting to note that, according to Craigie, the cost of publishing *DOST* (which Hemens found much too high) was, for setting Part XIII, 164 pages, £420 with £94 for corrections, whereas Part IV of volume III of *SND*, 134 pages, cost £1,100. At this time, as throughout its production, *SND* was published by the Scottish National Dictionary Association Limited and financed by subscription of its members. It was printed in Edinburgh, latterly by Constable.

The outcome of this initiative was the setting up in 1952 of the Joint Council for the Scottish Dictionaries with McIntosh as its Convener. McIntosh played a prominent role in all three major initiatives in Scottish studies of this period, the others being the creation of the Linguistic Survey of Scotland and the School of Scottish Studies. Thus, as it turned out, so far from being a time of disintegration, this was a period of both consolidation and expansion.

Dictionary production

From 1950 Craigie had begun to send materials, books and citation slips north to Aitken and in 1955, when Aitken took over from Craigie as Editor of *DOST*, its government and funding had altered radically. The DOST enterprise had become to all intents and purposes a department within the University of Edinburgh, overseen by the Joint Council representing the four universities and funded in part by them, in part by a variety of charitable foundations. Two years later, in 1957, Craigie died, aged ninety. He was a notable scholar in many fields, and one of a line of extraordinary Scottish lexicographers.

The financing of an adequate level of staffing was a perennial problem. In 1952 Aitken had received a small grant of £100 from the School of Scottish Studies Committee with which he had employed a part-time assistant, Miss Iona B. MacGregor. Aitken reported to the Committee the following year:

I have no hesitation in saying that she is well worth the 4/– [4 shillings] per hour which she is paid. Since she has arrived there has been a perceptible acceleration of the output of finished dictionary copy, which is directly attributable to her contribution. (*DOST* Archive)

Miss MacGregor was required to 'rough out the material for editing' which Aitken then completed. In the year for which she was contracted, he reckoned she would complete fifty of the dictionary's pages. She also reassigned citation slips to words further down the alphabet, sorting the material which had arrived from Craigie, and did some library research for Aitken. This accounted for £90 of the £100 grant. In 1953 the School Committee was not able to renew the grant. Aitken spelled out the precariousness of the situation in a letter to McIntosh:

I understand that this year the School's allotment of money is likely to be largely used up, and also that there may be other objections to making even a small non-recurrent grant to an enterprise which is not a responsibility of the School itself. (*DOST* Archive)

At this point, in February 1953, Aitken applied to Dr J. R. Peddie of the Carnegie Trust for support for his assistant. His letter makes it clear that a previous application made 'some years ago' had been successful in obtaining a grant of £300. On this occasion the Trust made a grant of £150, and, equally importantly, a connection that was to be crucial to the future of the dictionary was reinforced.

In 1955, when Aitken took over as editor, Hemens, wishing reassurance as to the value of the University of Chicago Press's investment in *DOST*, sought an opinion from C. L. Wrenn, Fellow of Pembroke College and Rawlinson and Bosworth Professor of Anglo-Saxon at Oxford. The Press was at this time underwriting a small publishing loss and wished to ascertain whether its money was well spent. It is perhaps worth quoting some of the points that Wrenn made in his extremely full reply. After praising the relatively recent integration of the organisation of *DOST* into the Scottish university system, and the staff, including the two newly appointed assistant editors, Betty Hill and Hans Meier, he went on to make some general points:

To some extent the value of the dictionary will ultimately depend on its association with the Scottish National Dictionary which is also being directed by the same Joint Dictionaries Council and there is an obvious advantage in the two Dictionaries being thus intimately related . . .

The Dictionary of the Older Scottish Tongue is a vital companion piece to the Ann Arbor Middle English Dictionary which relies on the existence of the former and has specifically excluded all Scottish material. Here again the importance of either Dictionary depends in some measure on the completion of the other . . .

The importance and worth of the Dictionary of the Older Scottish Tongue will continually increase with the fuller development of Scottish studies which is being pursued, for example, by the University of Edinburgh School of Scottish Studies. As these studies come more and more to take their proper place in the picture of N.W. European culture in the Mediaeval and Renaissance periods, it will more fully come to be realized how absolutely indispensable and admirable the Dictionary of the Older Scottish Tongue really is as a working tool. (*DOST* Archive)

Expansion

During this period Aitken put a great deal of effort into expanding the dictionary's corpus.[5] One aspect directly affected by the enlargement of the corpus was the scale of the dictionary. This had been problematical for years and had been one of the causes of Chicago's unhappiness about the project as far back as 1949. This situation had not changed when in 1953 Aitken tried to calculate the likely number of parts in the finished Dictionary by a comparison with the size of *OED*. He reckoned that for A–INDENTIT each of *DOST*'s parts of 120 pages corresponded to 376 pages of *OED*. This equation allowed him to calculate that, corresponding to the total of 15,487 pages in *OED*, *DOST*, when completed, would have 4,920 pages or 41 parts. Volume III (H–L), the first volume for which Aitken was responsible, was published in 1965.

The development of the infrastructure for funding and academic support and the expansion of the corpus led to an expansion of the project as a whole and set it on a new footing. The size of the staff increased, both editors who prepared edited copy and editorial assistants who carried out the various tasks required to prepare the raw slips for editing and afterwards the edited copy for the press. Aitken was the sole Editor until, in 1973, Dr James A. C. Stevenson, who had come to *DOST* in 1966 from a career in teaching, was appointed Joint Editor with him. In 1971 Aitken was appointed part-time Senior Lecturer in English Language in the University of Edinburgh and between that date and 1979 devoted only half of his working time to the dictionary. During this period he developed the teaching of Scots within the English Language Department and will be remembered by many for this aspect of his career.

Stevenson's meticulousness in the analysis of language was fully in keeping with the quality and attention to detail for which *DOST* was renowned. The attitude that the project was much more a matter of scholarship than a product to be got speedily into the market-place was characteristic of historical lexicographers from the time of Sir James Murray at least. *OED*'s original remit, for instance, had been to restrict the etymological material included, on the grounds that it was a historical dictionary rather than an etymological one. In practice this restriction was largely ignored. Coming from this tradition, Craigie's intention was to expand the history of Older Scots as fully as he could. So too in his turn Aitken saw the gaps in coverage and the need to fill them if the record of Scots up to 1700 were to be as close to exhaustive as might be. These perfectionist tendencies, which he confessed to in the paper '*DOST*: How we make it and what's in it' (1981: 46) about a later situation, were always evident, and the dictionary itself is all the better for them, even if the funding bodies felt plagued by this compulsion to edit to the absolutely highest standards. Stevenson fitted into a lineage of high scholarship with ease and, through the 1970s especially, developed the highly analytical style that is so evident in the volumes from that period on.

Completion and crisis

In 1969, Aitken expressed the hope that *DOST* might be completed in 1976, shortly after the scheduled completion of *SND* in 1974. In 1971, the year in which volume IV (M–N) was published, the fact that *SND* was approaching completion (it was completed in 1976) and the expectation that *DOST* would follow soon thereafter gave rise to a number of proposals for the future. An Institute of Lexicography dealing especially with an archive of computer-readable texts was suggested, as well as a project to produce an abridged dictionary. The Joint Council took the view that exploration of the former proposal should not be allowed to have a prejudicial effect on the production of the dictionary, though it merited further consideration. The latter proposal continued to be researched with the hope that it might come about on the completion of *SND*. This led ultimately to the production of the *Concise Scots Dictionary* (*CSD*) and its publication in 1985. As the completion of *SND* drew closer there was a further debate as to whether the Joint Council should be wound up and *DOST* supported until its completion by Edinburgh alone. However, by the end of 1976 the Universities of Aberdeen, Dundee, Edinburgh, Glasgow, St Andrews and Stirling had agreed to continue to fund the project. A Joint Council memorandum drafted in 1974 included the statement. 'The project was unquestionably a national enterprise and should be treated and be seen to be treated as such' (*DOST* Archive). This remains true, now as then; indeed, it is one of the most remarkable aspects of a remarkable project that it had the participation of the Scottish universities for almost fifty of its eighty years. However, such support did not put paid to financial problems, and in 1981 what was perhaps the most serious crisis so far blew up.

In 1980 the universities, disappointed of completion in the 1970s, threatened withdrawal of support if a firm end date were not established. The Conference of the Scottish University Courts made it clear that it would be unlikely that the Universities would continue to support the dictionary after 1988, a year after the Carnegie Trust had said it would terminate its financial support. It was undeniable that the editing was taking too long. The calculations of Aitken and Stevenson proved that this date could not be met following the traditional methods so they devised a plan to finish *DOST* by means of what they called the '*OED*-Dependent Method' where dictionary entries were based solely on the equivalent entry in *OED*:

> We accept OED's sense-analysis and definitions as given and simply
> assign our quotations as best we can to their places in the OED scheme,
> providing our own definitions only for those additional words and
> applications which we cannot fit into the OED scheme . . . And we
> propose to offer no etymological note and to undertake no research to
> ensure the precision of definitions or to provide encyclopedic notes and
> comments beyond those already in OED. But we would continue to
> provide exemplification at least as copious as now of all words, senses
> (according to OED's analysis), forms and collocations, with all their
> distributions. (Aitken 1981: 47)

The whole situation was explored at the Joint Council meeting in February 1981, when the following options were offered:

1. Consideration of a plan to complete the *editing* of the dictionary by 1994.
2. . . . to complete the editing of the dictionary by 1994 and allow for a further period of about a year for checking the press-prepared material and for proof-reading.
3. . . . to use a much lowered standard of lexicographical analysis which would present, for T–Z, only those Older Scottish forms and meanings not already recorded in the Oxford English Dictionary. This would therefore be an Older Scots supplement to the OED; it would enable the dictionary to be 'completed' [sic] earlier than 1994. (Joint Council Minutes, *DOST* Archive)

A further meeting was arranged for April to give Aitken time to complete his researches into the viability of these options, so that a final decision might be reached. In the meantime a crisis of another sort arose with the publisher, the University of Chicago Press. This exacerbated matters, though it did not actually cause the crisis as had the problem of publication in 1950. The basic problem was still the same: the scale of the dictionary had doubled, at least, in comparison with what was envisaged in 1929. By the point reached in editing in 1981, the relationship Aitken had calculated in 1953 of 120 pages of *DOST* for every 376 pages of *OED* had become closer to 176 pages of *OED*. So between February and April 1981, Chicago University Press withdrew as publisher. This news was announced to the Joint Council in April, when an emergency meeting was called to address the future of the dictionary. The following options were laid before the Council:

1. Completion of editing by 1994 with an increase of staff and replacement of editors when they retire.
2. Completion of editing by 2020–2030 by one editor and no replacement of staff when they retire.
3. Completion of editing by the Oxford English Dictionary-Dependent Method.
4. Abandonment of the whole project.

Aitken's assessment of option (3), which had now undergone a trial period, was that completion by this method would be two to two and a half times faster than by the other methods proposed, and that it would, therefore, be conceivable to complete the editing by 1987–8. He considered, however, that in larger entries there would be considerable loss of quality. The Joint Council invited a distinguished panel of lexicographers and scholars of Older Scots, Dr R. W.

Burchfield (*OED*), Dr A. Fenton (National Museum of Antiquities, Edinburgh), Professor D. Fox (University of Toronto), Mr P. G. W. Glare (Oxford University Press), Dr R. J. Lyall (University of Glasgow) and Dr J. L. Robinson (*Middle English Dictionary*), to report on the editorial policy of the dictionary and recommend a way forward. They reported in September that the *OED*-Dependent method of editing was a distinctly inferior option. The proposal had also been aired by Aitken at the Third International Conference on Scottish Language and Literature (Medieval and Renaissance). This Conference represented scholars with the most intimate knowledge of *DOST*, those best able to judge the losses that would be sustained were it to be completed according to the *OED*-Dependent method. On Saturday 11 July, their views were reported thus on the front page of *The Scotsman*:

> Sixty experts from all over the world . . . signed an open letter condemning the possibility of cuts in the project, which they said would amount to 'an appalling blot on Scottish scholarship'.
> The letter stated:
> For all our working lives we have looked on the *Dictionary of the Older Scottish Tongue* as one of the great enterprises of literary and linguistic scholarship and have looked forward to its completion according to its present plan and format as a major contribution to the cultural life of Scotland and the world.

As Aitken had expected, the outcry which their complaint unleashed was sufficient to ensure a return to autonomous editing, though with no guarantee that funding would continue beyond the working lives of the present staff. Indeed, part of the package of 1981 was that after the retirement of Stevenson in 1985 and Aitken in 1986 the universities would support only two posts, one editor and one editorial assistant. By November 1981 Aberdeen University Press (AUP) had expressed an interest in publishing *DOST* and in February 1983 acquired the publication rights. AUP installed a microcomputer in the *DOST* offices and from then until 1994 edited copy with a minimal level of tagging was prepared for printing in-house and recorded for the first time in electronic form.

1981–1994

Staffing

The 1980s started inauspiciously with the crisis of 1981 and promised worse with the imminent retirement of both the editors who had brought the project through the 1950s, 1960s and 1970s. When Aitken and Stevenson retired, the editorial staff consisted of Harry Watson and Marace Dareau. Volume V (O–Pn) was published in 1982 and VI (Po–Quh) in 1986. The whole of R and a considerable part of S had been edited but was not yet ready for publication. A completion date of 1988 was clearly out of the question.

In 1984 a charitable organisation, The Friends of the *Dictionary of the Older Scottish Tongue*, was set up to help with fund-raising. This initiative grew directly out of the concern felt by scholars that *DOST* might founder. By the end of the decade it had raised enough money to fund a part-time editor and a full-time editorial assistant/editor as well as providing a number of short-term clerical posts. During this period there were also a number of valuable private benefactions, one of which funded a further editorial assistant post. In 1986 the Royal Society of Edinburgh agreed to support the dictionary for three years at the rate of £4,000 per annum.[6]

Watson became Editor-in-chief in 1985 on the retirement of Stevenson. He had six years experience of lexicography, having, like Stevenson, come to it from teaching. The years between the crisis of 1981 and Watson's assumption of overall authority had seen no basic changes in editorial methodology or routine. The possibility of using word processing technology as part of the editorial process had been investigated, but it was quickly realised that on-screen editing was not feasible. It was recognised that the process of editing required the physical presence of citation slips, the pieces of paper on which individual quotations were recorded, so that all the quotations for a given word could be sorted and re-sorted with maximum ease. The most time-consuming aspect of lexicography is the thought and research that goes into the editing process, which only long years of experience can shorten. Watson applied the methodology passed on to him by Aitken and Stevenson, which meant that the conditions that had provoked the crisis of 1981 continued.

Dareau had returned to *DOST* in 1984 after a period as an editor on *CSD*. During the second half of the 1980s she became responsible for the revising stage of editing. From 1987 Lorna Pike became the third member of the editorial team. The anomalous situation with regard to responsibility for edited copy (Dareau) and overall responsibility for the dictionary (Watson) was recognised in 1988 when both were re-titled Senior Editor, with Watson retaining administrative responsibility and the title of Director.

Publishing

Volume VII (Qui–Roz) was published in 1990. In 1993 the collapse of AUP added renewed publication difficulties to the organisation's other problems. They were resolved with a return to OUP, *DOST*'s printer during the years with Chicago University Press, as publisher. Although the relationship enjoyed with AUP had been beneficial in every way, publication by the major publisher of reference works in the United Kingdom seemed to bode well for the final stage and there was a hope that the publication of the paper version might lead on to an electronic version similar to the electronic *OED*.

1994–2001: ACCELERATED COMPLETION

In November 1993 Dareau, in a letter to Dr Victor Skretkowicz of the Department of English in the University of Dundee, who had succeeded Professor John MacQueen as Convener of the Joint Council, took stock of the situation with regard to editing. At that date the first editing of S was almost finished. She suggested that twelve years would be required for the remaining eighty-four drawers of unedited slips for T–Z. Early in 1994, Skretkowicz instituted a Review of the editorial methods and management of *DOST* in relation to the costs for completion of the project. Its context was outlined as follows:

> The Review was required for the purposes of fund-raising by Professor Alexander Fenton, Chairman of The Friends of *DOST*. It provides a long overdue examination of the editorial policy and of the procedures of editing and production. The first Part of *DOST* was published in 1931. The only interim Review was in 1981. (Asher et al. 1994)

The Review was carried out in March 1994. The Review panel consisted of: Professor R. E. Asher, Professor Emeritus of Linguistics, University of Edinburgh; Mr T. Benbow, Director of Dictionaries, Oxford University Press; Dr C. Macafee, Lecturer in English, University of Aberdeen; and Dr Skretkowicz, with Lesley S. Brown, Editor-in-Chief of the *New Shorter Oxford English Dictionary*, as Consultant. The aims of the Review were:

> to fix a firm date for completion and make recommendations on how this might be achieved;
> to examine the organisation and working practices of the staff, and editorial policy;
> to make recommendations concerning staffing levels, and to consider replacement or addition of equipment. (Ibid.)

As regards the completion date, the panel found grounds to believe that funding might be easier to obtain if a date of 2000 was guaranteed. Dr Robert Burchfield, then editor of the *Oxford English Dictionary*, had served on the 1981 Review. On 18 February 1994 he wrote from New Zealand, '*DOST* must be finished somehow, and I very much hope that the means to do this by the year 2000 can be found'. Alexander Fenton, Chairman of the Friends, has also urged completion during that year (Ibid.).

Completion by 2000 thus became a cornerstone in the recommendations of the

Review. However, it was unanimously agreed that the volumes of *DOST* to be published after the Review must maintain the quality of those published before. The solution proposed in 1981, where the *DOST* entries would depend for their content and structure on those of *OED*, was not acceptable. It was hoped that the time saving required on the production side would be made largely by employing a data-entry agency to key the edited copy from slips. An extended trial conducted with SPI (Technologies) Ltd demonstrated the practicality of this approach and a contract covering the keying and three phases of corrections for some 180,000 citation slips (in the event the number ran to 204,000) was agreed. Although SPI is based in Manila in the Philippines and all the work was done there, the company's European technical and marketing office was in Irvine in Ayrshire. This enabled a close liaison to develop between the two organisations, and the effectiveness of SPI's contribution with regard to quality in relation to efficiency of production cannot be overstated. An important consequence of keying the material at a relatively early stage in the process was the capacity gained to sort the quotations electronically. The extensive verification of the quotation material required prior to publication was greatly expedited by the capacity to check all the quotations from a single text at the same time. However, the challenge of speeding up the editing still remained. The editors' response to the Review document, made in September 1994, indicates how they saw this:

> We have carefully addressed the specific points made by the Review and our responses will demonstrate to all those interested in the future of *DOST* our commitment to drive the project in a new direction to achieve completion by the end of the year 2000. (Dareau et al. 1994)

It was clear to the editorial team that there was no time to waste. As soon as the editing of S was completed in August 1994 a calculation was made, dividing the time available by the work to be done. This gave a figure of eighteen days as the time available for editing each half drawer of the eighty-four drawers of raw slips for T–Z. This crude calculation gave the target to aim at and the rate of editing to be sustained over the six-year period to 2000. (Previously, a similar amount of editing might have taken thirty or more days.) New editing guidelines were tested throughout August and September. The editors' response to the Review included a statement of what would be required if the 2000 deadline were to be met:

> To complete the fascicles of T–Z by 2000 we must edit two fascicles per year. This means one fascicle every eighteen months for each Editor. At present we are testing the hypothesis that this is possible by editing the first part of T in the fashion outlined above. By the second week of November when the period we have given ourselves for this test is up we should each have edited a sizeable sample of untouched material. If we can do this, and at present we believe we are on target,

then we can claim with assurance that we can achieve the desired end
date. (Ibid.)

There was certainly very little slack in the system, but some benefits arose from
suggestions made in the Review, namely that a Project Manager be appointed to
maintain an overview of the progress of the project as a whole; a production
schedule devised; and a system of performance indicators, assessment and
feedback adhered to. By the end of 1994, Professor William Gillies of the
Department of Celtic, University of Edinburgh, had been appointed Project
Manager. William Aitken, Secretary of the Joint Council and formerly Director
of Management Information Services in the University of Edinburgh, took on
responsibility for the budget. The production schedule drawn up by staff was
monitored and refined in collaboration with Aitken, who drew up a monthly, and
towards the end of the project, weekly, schedule. This operation demonstrated to
the Joint Council and the Universities that the demanding targets set in 1994 were
in fact being achieved. Aitken was also responsible for overseeing the increased
computing aspects of the project, while he and Gillies looked after much of the
day-to-day management of the project including fund-raising, thus freeing the
editors to concentrate fully on the editorial task.

The quality and size of the team were also critical. It consisted of the three full-
time editors and one full-time and two part-time editorial assistants (Eileen
Finlayson, Heather Bree and Marjorie McNeill). The team combined size and
experience to a greater degree than at any time in the past. The importance of
experience had been stressed by A. J. Aitken in a letter to McIntosh in 1980:

Some remarks [were made] . . . that one could buy three or more junior
editors for the price of two seniors and that younger people worked
faster than older. The implication of the former and the fact of the
latter are untrue in the context of *DOST* (or any other similar
dictionary, such as *MED*), at least if any regard at all is given to
quality. More experienced persons in fact produce acceptable results
much faster, because they already know much the junior has to find out
ad hoc, because they are more skilled at analysis and at the devising of
definitions and because they have confidence in their findings where a
junior hesitates and vacillates. (*DOST* Archive)

In 1996 a follow-up Review took place. Its outcome is summarised in the report
drawn up by the Review Panel, Professor Emeritus R. E. Asher (University of
Edinburgh) and Professor A. A. MacDonald (University of Groningen):

The high-level objectives of this review were to establish whether the
changes recommended by the previous review in 1994 had been
implemented and, in consequence, whether the target of completion in

2000 is likely to be achieved. The reviewers report that they were most favourably impressed with the progress made by the members of the DOST Team since 1994, and are pleased to state with confidence that:

1. the dictionary is now likely to be completed on time and,

2. the high quality of scholarship can be maintained throughout the remaining stages.

The Conclusion to this Review was as follows:

The reviewers found that the actions taken in response to the recommendations of the 1994 Review had been very effective. They were impressed by the realistic and constructive attitude of the staff and management of the project, both in terms of morale and commitment. The target for completion of *DOST* remains 2000. The reviewers believe this is an achievable target and, further, that this should include publication of one volume per year with the final volume appearing in 2000. This would be a most commendable monument to Scottish scholarship. (*DOST* Archive)

As a result of this Review the Universities affirmed their willingness to fund the project to completion. The funding situation was also eased when in 1999 the Management Team secured a grant of £155,000 from the Arts and Humanities Research Board (AHRB) and one of £34,000 from the Heritage Lottery Fund.

The punishing rate of editing was maintained from 1994–2000 but the internal structure of cross-referencing of variant spellings and the interdependency of U, V and W meant that the publishing schedule of one volume per year could not be adhered to. Volume VIII (Ru–Sh) was published in 2000. Editing was completed in early December 2000 and all copy for volumes IX–XII dispatched to OUP by mid-July 2001. Volumes IX and X were published in 2001 and XI and XII in 2002.

CLOSING REMARKS

From 1953 the work of the dictionary was carried on at 27 George Square, Edinburgh. Whilst support from all the participating universities (Aberdeen, Dundee, Edinburgh, Glasgow, St Andrews and Stirling) showed a generous and genuinely national effort, Edinburgh as the host university and employing institution also supplied support for the day-to-day needs of the project. The premises in George Square, charged at a rental well below commercial rates, ensured security of tenure and the many benefits of working in an academic environment with ready access to colleagues and services such as the Library and Computing Services. Most significant was the support from *DOST*'s nearest neighbour, the School of Scottish Studies, whose staff proved valued colleagues. From 1988 to 1992 the Director of the School, Professor John MacQueen, was Convener of the Joint Council, and his successor, Professor Alexander Fenton, was a founder, Honorary Secretary and Treasurer of the Friends of *DOST*. The Director during *DOST*'s final years, Dr Margaret A. Mackay, continued the tradition, always giving generous support not only to the work of the Dictionary but also to its staff as colleagues over the years of her tenure and especially in their more recent initiatives to find a future role for Scottish lexicography.

As completion approached, both the *DOST* team and the Joint Council gave thought to what would come next. A Colloquium of representatives of *DOST*'s user groups was asked to contribute to a discussion of where Scottish lexicography should direct its efforts at the beginning of the twenty-first century. These meetings, which received a warm response from a number of groups involved in the study of language and linguistics as well as related subjects in Scotland, led to a proposal for an Institute for the Languages of Scotland. This was conceived as an enabling agency which would foster work on many levels and within all the languages that are or have been contributors to Scotland's culture. It received wide support and remains an aspiration, so that the co-operation that is clearly desired by participants in so many fields can find suitable expression.

In a more local initiative a Liaison Group was set up to explore the possibility of integrating the data contained in *DOST* and *SND*. As a result of its deliberations, an application was made to the AHRB for funding to digitise *DOST* and *SND*. The successful outcome of this bid enabled the initiation of a joint project to make *DOST* and *SND* available in electronic form on the World Wide Web. This project (2001–4), carried out at the University of Dundee, allows easy access for anyone with an internet connection to the dictionaries as they are, and will facilitate revision, leading, we may hope, to the eventual creation of an integrated *Dictionary of the Scots Language* from the earliest times to the present.

It is fitting to pay tribute at this point to the Scottish Arts Council (SAC), which supported both *DOST* and *SND* and warmly encouraged their coming together. SAC's recognition of the national importance of Scotland's languages was a major influence in a strategy which led in 2002 to the inception of Scottish Language Dictionaries Limited, the body now responsible for the dictionaries and the furtherance of Scottish lexicography, and active in a wide variety of language support measures.

Thus it is with the sense of coming full circle that Craigie's letter to Grant is recollected. Craigie had hoped that *DOST* and *SND*, although dealing with the language in different ways, might be organised so as to allow the connections between the older language and the modern to be clarified. The developments now envisaged surely offer the best prospect for fulfilling Craigie's vision, and, although he could not imagine the unity of *DOST* and *SND* in 1916 at the point of their conception, such an outcome would no doubt have given him enormous satisfaction.

NOTES

1. Material from this section is included in Dareau (2002b) and in *DOST* XII, pp. ix–xix.
2. For a more detailed history of editorial policy see 'Editorial Philosophy', *DOST* XII, pp. xx–xxviii. For the editors, see the biographies in this volume.
3. George Watson joined the Clarendon Press in 1907 and worked as an assistant on *OED* till its completion, when he went to the University of Chicago as an Assistant Professor working with Craigie on *DOST* and the *Dictionary of American English*.
4. This phrase was used by Lesley Brown in her recommendations to the Review panel in 1994: 'that the *DOST* staff be fully apprised of the true grimness of the financial position'.
5. See The DOST Corpus, *DOST* XII, pp. clxiii–clxxiv.
6. See list of Funding Organisations, *DOST* XII, p. cclvii.

CHAPTER 4

'There is Nothing Like a Good Gossip': Baptism, Kinship and Alliance in Early Modern Scotland

Jane E. A. Dawson, University of Edinburgh

'There is nothing like a good gossip': the modern meaning conjures up the image of two neighbours talking over the garden fence or women on the telephone to their female friends.[1] The emphasis is upon the verb and the 'crack' which is taking place and very often the image is linked to that of a nosy female minding someone else's business! In early modern Scotland, by contrast, the word is usually found as a noun describing a person, often male and used within the context of social and political power. The complexities of the term 'gossip' created a problem whilst I was editing the *Campbell Letters 1559–83*. I was having difficulty identifying which two men were signing themselves and addressing each other as 'gossip' in a series of interesting letters written in the winter of 1565–6. The *Dictionary of the Older Scottish Tongue* provided the key definitions of the term 'gossip' as employed in Scotland during the early modern period, noting it referred both to people and to their relationships (s.v. *gossop, gossoprie*). The dictionary also offered a range of interesting references which linked the 'band of gossiprie' to bonds of manrent and so provoked me to start an investigation of these connections. Thanks in part to the *DOST* definitions, the two gossips in the *Campbell Letters* were identified as Colin Campbell, sixth laird of Glenorchy, and his friend and kinsman, John Campbell, Captain of Carrick Castle.[2] The tone and content of the letters clearly demonstrated there was a strong personal link between the two clansmen. A contract signed ten years before the letters had been written revealed that in the event of Colin's death, Carrick would have acted as one of the protectors for his wife and family.[3] However, it has not been possible to establish whether either man had acted as a godparent for the other's children or whether their parents had done so, thus making them 'font siblings'. In this instance it is not clear whether the term 'gossip' was describing a relationship created by godparenthood or more loosely used to indicate a close personal friendship.

In *DOST*, as in the *Oxford English Dictionary* (*OED*), the main definition of *gossip* refers to a person, the godparent or *god sib*, 'who has contracted spiritual affinity with another by acting as a sponsor at a baptism' (*OED*). As its core meaning, *gossip* was the godparent, covering either the godfather or godmother, who entered into a spiritual kinship with the godchild and his/her family at the sacrament of baptism. In the late medieval period, godparents played a very important role in the christening service. At the font they sponsored and named the child, took vows on his/her behalf and received the newly-baptised infant from the priest.[4] As well as playing a central role in the ritual, they were expected to continue to act on the godchild's behalf throughout their life, ensuring s/he knew the Apostles' Creed and the Lord's Prayer. In particular, they became the protectors and patrons of the child, smoothing his/her way in society.[5] To assist with this social nurture and to provide general support to the family, it was common to have a considerable number of male and female godparents. For both the parents and the child, the godparenting link offered an opportunity publicly to extend their kin group or reinforce existing ties within it.[6]

Baptism was the key socialising rite of passage for the individual child, introducing him/her as a new entrant to the Church and to the community, which in this period and context were understood to be co-terminous.[7] It was also an important event for the family and bloodkin, because the sacrament created a new type of kinship through the godparenting relationship which ran alongside and often overlapped with existing blood or marriage ties.[8] At the time of the christening, the kin group proclaimed its corporate existence and its place within society. The celebrations which followed the church service were the public demonstration of the solidarity of this newly enlarged kindred. The central importance of godparents is further indicated by the existence of a 'gossipis dance', which was probably a feature of the celebrations. There was also a 'gossip cup' which included making a toast, presumably to the child and her/his future.[9]

During the later medieval period, the social function and importance of godparenthood was regarded as flowing naturally from the sacrament. However, after the Scottish Reformation the Kirk held a different view of baptism. It regarded this sacrament as first and foremost an ecclesiastical initiation, the entry of the child into the fellowship of the faithful. By insisting that all baptisms be conducted 'in the face of the congregation', the Kirk retained and even strengthened the communal dimension of a christening. But the emphasis was exclusively upon entry into the spiritual community of the Church, rather than into the kin-based society. One consequence of this new understanding of baptism was a challenge to the traditional role of the godparents. The Kirk attempted to diminish their status and the part they played in the service, shifting the focus to the natural parents, especially the father who presented his child in church. Rather than major participants, godparents became witnesses to the sacrament. There was also a long struggle to reduce the number of godparents, which settled on the compromise of a maximum of four godfathers and four godmothers.[10] As in many areas where the theology ran counter to the perceived social need provided by a church practice, the Kirk was only partially successful in enforcing its interpretation upon everyone.[11] The continued use of the word 'gossip' is testimony that many of the old assumptions continued. As late as the nineteenth century in the Hebrides, it was normal for the first or chief witness at a christening to share their name with the child, indicating how practice and the understanding of its meaning had been adapted to conform to the demands of kinship.[12]

During the christening and for the general designation of godparent no gender distinction was made, with both godmother and godfather being equally godsibs or gossips. However, by the sixteenth century there appears to have been a split between Scots and English in the linguistic usage of the term 'gossip', especially when referring to the relationship between the natural and the god parent. In England, the word *gossip* became more closely associated with the godmother, her relationship with the natural mother and by extension with a range of specifically female activities. In particular, it was linked to the female friends who gathered during a mother's lying-in and were present at the birth of the child.[13] Men were normally excluded from the birth-room, which was traditionally regarded as a female area staffed by midwives assisted by other women. At the end of the mother's confinement, a similar group of female companions would accompany the mother in procession to the church for her 'churching', usually forty days after the birth. As that ritual of purification and thanksgiving often took place some time after the christening, it was not unusual for the natural mother to have been absent from her child's baptism. She would have relied upon her gossips to report the proceedings to her. By the middle of the sixteenth century in England the word *gossip* had been firmly linked to women and female chatter, producing the meaning which is dominant today.[14] This connection is illustrated graphically in an English print of c. 1600 entitled 'Tittle Tattle or the Several Branches of Gossiping', which shows women meeting and swapping news in a variety of social settings.[15]

By contrast, in Scots 'gossip' was more likely to refer to the godfather and to male activities. This was because there was another word 'cummer/commere' (from French *commère*) to describe a godmother. In his *Memoirs*, Sir James Melville of Halhill referred to the two terms, explaining that using *gossip* about a godmother was an English usage (Thomson 1827: 159; *DOST*). His observation can be confirmed by the clear gender distinction present in the terminology employed by the St Andrews Kirk Session when it recorded those present at an irregular baptism in 1566. The two men were described as 'gossopis' and the woman as 'cummer'.[16] In the more general sense of a very close friend, many of the references noted by *DOST* relate to men and 'gossip' was a common form of address between men in their correspondence.[17]

As *DOST* notes, closely connected to 'gossip' as a person, was the 'band of gossiprie', covering the relationships flowing from godparenthood. At the baptism a series of vertical and horizontal relationships was created. The primary vertical tie was the kinship between the godparent and the godchild, which lasted throughout their lives.[18] Such a spiritual kinship was as real and permanent as a blood tie. Having been created as a consequence of the working of divine grace bestowed through the sacrament, it did not depend upon human will or intention either for its inception or for its continuation. This was precisely why it was valued so highly. In the eyes of the Church and of society spiritual kinship brought similar obligations to blood kinship. The most striking example of the closeness and permanence of this affinity was that under canon law a godparent and godchild were prohibited from marrying, at least without a dispensation.[19]

In addition, there were two categories of horizontal tie. One encompassed the links between the godchild and his/her 'font siblings', the children of the godparents. They became a parallel set of brothers and sisters who could form a peer group for the future. However, at the time of the christening the most significant horizontal tie was forged between the godparents and the natural parents. A baptism offered a perfect opportunity for alliances to be made or cemented between different kin groups. The bond of *compaternitas* or co-parenthood was superior to, and distinct from, other forms of alliance because the sacrament provided the occasion and the means to sanctify such an alliance. Sacramental grace transformed the status of the child and his/her relationship with the community. As a consequence, it created ties of kinship and affinity between the godparents and the godchild, and by extension between the god-parents and the child's blood kin. It was this special sacramental dimension which gave such substance and durability to alliances made between natural and god parents. Being formed by divine grace and not human power, such ties were permanent. To break them was to risk divine as well as human sanctions.[20]

The seriousness with which society regarded the ties binding gossips was reflected in the terms in which a breach was described. In Scotland flouting the obligations of being a good gossip was a shocking offence and one which provoked comment and condemnation. It provided the framework for one of the most famous betrayals in Scottish history. Blind Harry's great poem on William Wallace retold the story of his hero's tragic fate. The poet was careful to point out on several occasions that Sir John Menteith and Wallace had been gossips, which made Menteith's betrayal even more heinous.[21] For late medieval people treachery to one's kin was as bad, if not worse, than treason to one's country. They assumed that whilst in this life such actions brought opprobrium, in the next they merited lasting punishment.

Although conscious of the eternal consequences of the kinship created at baptism, the main focus was normally the immediate situation. A christening was a chance to forge new alliances, cement established ones or make peace between feuding kin groups.[22] The use of the sacrament of marriage as the basis for alliance and peacemaking is well known. By comparison, baptism, which per-formed the same function, has been neglected. Such peacemaking could operate at the highest level. In 1566 at the christening of Prince James, Queen Elizabeth of England was invited to be his godmother. Among other considerations, this request was a formal move to reconcile Scotland and England after the complete breakdown in diplomatic relations following Mary Queen of Scots' marriage to Lord Darnley. The gesture of friendship was accepted and Elizabeth appointed Mary's half-sister Jane, Countess of Argyll, as her proxy for the ceremony.[23] James Melville, the diplomat sent to the English court, recorded, 'I requested her Majesty to be a gossip to the Queen' (*DOST*).[24] His phrasing demonstrates that at this juncture it was the present relationship between Mary and Elizabeth which was uppermost in everyone's mind, rather than the future one which James might enjoy with the English Queen.[25]

There were overwhelming advantages to reinforcing alliances between kin-groups by becoming 'gossips'. However desirable, such an alliance might be prevented by the practical problem of finding an unbaptised child. With christening normally following within weeks of the birth, the window of opportunity to become gossips was short! One solution was akin to a pre-nuptial contract, the signing of an agreement to become gossips once a child was available. In 1520 John Campbell of Cawdor and Alexander MacDonald of Dunivaig made a bond of manrent. They also agreed to complete the 'fynal concord' of their alliance 'quhat tym or howyr God sendis thame ony barnys that thae sal baptys the barn and be gossepis and aye and quhil the sayd gossepry be compleyttyt the sayd Sir Johne and Alexander sal keip leyl trewe and affald part to oderis as it var complettyt' (Innes 1859: 134; Wormald 1985: 255 [Cawdor 11]). The reference made to mutual loyalty created by gossipry and the obligations which gossips had one to another is clarified in a later letter of maintenance given by Cawdor to Alexander MacLeod of Dunvegan. It was agreed that 'quhen ewyr the caus iniuris to eithyr of us the saidis parteis fulfill the band of Gossaprie quhen ony of us beis chargit be uder party in stied and lawte as Gossapis suld do'.[26] The 'band of gossaprie' was here assumed to encompass all the obligations of blood kinship and a bond of manrent.

On occasion the parties did not choose to wait for a baptism. They could adopt the alternative solutions of fosterage or adoption, which also placed a child as the focus around which an alliance could be constructed.[27] Although the alliance lost the sanctification which the sacrament of baptism bestowed, these practices had strong social or legal obligations attached to them to underpin an alliance. Fostering, when a child was raised by another family, was widely practised, especially within Gaelic society.[28] Its prime function was to create alternative kindred for the child. With succession often depending upon besting one's closest relatives, it was recognised that being surrounded by the immediate family and blood kin was not necessarily the safest place for a noble child!

From a more positive perspective, fostering was viewed as a method of integrating the different branches or social levels within a clan. It also generated a much closer bond and a higher level of loyalty for the fosterling. One of many Gaelic proverbs on the foster bond sums up the relationship: 'A man's relation is beloved of him, but his foster sibling is as the pith of his heart'.[29] As with the gossip relationships of baptism, the kinship created between the natural and foster parents was also of importance. Without the permanency bestowed by the sacramental action, it was more subject to the vicissitudes of human alliances. The needs of the fosterling could on occasion be subordinated or sacrificed to the demands of the political relationship between the natural and foster parents. For example, Colin, the natural son of the 5th earl of Argyll, had been withdrawn from the foster care of Donald Gorm MacDonald of Sleat when Argyll and Sleat had fallen out and was only returned to Skye after Donald Gorm had been restored to the earl's good graces.[30]

It is noticeable, especially from the abundant evidence available from Campbell sources, that gossiprie was being expanded to include a wide range of alliances and relationships which focused upon a child through godparenting, fostering and adoption.[31] Such alliances were an essential part of late medieval and early modern Scottish society, as the general practice of bonds of manrent clearly demonstrates.[32] The formal adoption of a child was a similar practice to fostering, though it was formed within a legal framework with a heavy emphasis upon the terms of the contract. The adopted child did not necessarily go to live with his/her new family, though the legal absorption into that family was of crucial importance. In particular, it gave the adopted child inheritance rights, specifically the 'bairn's part' on the death of the adoptive parents. The legal language of adoption was frequently employed in the bonds made by the Campbells of Glenorchy. With the Glenorchy family also following the Gaelic practice of fostering their children, there is a problem distinguishing which relationship was really meant in such bonds. It is clear that this branch of the Campbells sometimes employed adoption simply as a device to secure a 'bairn's part' from some of their dependents, thereby increasing their own territories and regional control. When all parties to the bond were adults, this produced some bizarre scenes. Although in these cases the 'adoption' was purely a legal fiction to serve another end, the symbolic ritual which accompanied adoption was still enacted. In 1538 when John Cambell of Glenorchy was well into his forties, John MacGillespie took him upon his knee and called him his adopted son (Innes 1855: 182–3; Wormald 1985: 206 [Breadalbane 5]). In these and similar Glenorchy bonds, although the legal language remained, a child had ceased being the focus for an alliance which was itself reduced to a method of control and exploitation.

The central importance of alliances and the networks they produced is reinforced when Scotland's experience of gossiprie is compared to that of the Irish. Information concerning gossiprie was recorded in an attempt to explain to the incoming English and the government in London the different set of social customs which prevailed in Ireland. In Scotland, by contrast, where gossiprie was an accepted custom, there was no need to produce such an analysis nor any call to write it down. In a tract written in Ireland during 1598 by an anonymous author with the initials 'H. C.', the fourth book covers 'matters concerning the common weal of the country', including information about fostering and gossiprie.[33] The different types of fostering and gossiprid/gossipraed (the English equivalent of *gossiprie*) were treated as variants of the same basic custom.

The description in the tract was given in the form of notes upon a narration by an old man from the English Pale who characterised gossiprid as 'a moste pestylent monster to a common wealth' (Fitzsimmons 2001: 147). It received such a damning description precisely because gossiprid created deep and binding ties. They were sufficiently strong to overcome the profound racial divide within Ireland between Palesmen and Gaels. In the old man's opinion, these bonds had a devastating effect upon the security and cohesion of the Pale because they destroyed the racial unity of the English which had been their strength. In the past the Pale could not be broken because all the English had remained bound together, like a sheaf of arrows, individually fragile but strong when bound as one. Now, the old man lamented, the ties of gossiprid between Palesmen and Gaels had snapped that unity.

During the frequent military campaigns against the Irish Gaelic chiefs many Palesmen would make the fatal mistake of hesitating in the midst of battle. Their singleness of purpose was undermined because they would pause to consider 'how to make choyce of our enemies to fight with, many of them being our fosterers, gossips and allies' (Fitzsimmons 2001: 149). The ties of gossiprid had removed the simple boundaries between the two races leaving a complete confusion over who was a friend and who an enemy. From the perspective of the elderly Palesman, gossiprid was the fundamental cause for the dissolution of the deep, and to him essential, division between the two cultures within Ireland.

The old man had listed four methods by which ties of gossiprid were created: the font stone, or baptism; partaking of the eucharist together; breaking bread together, and lastly voluntary oaths. All incorporate sacramental or quasi-sacramental actions invoking divine power to create the new relationship of kinship or at least witness its formation. The sanctity of their setting allowed alliances to be made across the racial divide, overcoming the normal obstacles between the English and the Gaels. On the strength of such bonds, the elderly Palesman argued that the Gaelic Irish were able to demand protection, patronage and mutual support from their English allies. This broke down divisions between the two societies, in particular encouraging the learning of the Gaelic language in the Pale. An irresistible pressure also built up for intermarriage between Gaelic and English families. This, in turn, led to an intermingling of the races which the old man scathingly referred to as 'a confusion of septs'.[34]

From the Scottish perspective, the Irish evidence is important because it allows the workings of gossiprie to be revealed more starkly than in the relatively homogeneous Scottish situation. In both countries the band of gossiprie produced the same result; it could forge alliances of great strength and durability which were prized because they were able to overcome seemingly insurmountable obstacles.

Even when the obstacles were relatively minor, the resulting networks were of immense importance. The networks which lay at the heart of the social and cultural world of Edinburgh have been uncovered by Theo van Heijnsbergen's fascinating prosopographical study of the circle surrounding the Bannatynes. At the centre of this circle was the group who acted as godparents for the Bannatynes.[35] The preservation of the book listing these gossips is most unusual. It offers a tantalising reminder of those fundamental relationships which early modern Scots took so much for granted and about which so little is now known.

By the sixteenth century the term 'gossip' had stretched to cover a variety of people and their relationships, as can be seen in the quotations which *DOST* has gathered demonstrating the word's use in Scotland. Following Humpty Dumpty's famous definition, 'gossip' in early modern Scotland had become a 'portmanteau word', with two meanings packed up into one. With *DOST*'s help it has been possible to look inside the portmanteau of 'gossip' and begin to upack it, revealing a variety of new items which deserve more attention from scholars.[36] On the subject of 'gossip' we need to follow Humpty Dumpty's practice. 'That is a great deal to make one word mean', Alice said in a thoughtful tone. 'When I make a word do a lot of work like that,' said Humpty Dumpty, 'I always pay it extra.' 'Gossip' in early modern Scotland needs to be paid extra attention!

NOTES

1. This work-in-progress paper was presented to the Conference of Scottish Medievalists, Pitlochry, 5–6 January 2002, which celebrated the completion of *DOST*. I am grateful to those present for helpful comments, questions and suggestions, some of which were incorporated into the version printed in *Review of Scottish Culture* 15 (2002–3), pp. 88–95 (*ROSC*). It is reprinted here by kind permission of the editors of *ROSC*.
2. For details of Colin Campbell of Glenorchy and the 'gossip' letters, see Dawson 1997: 14–20.
3. Carrick acted as a witness to the contract between Lord Lorne (the future 5th earl of Argyll), Colin Campbell of Glenorchy and Katherine Ruthven his wife, in which Katherine was appointed the guardian of her children. Carrick and the other witnesses, all senior kinsmen of Colin and Katherine, would have been expected to protect and support Katherine. Contract, 8 April 1555, in Campbell and Paton 1913–22: VI, 1–2.
4. For a description of late medieval practice and the changes brought by Protestant and Catholic reformers see Bossy 1984a: 194–201; Hillerbrand 1996: II, 180–1.
5. In this context godparents were closely associated with the patronage of name saints, (Bossy 1977: 119–37; 1984a: 196).
6. See Bossy 1973: 129–43; 1984: 197–9.
7. In this study a comparison with early medieval practice has not yet been undertaken. In the time of the Church's expansion into non-Christian lands and in those instances where baptism was the consequence of adult conversion to the faith, the kinship relationships thus formed were rather different; see Lynch 1986.

8. In Scotland godparenthood seems to have taken precedence over distant kin ties as shown in the forms of address where 'gossip' was used to reinforce or supplement 'cousin', *DOST* in n. 17 below and cf. Bossy 1984a: 198.

9. For the dance see *DOST*, citing *Complaint of Scotland* 'thai dancit . . . fut befor, gossep'. For the cup see *OED*, citing Hart's *Diet of Diseased* (1633) where it was described as 'a cup of good ale, with some nutmegg, suger, and a tost, a good gossip cup I confesse'. At present I have few details on either dance or cup and would be grateful for further information.

10. For e.g. 29 June 1584 the St Andrews Kirk Session inveighed against 'the abuse enterit in the ower gret number of witnes or gossopis' (*RSTAKS*; Fleming 1889–90; II, lxxxviii–ix, 533). St Andrews attempted to keep the witnesses down to two or three, or at most two from each gender, but in 1626 the Order for Baptism had to concede four of each gender (*DOST*). The medieval Church had unsuccessfully tried to restrict the number of godparents, with concerns being raised at the Council of Basle in 1432 that the institution was getting out of hand. In a parallel move to the Protestant reformers, the Council of Trent also made strenuous efforts to reduce godparents to a single pair (Bossy 1984a: 195, 199–200).

11. For post-Reformation christening customs see the illuminating study by Margo Todd (2002), ch. 2.

12. I am grateful to David Sellar for this observation concerning later Hebridean practice. The patron saint, the third member of the name link in late medieval times (see above n. 5) had obviously gone, but the 'gossip' ties remained.

13. *OED* gives the quotation from Fuller's *Worthies* of 1661, 'They are as good evidence to prove where they were born, as if we had the deposition of the midwife, and all the gossips present at their mothers labours.'

14. *OED* gives a quotation from c. 1560, 'She is to her gossypes gone to make mery.'

15. See Fox 2000: Plate 6. The French term *commèrage* evolved in a similar way to 'gossip' (Bossy 1984a: 197).

16. 4 December 1566, *RSTAKS* I, 284.

17. For example *DOST* notes 'My lord and belowit gossep', from the *Waus Correspondence* and 'Your lordshopis loving cousin and gosseip' from the Elphinstone Family book. As well as the series of 'gossip' letters between Carrick and Glenorchy, George Johnson (alias MacGregor) signed himself to Glenorchy as 'your Masteris servant and gossaip' (Dawson 1997: 236).

18. The almost exclusive emphasis upon the religious role of the godparent, to supervise the education of the child in Christian beliefs and values, was a later development. The 'spiritualisation' of the godparent was an attempt by both Roman Catholic and Protestant reformers to distance baptism from its overtly social function in late medieval Europe (Bossy 1984a: 199–200; 1984b: 14–19). A vertical tie was also created between the priest and the child.

19. This in fact ran counter to one of the social functions of godparenting, that of providing for a suitable spouse for the child. In many Mediterranean countries it had been the practice to include children among the godparents with just such an aim in mind (Bossy 1984a: 198). For illuminating discussions of marriage customs, especially in Gaelic Scotland, and of the forbidden degrees see Sellar 1978–80: 464–93; 1995: 59–82.

20. Bossy described the model of *compaternitas* 'as a relation of formal amity, entailing honesty, absolute mutual trust and obligatory assistance, a sacred and specifically Christian relationship, an ideal to which natural kinship aspires but perhaps rarely attains' (1984a: 197).

21. *DOST* cites of Menteith 'Wallace his gossop was' and 'twys before had his gossep beyn'.
22. For feuds see Brown 1986; Wormald 1980: 54–97.
23. The Countess was subsequently in trouble with the General Assembly for participating in a baptism according to Roman Catholic rites (Thomson 1839–45: I, 114, 117).
24. The Secret Council sent out invitations to all the Scottish nobility to come to the baptism to act as 'witnesses and gossips' (Burton et al. 1877–1970: I, 485; Lynch 1990: 1–21).
25. This did not prevent the adult James VI reminding Elizabeth of his spiritual kinship with her, whenever it suited him.
26. 10 November 1533 (Innes 1859: 159; Wormald 1985: 56 [Cawdor 19]).
27. Another relationship which often had a child (at least in the legal sense) at its centre, was ward, marriage and relief. Being a feudal obligation which was frequently transferred by financial transactions or via patronage, this did not have the same connection with forming alliances between equal partners. However, wardship could create important relationships and provides information concerning the political networks of early modern Scotland. I am grateful to Margaret Sanderson for her perceptive remarks on this topic.
28. This ancient tradition was being regulated in the early Irish law texts of the seventh and eighth centuries.
29. 'Is caomh le fear a charaid, ach is e smior a chridhe a chomhdhalta' (Newton 2000: 122).
30. Bond between Argyll and Sleat, 21 April 1571, Argyll Transcripts (made by Niall 10th duke of Argyll, copies in Argyll MSS at Inveraray Castle and Dept. of Scottish History, Glasgow University), VI, 160–2; Wormald 1985: 186 [Argyll 44]; Dawson 2002: 207.
31. Because they were great creators, collectors and preservers of written records, Clan Campbell archives provide the richest source of information about Highland society during the early modern period (Dawson 1997: 1–2, 20–2).
32. For the seminal discussion of bonds see Wormald 1985.
33. The following discussion relies upon Fitzsimmons 2001: 138–49 [extracts from H. C.'s tract 144–9].
34. This was the 'degeneracy' which had been the fear of the English in Ireland throughout the medieval period provoking the Statutes of Kilkenny in 1366 to legislate against any alliance between the English and the Irish by 'marriage, gossiprid [and] fostering' (Fitzsimmons 2001: 144, 146).
35. On networks, see, for example, van Heijnsbergen (1994). I am grateful to Alasdair MacDonald for reminding me of the godparenting link. Studies of godparenthood in England and other parts of Europe have been able to investigate the composition of such networks; see brief summary in Hillerbrand 1996: 180–1.
36. Godparenting in England is the subject of an important study by W. Coster (Coster 2002). Unfortunately, this book was published too late for its findings to be incorporated into this article.

CHAPTER 5

'Wyne Confortative': Wine in Scotland from the Thirteenth till the Eighteenth Centuries

Alexander Fenton, European Ethnological Research Centre, National Museums of Scotland

INTRODUCTION

This paper examines the history of the drinking of wine in Scotland as an exercise in using entries in the *Dictionary of the Older Scottish Tongue*. Wine is not native to Scotland and so had to be imported as an object of trade. It was expensive, and remained as a drink of the better off until surprisingly recent times. As a personal reminiscence, I remember the very unflattering reception given in the 1950s to a bottle of claret that I brought from France to a croft in the north-east of Scotland. There, the expected drinks were beer and whisky for men, and sherry for the women. Wine was found on the tables of the professional classes, though not necessarily with any degree of regularity, and in the homes of the lairds. There has now been a revolution in wine drinking. The influence of travel, of programmes on the radio and television, of articles in women's books and magazines, of eating out, and of the easy availability of wines at relatively low prices, especially in supermarkets, which have a high percentage of the trade, have led to a great popular widening of the taste for wine, as part of the process of globalisation that marks the lives of everyone at the present day.

DOST deals with Scots up till the year 1700. However, in this paper, the story is continued up to the end of the eighteenth century in order to assess the situation immediately beyond the time-scale of the Dictionary. Details of more recent history can be found in, for example, Kay and Maclean's book, *Knee Deep in Claret* (Kay and Maclean 1985).

The title of this paper comes from a poem by William Dunbar (c. 1460–c. 1520), 'Dumbaris Dirige to the King', that is James IV, in which he jocularly contrasts the 'purgatory' of Stirling with the 'myrrie town' of Edinburgh, where could be got

> . . . the new fresche wyne
> That grew apone the revar of Ryne,

> Fresche fragrant clarets out of France,
> Off Angeo and of Orliance
> (Bawcutt 1998: I, 274–5)

By this date, the end of the fifteenth century, wine was an established item of trade in Scotland. There was a range of varieties from different parts of Europe, transported by sea in containers of different sizes, and subject to controls and payments that produced income for the burghs and the nation. Examination of the terminology in *DOST*, starting with 'wyne', can produce a remarkably detailed picture, which can then be filled out by consulting the numerous illustrative references provided under the dictionary entries.

EARLIER HISTORY

In Britain, wine was nothing new. The Romans were growing vines in the south of England in the early years of their occupation. The skills they had already developed in warmer climes are indicated by a writer such as Columella in the early first century AD. He listed a number of varieties of grapes for eating and for wine-making, related the resulting types and qualities of wine to soil and situation (level ground, whence quantity; hill-slopes, whence better quality), and examined the economics of vine-growing. Though vines in present-day vineyards are universally self-supporting, it is likely that those grown in England, as in Italy, were supported by stakes or props, of which there were numerous forms (White 1970: 241–2; White 1975: 119–23).

In the eighth century, the Venerable Bede reported the growing of vines in some places in Britain: 'vineas etiam quibusdam in locis germinans' (Plummer 1896: I, 10), and the Domesday Book of 1085–6 recorded just under forty vineyards in southern England (Wilson 1976: 294, 328–9). English wine production flourished for a time, but declined as close connections with France led to the import of cheap, plentiful and better quality wines from that quarter, particularly under Henry II (1133–89), who held the duchy of Normandy and was Count of Anjou, and added Poitou and Guienne to his lands in 1152 on marrying Eleanor of Aquitaine. Before that, wines had come mainly from the Moselle valley, the Rhineland and northern France; now great quantities started to come via Bordeaux from Gascony, Poitou, Burgundy and Languedoc. London was one of the chief trading points of the Hansa, and the merchants of Cologne were already selling wine there in the twelfth century. Indeed, Henry granted them in 1175–6 the same favourable conditions as the French for selling wine in England.

TWELFTH TO EARLY EIGHTEENTH CENTURIES

Wine reached Scotland also. The Assize of Wine in the Acts of the Parliament of Scotland, attributed to David I (1124–53), already sought to regulate retail prices in relation to wholesale prices, in such a way that 10 shillings on a tun gave 1d. on a gallon. This meant that 120 gallons of wine would sell at the price of a wholesale tun (Gemmill and Mayhew 1995: 215–16). By the mid-twelfth century it was being imported to Berwick for the use of Jedburgh Abbey, where it would have been an element in the Eucharist. It would have graced the Abbey's top table at meals, especially when distinguished guests were being received. It continued in use after the Reformation at the celebration of Holy Communion or the Lord's Supper. In the thirteenth century, French wine came from Normandy and Maine, then increasingly from Gascony by way of Bordeaux. By 1246 Perth merchants were recorded as having debts in that town and London vintners were selling wine in Scotland directly or through Scottish merchants such as John Rufus of Berwick (Duncan 1975: 508).

Though burgh regulations concerning taverns demonstrate that the selling of wine to those of the wider public who could afford it was carried on through these establishments, the major single customer was at first the royal household. This was also true of England, and of other countries to which wine had to be imported, such as Denmark, Norway and Sweden (*KLNM* 1976: XX, s.v. *vin, vinhandel*). In 1263, for example, Alexander III bought 178 tuns of wine, of which some was Gascon, and 67 tuns in 1264 (Duncan 1975: 509). Regular suppliers were established. The royal example made wine a prestige drink, and therefore something to be emulated by those who could afford it. The higher echelons of society could drink wine every day, and taverns in towns stood ready to satisfy a more occasional and socially wider demand, as and when supplies arrived in the trading vessels. This was a seasonal occurrence, since there were no preservatives to make the wine keep and the new vintage would turn sour after the first few months, after which unscrupulous vendors might use it to dilute fresh wine. They might also mix dearer with less expensive wines. In general, there was a broad class division, marked by the drinking of wine by the upper orders, of ale by the burghers and lairds, and of small beer by the commons (Innes 1867: lxxv).

Another aspect of wine consumption was that, since it was not always new and fresh, it might be drunk with spices, and probably also hot. Sugar was used with wine too: for example, the *Household Books of James VI and Anne* record sugar for His Majesty's sack in 1597. A posset made with sack, sugar and milk is mentioned in 1665, and in 1690, a pint of wine sack is paired with four ounces of sugar. The spicing and sweetening of wine may have been to disguise fading quality, but it is certain that the combinations also suited the taste of the period and may have been considered as having medicinal qualities. From at least the fifteenth century, spice and wine are frequently paired in the sources, and a new brother, on being elected to a guild, for example, was expected to provide wine and spice as well as a sum of money. In this kind of way, wine developed a secular as well as a sacramental function (*DOST*, s.v. *spice, spicery, succar*).

Because wine was expensive, partly because it did not keep, the burgesses took care to maintain a monopoly of the trade, and they themselves were subject to controls. For example, according to the Statuta Gilde for 1281, every burgess should give full 'drawage' for every cask of wine placed in his booth, put aboard ship or taken off a ship. For moving a cask from one cellar to another, he should pay 2½d., that is 1d. to the town and 1½d. as drink money. For a cask for his own drinking, he should pay 1d. in drink money (*Ancient Laws* 1868: 83–4). The less scrupulous, as ever, clearly found ways to extend profit, for regulations were made against selling wine without tasting, using measures that had not been approved, mixing good with 'corrupt' wine, and not sticking to the price set by the tasters. Not only was wine that was going off used to adulterate wine but also, according to a source referring to Edinburgh, milk, brimstone and other ingredients. To counteract fraud and maintain standards, tasters or 'cunnars' were appointed to check both wine and ale. They also set the prices, and were required to go through the town four times a year (as reported in 1571) to carry out their tests (*Ancient Laws* 1868: 145; *DOST*, s.v. *wyne, cunnar*).

Wine continued to be a favoured royal drink. It was regarded as a suitably valuable gift for presentation by one king to another. Louis XII of France sent 100 puncheons of new wine to James IV on 1 November 1512 (Bawcutt 1998: II, 492, nn. 55–8).

Wine came to play a role in royal etiquette. In his *Buke of the Governaunce of Princis*, 1456, Gilbert of the Haye gave advice on what a prince should know about wine and how he should behave in relation to it. The best, dry, wines, from sun-facing hill slopes, were not good for young men of hot blood or such as were of a choleric nature. Wines that were too sweet did not aid the digestion and engendered 'ventositeis' (flatulence). Medium sweetness wines, grown between the high and the low lands, were to be preferred; they had a good colour between red and yellow, this being described as 'claret wyne' (which was not then a red wine only). Such wine should be drunk in moderation, according to the age of the drinker, the time of year and the nature of the season. By aiding digestion they also aided mental well-being, though over-indulgence had the opposite effect (Glenn 1943: 107–8).

Churchmen too helped to keep the trade active. For instance, 'my Lord of Holyroodhous', Abbot Robert Bellenden, had four puncheons of the wine of Orleans shipped to him in the *Julyan* from Middleburgh in the Netherlands in February 1496, and two puncheons of claret wine were brought from there to the Archdeacon of St Andrews in the *Gylbert Edmeston* (Innes 1867: 15, 249).

Luxury items of this nature tended to reach Scotland from France and England, and later from the Low Countries. From the first half of the fourteenth century till the time of the French Revolution, a number of towns in the Low Countries, especially Flanders, acted as the Scottish staple or trading centre – Middleburgh, Bruges, Antwerp, Campvere (*DOST*, s.v. *stapill*; Innes 1867: liv–

lv). Through these centres, wine also reached Scotland: claret wine in 1495, malvoisie wine in 1493, Ryns wine and claret gaston in 1496, claret wine in 1499. The following table lists wines mentioned in *DOST*, though not all of them have been identified. Wherever possible, the first date of occurrence is given.

Table 5.1 Wines referred to in *DOST*

Name	First date	Source and description	Price
Allacant	1538	Spanish, from Alicante	
Amzerk	1556	s.v. *scherand*	pint, 10d.
Bastart	1457	Spanish, sweet	
Binzac	1553	s.v. *scherand*	
Boyane	1596	French, Beaune, s.v. *punschioune*	
Burdeaux	1552	French, Bordeaux	tun, £50 (1579); pint, 3s. (1580); pint, half a merk (1594)
Burdeous	1552	France, from Bordeaux	tun, £17 (1552); tun, £24 (a. 1578); pint, 5s. (a. 1578)
Canarie	1604–5	Canary Islands	
Chirrie seck	1661	Sherry	
Claret (wine)	1456	France, red	pint, 8d. (1517)
Frontiniac	1680	Frontignan, South France	
Hoypis	1553	?	
Hullok	1598	Spanish, red; Sp. *(h)aloque*	
Leaticke	1632	s.v. *wyne*	
Libnon	1553	?Lebanon	
Malaga	1612	Cf. sack	
Malvesy	1412	Malvasia, in the Morea	butt, £6. 16s. (1493); butt, £5. 15s. (1499); half gallon, 4s. (1508); pint, 30s. (1633); quart, 8s. 8d. (1554–5)
Muscade	1548		
Muscadel	1434	sweet	pint, 10s.
Muscaldella	1632		
Muscaldy	1513		gallon, 16s. (1513)
Musticat	a. 1578		
Nanse wine	1689	France, Nantes	chopin, 10s.
Osay	1426	Alsace, Auxois	pint, 2s. (1545–6)
Portaick wine	1680	Portuguese	chopin, 12s.
Ranische	1624	Rhenish	
Rinis	1654	Rhenish	
Rins	1468	Rhenish	quart, £34 (1488)
Romany	1531	of Greek origin	pint, 2s.
Sek	1608	Spanish, Canary Islands	white pipe, 10s. (1608); quart, £3. 4s. (1670); butt, £41. 15s. 6d. (1694)
Wine sek	1543/4	Spanish, dry	pint, 7/- (a. 1578); kag, £12. 4s.; pint, 10s. (1591); pint, 6s. 6d. (1574–5)

Rochell	1562–3	France, (La) Rochelle	
Tent	1376	Spanish, red, Sp. *tinto*	pint, 16s. (1609)
Turke	1475	Turkish	
Wormit wine	1662–3	flavoured with wormwood	mutchkin, 5s. (1680)

The following range of imported wines was listed for customs' purposes in 1612:

Impost to be payed for wynes brought in Scotland by Scottismen or Strangearis

Gascoigne and French wynes and all vther wynes of the Frenche Kingis Dominionis in Impost fer euery tun thairof Threttie sex pundis quhairof thair is to be rebatted to the marchand for his lekkage the tenth penny extending to thrie pundis tuelf shillingis sua restis to be ressauit frie to the Kingis Majesteis vse of euery tun . . . xxxii lib viii s.

Muscadels Maluaseis and all vther wyns of the grouth of the Levant seas in Impoist for euery tun thairof Thretty sex pundis quhairof thair is to be rebaitted to the merchand for his lekkage the tenth penny extending to thrie pundis tuelf shillingis sua restis frie to be ressauit to the Kingis Maiesteis vse of euery tun . . . xxxii lib viii s.

Sackes Canareis Malagas Maderais Romneyis Hullokis Bastards Teynts and Allacants in Impoist for euery tun or tuo pypes or butts thairof threttie sex pundis wherof thair is to be rebaitted to the merchand for lekkage the tenth penny extending to thrie pundis tuelf shillingis sua restis frie to be ressaued to His maiesteis vse of eueri tun . . . xxxii lib viii s.

Rhenish wyne the awme in Impoist . . . vi lib. (Innes 1867: 334–5)

Wine was transported or stored in a variety of containers and was sold according to various measures:

Table 5.2 Containers and measures for wine

Container	Date	Amount/description
Barrelkin	1583	
Barrikin	1567	
Bos	1380	Leather bottle for wine etc.
Bote	1426	Butt, cask
But(t)	1606	Equivalent to a 'sek'
Chapin	1646	Half a pint Scots
Chopin	1546	Half a pint Scots
Flaccon	1513	Flagon
Gallon	c. 1420	
Ham	1495	Between 37 and 41 gallons; Dutch *aam*
Hoghead	1490	'Westland hoget', 15 gallons
Hogsheid	1557–61	

Muchkin	1643	Quarter of a pint Scots
Pece	1581	Quarter of a tun
Pint	1384	
Pipe	1264	2 puncheons or 4 barrels
Punshion	1512–13	
Point	1488	
Rub(b)our	1373	5 gallons (1513); one gallon. Sp. *arroba*, liquid
Rude	1495	A measure of wine; Du. *roede*, rod for measuring the amount of wine in a cask or other container
Stoup	a1500	Quart and pint (1502)
Stek	1433–4	3 'ham' and 1 'strif' (1495)
Strif	1495	Rhenish wine, 1/24 of the Du. *aam*. A stek could variously hold 3 ham and one strif, 4 ham and 12 strif, or 4 ham and 18 strif (*DOST*, s.v. *strif, ham*; Innes 1867: 22, 25, 90)
Terce	1667–8	1/3 of a pipe
Tersell	1544	
Tertang	1447	24 gallons
Tre	1497	
Tun	1375	Equal to 2 butts, 2 pipes, 4 hogsheads, 6 tierces, 3 punchions or tertions, or 8 quarter casks.

Timber containers were subject to leakage, so an allowance was made for this in charging duty, stated in 1590 to amount to one tun in every ten. The quantity required to replace leaked contents was known as 'ullage' (*DOST*, s.v. *lekkage, ulage*).

Wine, as also ale, beer, brandy and mead, was sold in taverns run by burgesses or guild brethren. The personal name Taverner dates back to 1361, and women taverners were not uncommon by the mid-sixteenth century. Publicans and innkeepers were known as 'tappers', 'toppers', 'tapstars' or 'topsters', so called because they tapped or drew wine or ale from barrels for retailing purposes (*DOST*, s.v. *tapper, tap(p)ing, tapstar, tavern, tavernar*); this job too was frequently done by women. Wine and ale were often taken with bread in the form of a loaf, a bun, a cake or a bap.

As in countries where vines grow naturally, wine keeps better if stored in a cool place. Wine cellars are referred to from 1375, and wine caves from 1538. There were masters of the wine cellar in royal and high-level households, looking after barrels of sack and other wines, and generally maintaining supplies. The officer in the royal household who was responsible for selecting and supplying wine was the 'symolier', frequently referred to from the mid-sixteenth century (1562). He had an important function. When a ship arrived with a consignment of wine, it had to remain on board the ship until it had been examined, tasted and chosen by the royal symolier (*DOST*, s.v. *cave, sym(o)lier, wyne-sellar*). To sell wine, or to open a cask for the purpose of retailing it, was to 'vent' it, and the action was 'venting' (1548). Broachers of casks and sellers of wine were 'ventars' (1548) or 'ventenars' (1508). The word could also be used as a personal name (Thom Ventnare, 1524)

(*DOST*, s.v. *vent* [both entries], *ventar, ventenar, venting* [both entries]). When the cask had been opened, the wine was described as 'running'; for example, the *Register of the Privy Council* spoke in 1601 of losses sustained by the venters of wine by the 'continuall lekage thairof and fraud and desait of thair servandis having the chairg of the selling and rynning of thair wynis'. A 'rinnar' was one who sold wine in small quantities from a barrel or similar container (*DOST*, s.v. *rin, rinnar*).

Wine, like other alcoholic beverages that were sought after, was used as a means of extracting dues at various points on its journey from the producer to the consumer. As mentioned above, payments were made when moving casks on or off ship ('drawage'), between cellars or for personal use. Some of these payments were in the form of gratuities, 'drink money' (1646) or 'drink silver' (1453), a practice said to have been very common in the sixteenth century (*DOST*, s.v. *drink-money, drink-silver*). The Burgh Records are a fertile source of information on other dues and payments and procedures. In Edinburgh, it was stated on 3 December 1508 that if any stranger arrived with wine, the vintners should choose four to six persons from their own faculty, and buy the whole stock. They would then set a price, which would be equally divided among the taverners, 'the Kingis hienes being first servit' (*ERBE* 1869: 119).

In pre-Reformation times, sellers were expected to be members of the religious brotherhood of St Anthony, and to contribute a chopin of wine out of every puncheon in a consignment to the upkeep of his altar in St Giles. In fact, no one was allowed to sell wine who was not a member of the 'confrarie'. This practice continued after the Reformation. Before that:

in tyme of ignorance and blindnes, thair wes ane choppin of wyne granttit and gevin for the mantenyng the wikitnes and idolatrie of Sanct Anthonis Ile, of the tvn of wyne: now of every tvn of wyne thair be vpliftit be the dene of gild present and to come xijd allanerlie, to be put in ane box and disposit for sustenyng of the pure and fallit brethering merchants and craftismen of this burgh.

In 1567–8, the wine duties belonging to the 'alterage' of St Anthony, at a chopin per puncheon, were auctioned (*DOST*, s.v. *confrarie*; *ERBE* 1875: 106, 245). Thus Roman Catholicism gave way to social welfare. But this was not the only source of support. It was part of a general custom of collecting the value of a chopin from every puncheon of wine sold, the money to be put in a locked box with three keys, and to be kept by the dean of guild and two masters. It should be checked and counted twice a year, and used in support of needy brethren (*ERBE* 1875: 180).

Prices were regulated regularly to take into account the levels of supply and are given in the burgh records as the maximum allowable. Fresh wine at the end of the year, for example, was obviously worth more than the ageing wine of earlier vintages.

Table 5.3 Wine prices and dates of sale, 1517–87

Source	Page	Date	Wine	Price
ERBE 1869	172	Sept. 1517	Claret	pint, 8d.
	197	June 1520	Claret, white wine	pint, 6d.
	223	Oct. 1525	Wine	pint, 12d.
ERBE 1871	114	Dec. 1543	Wine	pint, 24d.
	115–6	Dec. 1543	Romany wine	pint, 24d.
	115–16	Dec. 1543	Claret, white wine	pint, 16d.
	120	Jan. 1554–5	Claret, white wine	pint, 18d.
	123	Oct. 1546	Malvysie	pint, 24d.
			Romany and Osay	pint, 17d.
	125	Dec. 1546	Rens wine	pint, 20d.
			Romany	pint, 16d.
			Malvasy	pint, 24d.
			Claret, white wine, Bordeaux	pint, 24d.
	127	Jan 1546–7	Rochelle white wine	tun, £22
			Claret, Bordeaux	tun, £27
			Romany	piece, £16
			Osa	£17
			Allacant	£22
	127	June 1547	Bordeaux wine	pint, 10d.
	134	June 1548	Claret, white wine	pint, 12d.
	147	Jan. 1549–50	Wine	pint, 14d.
	185	Dec. 1553	Bordeaux	tun, £22
			Hoypis, Libnon	tun, £20
			Scherand, Rochelle, Binzak	tun, £16; pint, 8d.
			Bordeaux, hoypis	pint, 10d.
ERBE 1875	89	Nov. 1560	Bordeaux, scherand	pint, 16d.
	132	April 1562	Wine	pint, 12d. and 13d.
	191	Dec. 1564	Bordeaux	tun, £36; pint 26d.
	198	June 1565	Wine	pint, 14d.
	224	Oct. 1566	New wines	pint, 12d.
ERBE 1882	48	March 1576	Bordeaux	pint, 30d.
			Rochelle, Cherane	pint, 26d.
	55	Dec. 1576	Wine	pint, 36d.
	62	Dec. 1577	Wine	pint, 40d.
	88	Nov. 1578	Rochelle, 'small wynis'	pint, 20d.
	129	Dec. 1579	Wine	pint, 36d.
	135	1579	Old wine	pint, 32d.
			New wine	pint, 36d.
	311	Dec. 1583	New wines	pint, 32d.
	484	Feb. 1586–7	New Bordeaux wines	pint, 32d.
			Smaller, meaner wines	pint, 68d.

On the basis of the example of Edinburgh, the Table shows that wines became progressively more expensive as the sixteenth century wore on. Nevertheless, prices were controlled. They were based on wine quality and type (Bordeaux wines were dearer than the 'smaller' wines), purchase price and freight cost, leakage, cellaring and legal dues set by Act of Parliament. By 1579, auctioning of the duty on wine coming in at the ports was beginning. The successful bidders, the 'fermoraris', uplifted the price of a pint out of every tun, this to be paid quarterly to the collector of the annuals (*ERBE* 1882: 73, 125; *DOST*, s.v. *fermorar*, 'a farmer of dues or imposts'). Measures for drink had to be authenticated with the 'town's mark'. All 'neighbours' sending for wine to any tavern had to have their pints or stoups duly certified as being of 'just measure', and marked by an official at the tolbooth. The measures should also have a bung or stopper in the neck, placed an inch below the lip, and the measure was to be filled up to this point (1543–4, 1554–5), (*ERBE* 1871: 112; *DOST*, s.v. *mesure, tapon*). There could also be personal marks, for identifying an owner: 'Ye sall resaiu . . . a boit of malwesy markit with your mark' (1502) (*DOST*, s.v. *mark*).

LATE SEVENTEENTH TO EIGHTEENTH CENTURIES

The customs books for Leith in 1688–9 help to indicate the organisation of the wine trade. At this date, there are 103 entries, naming 43 individuals. The wine was carried in thirteen ships registered to various ports in Scotland – Aberdeen, Burntisland, Fisherrow, Kirkcaldy, Leith, Pittenweem, Prestonpans, Queensferry – all discharging their cargoes at Leith. The amount of wine detailed was 534 tuns of French wine and 358 butts of Spanish wine, which together had a customs value of £71,602, at £96 per tun for French wine and £57 per butt for the Spanish. Only a small group of merchants was involved. In that year, five men accounted for 35 per cent of the French and 33 per cent of the Spanish imports. The risk of loss at sea was minimised by the practice of having single cargoes in the names of several merchants; for example, the *Sophia* of Pittenweem discharged 76 tuns of French wine for thirteen merchants, and the *Lyon* of Leith 125 butts of Spanish wine for fifteen (Dingwall 1994: 174–5).

There was a good deal of movement of wine along the east coast in the seventeenth century. The imposts having been paid, coastal re-export was frequent. Merchants sent wine from Aberdeen to Banff, Bowness (Bo'ness), Cowie, Findhorn, Fraserburgh, Moray, Peterhead and Stonehaven. Wine reached Aberdeen from Leith, Dundee, Montrose, Newburgh, and also from France and Flanders. The boats used were sometimes fishing boats, doubling up as trading vessels. On 4 January 1650, John Anderson arrived from France with four score tuns of wine at 4s. 6d. the tun, making a total of £18. From information in the *Aberdeen Council Letters*, it appears that in the official view, this would keep the town going for that year and also for the one following. Indeed, in the following year, 1651, only 41 tuns were imported, and all in small lots from neighbouring ports (Taylor 1972: 320). Information of this kind points to the assumption that the trade in wine was limited in scale and was reasonably predictable from year to year, and furthermore that the greater part of the sales was still largely confined to the upper echelons of society.

The accounts of Lord Fountainhall for 1670–5 show that he drank Rhenish wine, seck and malaga, as well as ale and brandy. On one occasion he bought *tent* (Spanish red wine) 'to my wife', which may imply a medicinal purpose (Crawford 1900: 240–1, 246–7, 249–51, 256, 262, 267). The range of wines drunk in this household, however, appears to have been fairly limited.

In the late seventeenth and eighteenth centuries, wine was the most expensive drinks item in the household budgets of the big houses. For example, at Hamilton Palace, the family and even the children regularly drank wine at mealtimes. In the 1690s, over 500 bottles of claret, about 200 bottles of canary, and several dozen bottles of Rhenish and Madeira wine were drunk each year. In 1638, the Marchioness of Hamilton actually sent to Spain for wine for which she paid £133. 7s., but Scottish merchants were the usual sources of supply. The Duke of Hamilton normally supervised the buying of wine himself, selecting hogsheads in Glasgow. These were moved to the Palace cellars where they were bottled. Two or three hogsheads would be bought at a time (Marshall 2000: 100).

At Ravelston, on the edge of Edinburgh, Sir John Foulis regularly indulged in a wide variety of wines, which suggests that he was something of a connoisseur. Those specifically mentioned are alacant, Barcelona, canary, claret, Florence (white Florence), French, frontiniack, Hamburg, Hungarian white, Montifiaslolie [sic], Nance or Nantis, Ranish, new rochell, tent, new seck, portaick, wormit and white. They were drunk with a variety of edible accompaniments, bread playing a notable part, as in the following list:

Table 5.4 Wine and accompaniments in Sir John Foulis's household, 1679–1706

Drink	Accompaniment	Date	Page
Wine	Broth	24 Dec. 1679	17
Mutchkin wine	Broth, loaf	10 Jan. 1680	19
Mutchkin wine	Broth	4 Feb. 1680	22
Chopin wine	Broth, bread	5 Feb. 1680	22
Claret wine, or seck	Cheese	10 Sept. 1690	128
Wine	Oysters	12 Sept. 1691	139
Chopin new rochell	Sugar	2 Apr. 1694	165
Seck	Nackit	28 Sept. 1694	171
Wormit wine	Figs	14 Oct. 1696	199
Wine	Bread, oysters	8 Jan. 1698	221
Mutchkin seck	Roll	25 Feb. 1698	224
Wine	Bread, oysters	8 Jan. 1698	231
Sack, claret	Oysters	7 Nov. 1698	241
Mutchkin seck	2 lemons	30 Dec. 1698	245
Pint nanss wine	Sugar	27 June 1701	294
Nanss wine	Sugar	26 June 1702	306
Mutchkin seck	Oysters	30 Sept. 1702	309
Wormit wine	Figs	19 Jan. 1703	314

Wine	Bread	26 Apr. 1702	321
Chopin nantis wine	Sugar	15 July 1703	328
Wormit wine	Oysters	7 Jan. 1703	337
Wine	Hot, sugar, spiceries	13 April 1704	343
Wormit wine	Bread	9 Aug. 1704	355
Wine	Oysters	4 Oct. 1704	357
White wine	A loaf	21 Nov. 1704	359
Ranish wine	Sugar	27 Dec. 1704	362
Wine	Cookie	14 Feb. 1705	366
White wine	Bread, oysters	3 Apr. 1705	372
White wine	Cookie	11 Apr. 1705	373
White wine	Bread	13 Apr. 1705	373
Pint wine	Babie (halfpenny) loaf	30 Apr. 1705	376
White wine, ale	Bread	7 May 1705	376
White wine, ale	Bread	14 May 1705	378
White wine, ale	Bread	19 May 1705	379
White wine, ale	Bread	24 May 1705	380
White wine	Bread	20 June 1705	386
Wine	Babie loaf	8 Oct. 1705	403–4
Quart claret	Babie loaf	18 Oct. 1795	405
Pint wine	Loaf	31 Oct. 1705	406
Wine	Loaf	9 Aug. 1706	443
Wine	Bread	6 Nov. 1706	452

(Hallen 1894; *DOST*, s.v. *nakket*, 'a small loaf' 1596)

On 9 February 1673, an entry specifies seck and white wine for possets. A posset was a drink of hot milk curdled with ale or wine. Sugar, spices and other ingredients could also be added. It was evidently popular at higher social levels, since posset-cups, pots and dishes of some quality – brass, earthenware, silver – are referred to in the sixteenth and seventeenth centuries (*DOST*, s.v. *posset*).

On 26 March 1680, three pints and three mutchkins of claret wine were given to the 'cummers' and 'gossips' who attended the lying-in of Sir John's wife, and on 17 April, twelve pints to the gossips who had come to see his wife. A cummer was a godparent or female intimate, in relation to the parents and other god-parents, so eligible to attend a birth. A gossip could be of either sex, and functioned in relation to a child or its parents or to each other. Cummers and gossips formed part of the intricate social network in earlier times, involving relationships which could be as tight as the ties of blood (see Chapter 4). For other occasions, a bride was toasted with a chopin of canary wine on 6 December 1704, at £1.4s., and the custom of foot-washing on the night before a wedding was marked by four chopins of new wine at £4 on 14 December (*DOST*, s.v. *cummer, gossop*; Dawson 2002–3: 88–95).

Wine was drunk as a medicine at times of sickness, as when a chopin of sack was bought for £1.4s. on 29 January 1680. A mutchkin of new seck cost 10 shillings on 3 March 1680, when Lady Foulis was sick, and on 17 September 1689, it was described as her 'diet drink' (Hallen 1894: 21, 25, 115).

It seems that Sir John Foulis bought wine in quantity, and bottled it at Ravelston, for two dozen bottle corks were bought on 29 July 1680, at 6d. each; seventeen dozen and five chopin bottles and one dozen and ten pint bottles on 19 April 1689; six dozen corks on 1 April 1690; six dozen glass bottles from Leith on 11 May 1696, and a gross and a half of corks with another gross on 16 September 1697; a gross of chopin bottles and four dozen mutchkin bottles on 9 April 1698; thirteen bottles at £1.19s. and corks at 1s.6d., carried from the glass works to the cellar, a half gross of bottles from Leith on 7 March 1702; one and a half gross chopin bottles, a half gross mutchkin bottles and three gross corks on 7 March 1706 (Hallen 1894: 46, 111, 121, 191, 214, 227, 251, 424).

A manuscript volume for 1754–5, from Hopetoun House near Edinburgh, provides a good deal of information on alcoholic drinks taken there. There were clarets, ports (mostly red, but occasionally white), and other wines named Lisbon, Vidonia, French Wine, St Lorain, Madeira, Malaga, Canara and Mallmasey. These appear to have been drunk mainly by the family at the first table, but sometimes wine was given to individuals who would not normally have drunk it, chiefly as a reward for good services. Claret was frequently consumed, though the white wine from Lisbon was nearly twice as common and was drunk throughout the year. 'Orange' wine was drunk in summer; Madeira tended to be more a winter drink (Robertson 1987: 61–3; Scott-Moncrieff 1911: 90).

By the mid-eighteenth century, wine was no longer confined to the landed classes. The Day-Book of Professor James Beattie at Aberdeen University, 1773–98, throws much light on the quantities drunk in at least this professional household. The pattern was different from that of the big houses, for the main wine drunk was white, and there was also some claret. The fortified wines, red port and to a lesser extent sherry, were common. Up to eighty-four bottles of port were bought at a time. Wine, however, was in balance with spirits (whisky, rum, gin), and ale, beer and porter, the last being bought in considerable quantities from local breweries. As a university professor, Beattie would have done a good deal of entertaining, and the poor quality of the water supply at that time would have encouraged the use of ale and porter as an alternative. The costs of household drinks over the twenty-five-year period from 1773 till 1798, which do not take into account what was consumed convivially outside the house, were: wine, £268. 11s. 9d.; spirits, £62. 9s. 2d.; brewery items, £138. 11s. 5d. (Walker 1948).

On the evidence of this selection of households, there was much variation in individual practices in drinking, and in the range that was consumed. Several of the named wines continue from the earlier period, but there are also new ones and the sources of origin are becoming wider. Though much more detail remains to be filled in for these periods, *DOST* entries and the associated references have provided a good skeletal framework as a basis for further research.

CHAPTER 6

Law and Lexicography: *DOST* and Late Medieval and Early Modern Scottish Shipping Law

A. D. M. Forte, University of Aberdeen

INTRODUCTION

This essay considers the value of the *Dictionary of the Older Scottish Tongue* from a lawyer's perspective. To assess the significance of *DOST*, however, requires one to understand the role of dictionaries generally in the interpretation of legal language. From this exercise it will become apparent that the lexicographer's conception of the significance of the dictionary is not one necessarily shared by the modern lawyer. However, the value of dictionaries to the contemporary lawyer may, in turn, be contrasted with their usefulness to the legal historian. As I have worn both hats for most of my professional career, writing this piece, in order to salute the completion of a truly magisterial work, has presented me with several opportunities. The first is to provide lexicographers with a perspective of how their work is treated by lawyers. The second is to demonstrate the significance of *DOST* to the work of the legal historian. The third is to offer my interpretation of a few terms which are not defined in its volumes.

LAW AND LANGUAGE

The importance of language to the law can scarcely be overestimated. Whether the context is the interpretation of words in a juridical act, such as a contract, or the construction of legislation, the meaning of the wording employed and sometimes the effect of grammar also can be of crucial significance. For example, in one recent case, the issue of whether or not an insured party was entitled to compensation under an insurance contract turned on the appropriate construction to be put on the word *storm*.[1] The policy covered the insured against loss or damage caused by 'storm or tempest'. A claim was made on the policy after the roof of a building owned by the insured collapsed under the weight of a heavy accumulation of snow which had fallen persistently over several days. The insurers rejected the claim, arguing that a gradual accumulation of snow did not constitute a storm and that the loss suffered was not, therefore, due to storm damage. In another insurance case, the liability of insurers to meet a claim turned upon the grammatical meaning of the words 'I am a total abstainer from alcoholic drinks and have been since birth'.[2] These were contained in a declaration made by the insured which was incorporated as a term of the policy. True when made in 1961, a decade later, having drunk a small amount of lager, the insured crashed his car, killing his passengers. The insurers argued that the declaration constituted a warranty as to the future, in terms of which the insured had promised never to drink alcohol. The insured maintained that the wording of the declaration, and the tenses used therein, could only be construed as a warranty of his temperance at the time he made the declaration.

In the first of these cases the court decided that intense snowfall accompanied by some wind could be construed as a 'storm'; and that the insured was covered. It was noted that the definition of *storm* in the *Shorter Oxford English Dictionary* did not always require wind or some element of violence to be present. However, while the court did take into account the dictionary definition here, the decision itself was based, ultimately, on the view that the circumstances themselves were decisive and that damage caused by heavy, persistent downfalls of snow, when considered objectively 'by a person of ordinary common sense making the ordinary use of language',[3] constituted 'storm' damage. In the second case, the court took the view that words expressed in the present or past tense could not be given future meaning.

Both of these decisions can be read as suggesting that, when considered judicially, ordinary words are given their ordinary grammatical meaning. Indeed, it has been said that 'most expressions . . . have a natural meaning, in the sense of their meaning in ordinary speech'.[4] However, against this one must juxtapose the opinion, again judicial, that, while the 'meaning of words is a matter of dictionaries and grammars', words used in legal documents cannot be assumed to bear a meaning referable to everyday speech.[5] Essentially, therefore, an objective approach to meaning based on legal context is to be preferred to meaning in ordinary non-legal usage.[6]

Even normal grammatical conventions may be departed from where the language said to reflect the parties' intentions warrants an alternative interpretation. For example, it does not follow that because an insurance policy against accidental injury requires the insured to take reasonable precautions, there will be no cover if he or she acts negligently.[7] Moreover, wording which might normally be thought to connote future effect may nonetheless be interpreted as indicating only present intention where the factual matrix so warrants. So where a parent company was asked to guarantee the debt liability of a subsidiary to a bank and refused to do so, also refusing to incur joint and several liability with the subsidiary, or to provide an indemnity, all alternative ways of guaranteeing repayment by the parent, it was decided that the words 'It is our policy *at all times*' to ensure repayment of the subsidiary's debt, found in a comfort letter[8] granted by the parent to the bank, did not place any obligation on the parent to ensure repayment once the comfort letter was granted.[9] Having rejected all attempts to extract some form of accessory liability, the circumstances surrounding the granting of the comfort letter could not be disregarded when it came to deciding the effect of the letter itself.

LEGAL LANGUAGE AND DICTIONARIES: CONTEMPORARY ATTITUDES

In the past, the rules regarding the interpretation of juridical acts clearly conceded a role for the dictionary. More recent judicial thinking, however, and proposed new statutory rules for interpreting juridical acts, would appear to reduce, though not abolish, this avenue of recourse. But even the older approach is characterised by caution and might appear to the non-lawyer to be counter-intuitive. As we have seen, it does not follow that the dictionary definition of a word found in a contract will necessarily be accepted as determining the meaning to be ascribed to it.

The other context in which resort is had to dictionaries is that of statutory interpretation. Most modern statutes contain an interpretation section in which the main terms employed in the statute are defined. From time to time, however, the courts are still faced with questions as to the meaning of words in legislation. For example, in *Mills* v. *Cooper*,[10] a person was charged under the Highways Act 1959 with the offence of camping on a highway without permission or lawful excuse. The success of the prosecution depended upon it being proved that the accused was a gipsy – a term which was not defined by the statute. The court was most explicit on recourse to the dictionary definition of *gipsy*: this was not to be followed since a definition which pointed to racial origin, and made reference to physical appearance, was simply unusable in the context of the legislation. The statute was not directed at 'member[s] of a wandering race (by themselves called *Romany*) of Hindu origin . . .' as defined in the *Oxford English Dictionary*. The purpose behind the legislation was to prevent 'a person without fixed abode who leads [a] nomadic life, dwelling in tents and other shelters, or in caravans or other vehicles' from setting up roadside encampments.[11] This highly contextual, judicial definition of *gipsy*, reflecting colloquial usage, was felt to represent the true intention of Parliament in enacting the statute.

The above case clearly indicates once more that, while dictionaries can be a valuable resource in the interpretation of legal language, they cannot be regarded as always determining the meaning of words in a legal context. Indeed, despite the fact that modern dictionaries such as the *OED* will often include legal usage in the definition of words, two modern legal writers on the topic have ventured the opinion that dictionaries are generally unhelpful in this context (White and

Willock 2003: 256).[12] While this somewhat overstates the position, there can be no doubt that the judicial attitude towards the use of dictionaries is extremely cautious. In the course of one speech in a Scottish appeal before the House of Lords, the view was somewhat pointedly expressed that the courts exhibit a 'marked preference . . . for citing judicial in preference to lexicographers' definitions of ordinary English words *even when they are not legal terms of art*'.[13] A further brake on the use of general dictionaries is the view that these should only be resorted to when the word whose meaning needs to be ascertained is not one included in a judicial dictionary, that is, 'a dictionary of words which have been defined by judges in the past' (Wilson 1984: 97). Related to judicial dictionaries are legal dictionaries, in which the meanings of legal terms and words are explained. These have a venerable history in Scotland, beginning in 1597 with the publication of Sir John Skene's *De Verborum Significatione*, in which he sought to explain the most 'difficill wordes' and terms found in the fourteenth-century treatise on Scots law known as *Regiam Majestatem*.[14] Others include an unpublished manuscript of a *Scots Law-Lexicon* by John Spottiswoode, written in the early eighteenth century, and Robert and William Bell's *Dictionary [and Digest] of the Law of Scotland*, published in the first three decades of the nineteenth century.[15] This genre has continued to be produced down to the present day (see, for example, Stewart 1995). In addition to such dictionaries are books of legal maxims.

The reserve which most lawyers exhibit towards general dictionaries is, however, matched by an objective and sophisticated appraisal of their merits when these are considered. Most would agree that the lexicon of choice is the *OED*. However, consultation is not confined to this work. Where, for example, the meaning of the term 'house-porter', used in eighteenth-century legislation,[16] fell to be considered by a twentieth-century court, the 1824 edition of Dr Samuel Johnson's *Dictionary* (first published in 1755) was happily resorted to by Lord Mackenzie as being the nearest in date to the statute to which the court had been referred.[17] The same dictionary, however, though lauded in one case for the 'anxious precision' taken by its compiler,[18] is deeply rooted in the language and literature of the seventeenth and eighteenth centuries, and was quite properly criticised in another case as being of doubtful value in interpreting modern fiscal statutes.[19] But what of specifically Scottish dictionaries?

Scottish judges have been rather positive about *Chambers' Dictionary* and John Jamieson's *An Etymological Dictionary of the Scots Language*. The former has been judicially commented upon as 'a very good working Scottish book',[20] and one illustrative of specifically Scottish usage of words.[21] Because of its Scottish provenance, however, the English courts have displayed a certain aversion to its use (Wilson 1984: 98). It is interesting (and pleasingly mischievous) to speculate what English attitudes to the *OED* might be were it generally realised that much of this is based on the pioneering efforts of the Scottish lexicographers James Murray and William Craigie.

Jamieson's work has been relied upon in a case of taking fish from a reservoir.[22] The accused was charged under the Theft Act 1607 *c*. 3, which made it a crime to take fish from 'proper stanks and lochs'.[23] The question before the High Court was whether or not a reservoir was a stank. Lord Ardwall, referring to 'Jamieson's Scotch Dictionary', which defined a stank as a 'pool or pond . . . said to be used to denote a fishpond', came to the view that a stank was a private fishpond. It has recently been suggested, however, having regard to the definition in *The Scottish National Dictionary*, though acknowledging that this deals only with usage after 1700, that a stank includes any pond containing fish and not just one which has been custom-built for that purpose (Rodger 1993). Had the relevant volume of *DOST* been available a decade ago, reference to it would have been most appropriate.

So far as I am aware, no Scottish court has ever been invited to consider the meaning of a word on the basis of that ascribed to it by *DOST*. Indeed, it may be ventured that the scope for so doing is somewhat circumscribed by a combination of *DOST*'s cut-off date of 1700 and the fact that most, though not all, of the pre-1707 Scots Acts have either been formally repealed by specific modern statutes or generally culled by statute law revision acts. Moreover, any Acts of the old Scots Parliament which have not been specifically abrogated may well have fallen into desuetude. (Under this doctrine such statutes are no longer treated as being in force if they have not been applied by the courts for a very long time, or if their contents are no longer compatible with modern life and conditions.) Of course, this does not preclude reference to *DOST* for the meaning of words found in a non-statutory context, for example in a contract, or disposition conveying heritable property, or a will. However, it is submitted that such reference should only be made where the purpose of the exercise is to establish Scottish usage at some time during the period covered by *DOST*. This view seems to be confirmed by *Glasgow Training Group (Motor Trade) Ltd*. v. *Lombard Continental plc*, described above, where the meaning ascribed to 'storm' was crucial to the outcome. There the argument was advanced that, since the insurance contract was governed by Scots law, then the Scottish usage of 'storm' had to be considered. Counsel argued that in addition to the Scottish usage given in the *Shorter Oxford English Dictionary*, the court should also consider the definition in the *Concise Scots Dictionary*. However, Lord Clyde, noting that the secondary meaning of 'storm' (as 'fallen snow, especially when lying on the ground in some quantity for a long time' or 'a period of wintry weather with alternating frost and snow') in the *Concise Scots Dictionary* was said to be confined now to north Perthshire, refused to adopt this definition as it did not appear to reflect 'modern, general usage'.[24] Since the judge indicated his preference for the primary meaning of the word given by the *Shorter Oxford English Dictionary*, he must, implicitly, have also rejected the Scottish usage in that lexicon. Moreover, as the latter's secondary definition of 'storm' is remarkably close to that in the *Concise Scots Dictionary*, this probably suggests that the judge's rejection of it was based on the same ground.[25]

LATE MEDIEVAL AND EARLY MODERN SCOTTISH SHIPPING LAW: *DOST* AND THE LEGAL HISTORIAN

Whatever circumspection must be observed regarding dictionaries, Scottish or otherwise, by the lawyer concerned with contemporary practice, the legal historian is happily free to consult these at will. For the period before 1700 *DOST* has become an indispensable tool. This is not, however, solely because the compilers of *DOST* have made such impressive use of legal material whether in printed or manuscript form, but also because, as William Craigie, the work's originator, envisaged, a 'large number of the words it contains are of historical and legal interest' (*DOST*, I, *Preface*: viii; see also Dareau 2002a). It is I would suggest impossible to work on any aspect of Scottish shipping (and many other areas of law) in the late medieval and early modern periods without initial and recurrent resort to *DOST*. In the remainder of this essay, therefore, I should like to give some examples of how *DOST* can be used by the legal historian and a few examples of words not presently found within its pages.

Kennings

In establishing the juridical significance of the word *kenning*, which appears in a jurimetric context in a late sixteenth-century manuscript,[26] as well as in near-contemporary passages in Balfour's *Practicks* and Habakkuk Bisset's *Rolment of Courtis* (McNeill, 1962–3, vol. 28, *c*. XI, 616, *c*. XXIII, 619; Hamilton-Grierson, 1920–6, vol. 2, 242 [fol. 315], 256 [fol. 323]), *DOST* was critical in establishing that one sense in which the word was used at the time was to denote sight or vision, particularly in relation to navigation. One may, however, quibble with the inclusion of the references to Balfour and Bisset (the MS passed unnoticed) in the context of the unit of measurement known as a *land-kenning*. A land-kenning represents the distance from which land is visible to a vessel at sea, but its use in the legal texts referred to is not in that sense. In these texts a kenning, not a land-kenning, denotes a unit of measurement which allowed (a) the calculation of freight *pro rata itineris* and (b) the calculation of seamen's wages as ships proceeded along a coast and not away from it. Moreover, the subsequent definition of a land-kenning refers to legislation which seems to indicate that this unit of distance was twenty-eight miles. Examination, however, of the text of the Record Edition of *The Acts of the Parliaments of Scotland* does not appear to accord with the quotation in *DOST*. These points notwithstanding, *DOST* has provided a fulcrum around which one can construct an explanation as to how a precise legal formula might actually have been applied by a Scottish admiralty court. Moreover, it also allows us to construct a late medieval world in which the symbiosis between law and maritime practice – the 'use and prettik of the seyfayr', or the 'use and consuetude' of mariners[27] – can be further demonstrated (Forte 1998a).

Farcosts and caumfers

In north-west Europe during the later medieval period the diversity of vessels used was considerable. Consequently, a number of taxonomic studies of the ships of the period exist (Burwash 1947: ch. 4; Friel 1995; Gardiner 1994; Mitchell 1994; Unger 1980). Characteristic of this research is its lack of dependence upon any one discipline to provide answers: iconography is one rather obvious source of information, as are archaeology and ethnography. Although it may seem an unpromising source of information at first, the legal record too can contribute to the debate. Thus construction techniques which have evolved to ascertain the meaning of legislative language, and that found in juridical acts, can be applied to documents dealing with ships (Forte 1998b).

In several charters granted during the period 1428–82 the Crown remitted in favour of the royal burgh of Edinburgh the right to levy toll and (later) anchorage charges on vessels using the port of Leith.[28] These charges varied in accordance with the type of vessel named and were clearly related to size. Barges, balingers and crayers were each levied at 5 shillings and, while clearly larger than, for example, farcosts, which were only charged 12 pence, all were smaller than hulks and 'forecastled' vessels, which attracted harbour dues of 10 shillings each. By 1482, however, these vessels, except for farcosts, were no longer specifically mentioned in the charters. The charter of that year, however, included for the first time a reference to anchorage charges, suggesting that the vessels listed as incurring these were too large to berth in the harbour itself and therefore had to remain anchored in the roads outside Leith while their cargoes were loaded from, or unloaded into, smaller boats. Of these vessels, three are simply described in terms of size, starting with the largest, a 'grete schip single or double forcastellit', and charged on a decreasing scale from a little over 13 shillings to just under 7. However, the smallest anchorage charge, of 5 shillings, was levied on vessels which were specifically identified by the name 'caumferis'. What were caumfers?

In the *De Verborum Significatione* Sir John Skene wrote that farcosts were 'inferiour in birth and quantitie to ane schip': a point of view confirmed by the charters. Ignoring Skene, J. D. Marwick, who edited the charters, and to whom *DOST* was obviously not available, states in his glossary that farcosts were merchant ships whose name, literally, meant 'going to foreign countries' (Marwick 1890: 10). He produced no evidence to support this definition, though had he at least referred to the edition of Jamieson's *Etymological Dictionary of the Scots Language* published a decade earlier he would have seen that the word was there defined as meaning 'a coasting vessel . . . one that fares along the coast'. Clearly contextually correct in the charters themselves, earlier laws *in pari materia* also indicate the smallness of the farcost. For example, a joint 'decree' of the burghs of Berwick, Edinburgh and Stirling in 1295 refers to 'schippis, forcastis and boats' (respectively *naues, nauicule, batelle*).[29] The thirteenth-century *Custuma Portuum* also refers to the charge to be levied on the farcost which is described as a 'litill schip'.[30] Much other evidence besides also supports the definition of a farcost now given by *DOST* as 'a small cargo vessel'.

Doubtless emboldened by his pioneering definition of *farcost*, Marwick then turned to *caumferis*. If the farcost went to far-off countries, the caumfer must have been a vessel which came from far-off countries (Marwick 1890: 9). Farcosts and caumfers must, he therefore concluded, have been one and the same – farcost out, caumfer home. The problem with this conclusion, however, is that it completely disregards the structure of the language in the charters. In each of the charters from 1428 to 1482, farcosts incur only harbour dues of 12 pence. Caumfers, on the other hand, do not incur harbour dues, only anchorage charges, and those charges are five times greater than for farcosts. No contemporary royal draftsman would have countenanced the use of such ambiguous terminology as Marwick's definitions require us to believe. That would have seen skippers argue that their caumfers were really farcosts in order to pay the substantially lower of the two charges. But if Marwick's definition of the caumfer must be rejected, does an alternative exist? Here we are without *DOST*'s help. For although in defining *mydlest* it refers to the passage from the 1482 charter in which caumfers are mentioned, and despite its many excellent entries for other ship types, no definition of *caumferis* as such is given. It is with some diffidence that I will proffer one.

At the point in the fifteenth century that 'caumferis' make their appearance, Scottish trade with the Low Countries was reorienting itself away from Bruges, whose port of Sluis was silting up. Eventually, after flirtations with Middelburg and Bergen-op-Zoom, a staple was established in Veere (on the island of Walcheren in Zeeland), which had a fine deepwater harbour. Is it not possible, then, that the caumfer is toponymic in origin, signifying any vessel which plied the seas between Veere (or Camp Veere as it is sometimes referred to) and Leith, and possibly to other Scottish ports? There are numerous references to Camp Veere and its variant spelling in other entries in *DOST*. For example, under *stapil*, we find *campvere, campueere, campweer, camfeire* and *campheir*. Under *met*, reference is made to a unit of measurement employed in 'Camfer' and elsewhere.[31] A broadly comparable case is that of the Dutch *fluit*, which appears in the seventeenth-century records as *straertsvaerder, oostervaerder* and *noortsvaerder* depending upon whether it sailed to the Mediterranean, Baltic or Norway (Unger 1994: 126–7, 130).

Caplagen

This word appears in an early eighteenth-century manuscript style of charter-party, used in Aberdeen, for the hire of a ship.[32] It also appears as *coplagen* in a charterparty for a return voyage between Leith and Norway.[33] At first glance, therefore, the word appears to fall outwith *DOST*'s chronological remit. However, three things point to its use in at least some seventeenth-century Scottish charterparties. The first is its occurrence in a charterparty in George Dallas's printed stylebook of 1697 (Dallas 1697: 823) and in the unpublished 1687 manuscript of one by James Dewar.[34] The second is that the styles used in the early eighteenth century were carry-overs from those used in the preceding century. The third is that the collection of Aberdeen styles containing the charterparty just mentioned was compiled in the aftermath of a fire in the Aberdeen Commissary Clerk's office in late 1721 which had destroyed 'the haill records and papers therein'. There was, therefore, a need to collect, quickly, as many styles and forms relevant to legal practice in the city as possible. Included in this collection were styles which referred to procedures no longer competent by 1721. Other styles, including the charterparty, contain archaisms copied from earlier styles. All in all, therefore, this charterparty (and the others) points to the use of a word more current in the seventeenth than the eighteenth century.

The word itself is Dutch in origin and a composite of *kap* (hood or cap) and *laken* (sheet or cloth).[35] This translates best as 'hat money',[36] which, in turn, approximates to the legal term *primage* (Bell 1858: I, 426; 1893: § 420; Watson: 1890, s.v. 'Hat-Money'). Caplagen, then, was paid by the charterer to the master as an incentive, over and above payment of the freight charges, to ensure that cargo was loaded and unshipped safely. *DOST* does indeed note this meaning of *primage* (or *prymage*) giving examples of its occurrence, *inter alia*, in Alexander King's *Tractatus Legum et Consuetudinum Navalium*,[37] written towards the end of the sixteenth century. It does not, however, refer to the loan-word *caplagen*. Recently, however, highly detailed research on the development of insurance law in the Netherlands has suggested a new significance for this term (van Niekerk 1999).

Insurance as the principal means of protection against maritime risks developed relatively late in Scotland, assuming real significance only around the mid-eighteenth century (Forte 1987). The major impetus for this practice came from the Netherlands where its use was fairly widespread from the late sixteenth century on. It is, however, also clear that insurance was sometimes used by Scots in the seventeenth century, and Robert Mylne's *Sea Lawes* contains copies of Dutch legislation on marine insurance.[38] Van Niekerk, however, has demonstrated that in the sixteenth and seventeenth centuries Roman-Dutch law prohibited the master and crew from insuring their own wages: a *placaat* of 1550, for example, forbade insurance of wages against capture by Scottish pirates.[39] But if wages could not be insured, what incentive was there to deliver cargoes safely and in good condition? The answer was a contractual entitlement to *kaplaken* (or primage) if this was done.

What are we to conclude for Scotland here? This must be very tentative at this stage and more work requires to be done. However, the fact that the term *caplagen* seems to make an appearance in seventeenth-century Scottish charterparties, but disappears at some time in the early eighteenth century, may constitute further evidence of the impact of Roman-Dutch law on Scottish shipping law in the seventeenth century, which was to diminish after the Union of 1707. Indeed, the Dutch word, in Scottish form, may have entirely displaced *primage*, which had previously been used in charterparties and would be again. Of equal significance, however, at least for the legal historian pondering the embryonic law of insurance in seventeenth-century Scotland, is that the word points to the possibility of Roman-Dutch influence here also. The only statement about insurance law in Scotland at this time is in Stair's *Institutions*, where he classified it as a species of exchange contract: which was exactly how the great Dutch jurist, Grotius, viewed it.[40] Perhaps, then, the adoption and use of this Dutch word suggests that Scots law, too, saw the master's and crew's wages as uninsurable. If correct, this is another small piece of evidence for the use of insurance in Scotland in the seventeenth century.

APPRECIATION

If Scots law can in some way be seen as a manifestation of Scottish culture and social values, then *DOST* has an important role to play in understanding our law in its historical and developmental contexts. This is something of which a former Editor, Dr J. A. C. Stevenson, would probably have approved (Dareau 2002a: 80). And even if its use in contemporary practice is likely to be somewhat limited, the level of scholarship evidenced in its pages is a reminder that the lawyer should not lightly dismiss the work of the lexicographer. For the legal historian, however, *DOST* is quite simply a treasure beyond compare. On finding an unfamiliar word in a manuscript or early text which is not to be found in *De Verborum Significatione*, it is a considerable relief to find that successive *DOST* teams have gone before to illuminate the way so richly. Omissions (rare in my experience) always provoke anxiety and show how much we have come to rely on the work of these splendid Scottish lexicographers.

NOTES

1. *Glasgow Training Group (Motor Trade) Ltd.* v. *Lombard Continental plc*, 1989 SLT 375. Insurance cover against 'flood' damage does not apply where damage has been caused by natural seepage of water: *Young* v. *Sun Alliance and London Insurance Ltd* [1977] 1 WLR 104.

2. *Kennedy* v. *Smith*, 1975 SC 266.
3. 1989 SLT 375, at 380 per Lord Clyde.
4. *Charter Reinsurance Co. Ltd* v. *Fagan* [1997] AC 313, at 384 per Lord Mustill. See also *Bank of Scotland* v. *Dunedin Property Investment Co Ltd*, 1998 SC 657, at 661 per Lord President Rodger.
5. *Investors Compensation Scheme Ltd* v. *West Bromwich Building Society* [1998] 1 WLR 896, at 912–13 per Lord Hoffman.
6. The Scottish Law Commission has broadly recommended the adoption of this objective approach: *Report on Interpretation in Private Law*, Scot Law Com No 160 (1997). The Scottish approach to the interpretation of juridical acts is explored in Clive 2000: II, ch. 2.
7. *Fraser* v. *BN Furman (Productions) Ltd, Miller Smith & Partners, Third Parties* [1967] 3 All ER 57.
8. A comfort letter is usually taken when all attempts to obtain a guarantee or pseudo-guarantee have failed. Such instruments reflect an element of moral (not legal) compulsion on a parent company to honour the debts of its subsidiaries.
9. *Kleinwort Benson Ltd* v. *Malaysian Mining Corp bhd* [1989] 1 All ER 785. Emphasis added.
10. [1967] 2 QB 459.
11. [1967] 2 QB 459, at 468 per Diplock L. J.
12. Other recent works on Scots law dealing with the use of dictionaries are: Paterson and Bates 2003: 357–8; D.M. Walker 2001: 426; Wilson 1984: 97–8. Wilson never published a projected work on statutory interpretation, for which a manuscript does exist, before his death. See Maher 1996.
13. *Haigh* v. *Charles W. Ireland*, 1974 SLT (HL) 34, at 41 per Lord Diplock. Emphasis added.
14. Skene sat as a judge in the Court of Session. *De Verborum Significatione* was published as an appendage to his collection of *The Lawes and Actes of Parliament*.
15. The editions compiled by Robert appeared in 1807 and 1815 under the title *Dictionary of the Law of Scotland*. His son, William, retained this title for the edition which appeared in 1827 but changed it to *Dictionary and Digest of the Law of Scotland* for the edition published in 1838.
16. 17 Geo III Cap. 39.
17. *Governors of George Heriot's Trust* v. *Matson*, 1920 JC 34, at 45 per Lord Mackenzie. *Murray's English Dictionary* of 1901 was also used.
18. *Spillers Ltd* v. *Cardiff Borough Assessment Committee* [1931] 2 KB 21, at 42 per Lord Hewitt C. J.
19. *Reed International* v. *IRC* [1976] AC 336, at 343 per Roskill L. J. The House of Lords turned for the meaning of the term 'funded debt' to *Palgrave's Dictionary of Political Economy* (1896).
20. *Lord Advocate* v. *Mirrielees' Trustees*, 1943 SC 587, at 612 per Lord Mackay.
21. *Rutherford & Son* v. *Miln & Co*, 1941 SC 125, at 143 per Lord Mackay.
22. *Pollock* v. *McCabe*, 1910 SC (J) 23.
23. The Act was originally entitled 'Act Anent woddis parkis planting dowcattis &c': *APS*: IV, 373, *c*. 6. It was given its new title by the Statute Law Revision (Scotland) Act 1964, s. 2, Sched 2. As regards the theft of fish, the 1607 Act was repealed by the Salmon and Freshwater Fisheries (Consolidation) (Scotland) Act 2003, asp. 15. The statute remains in force, however, so far as it relates to the theft of bees.
24. 1989 SLT 375, at 378.
25. Any other interpretation would suggest that Scottish usage generally is to be denied effect, which, on the basis of several of the cases cited in the text, is incorrect.

26. NLS Adv MS 24.6.3(3).
27. The phrase is one found in the records of Scottish admiralty cases in the latter part of the sixteenth century. (Callender-Wade 1937: II, 15, 31, 80, 86, 125.)
28. The charters were granted in 1428, 1445, 1454, 1471 and 1482. See Marwick 1871: 63, 66, 74, 133 and 165.
29. *Fragmenta Collecta*, 20, in Thomson and Innes 1814–75: I, 724.
30. *Custuma Portuum*, 4; *APS*: I, 672.
31. A toponymic element in vessel nomenclature is observable in the case of the 'Fifie'. This particular design of fishing vessel evolved, as the name suggests, in Fife. However, though used in the late nineteenth and early twentieth centuries, from Aberdeen to Eyemouth, the vessels were always referred to as 'Fifies'.
32. AU MS 3550. An edited version is to be found in Meston and Forte 2000: vol. 47, Style no. 42, 75–6, 'Ane Charter pairtie betuixt a Skipper and tuo persons'.
33. NAS Pyper MSS, 226. Reproduced in Smout 1963: 293.
34. NLS Adv MS 32.4.13, fol. 158.
35. *Woordenboek der Nederlandsche Taal* (S'Gravenhage, Leiden, 1926), s.v. *kaplaken*. Note also, J. de Vries, ed., *Nederlands Etymologisch Woordenboek* (Leiden, 1971), s.v. *kaplaken*.
36. NLS Adv MS 25.6.15, fol. 50 v. This is a late sixteenth-century stylebook written in a very difficult hand.
37. NLS Adv MS 28.4.7. Here 'primage' is one of the terms found in charterparties for which an explanation is given.
38. NLS Adv MS 6.2.2. This was probably written around 1706.
39. *Placaat* 29 January 1550 s. 21.
40. D. M. Walker 1981: I, 10, 12; H de Groot, *De Jure Belli ac Pacis*, II, 12, 5.

CHAPTER 7

Cereal Terms in the *DOST* Record

Iseabail Macleod, Scottish Language Dictionaries

INTRODUCTION

What does the terminology of cereal crops and their products in the *Dictionary of the Older Scottish Tongue* tell us about the language and diet of Lowland Scotland in the period? Evidence suggests that up until the middle of the sixteenth century, cereals played a secondary role to meat and dairy products in the Scottish diet, especially in the pastoral areas of the Highlands and the Southern Uplands. Fish was also important, especially on 'fish days' (in accordance with the fast days of the Church). Cereals were always important and after 1550 became dominant, as the most economic way to feed a growing population. The earliest staple crops were oats and bere, the former with greater emphasis in the Lowlands and the latter in the Highlands. Bere is a hardy four- or six-row variety of barley (the usual barley being two-row in more recent times). It had been a vital crop since prehistoric times and is still grown in a few places. Bere bannocks from the Boardhouse Mill near Birsay in Orkney are on sale there at the present time, and also furth of Orkney. With the agricultural improvements of the late eighteenth and early nineteenth centuries, oats gradually became the main staple crop. Wheat appears early in the record, but in the medieval period it was clearly the food of the privileged, a cash crop and not normally consumed by ordinary people. Rye bread is now found mainly in delicatessens, but rye did have a role in medieval times, partly, but by no means only, as fodder for livestock. In any discussion of the ingredients of bread and cakes, there should also be mention of legumes, as flour was also made from pease and beans, sometimes grown and ground together and along with grains.

DOST is rich in sources for these terms in all their variety. General histories of course make some mention of crops, but the best sources are administrative documents, including court and burgh records, and the Treasurer's Accounts. Literary works also produce instances, as in Robert Henryson's Fable, 'The taill of the paddok and the mous' (a. 1500):

'Seis thow', quod scho, 'off corne ʒone ioly flat,
Off ryip aitis, off barlie, peis, and quheit?'

There are a few specialist sources, such as *The Baxter Books of St Andrews* (Macadam 1903), the records of the incorporation of baxters there from 1548 to 1861. University records include diet lists and accounts for food and though some are in Latin, others are in the vernacular. Later in the period personal records such as letters, diaries and estate account books contribute.

THE VOCABULARY OF CEREAL VARIETIES

Corn

Corn in modern usage tends to refer to the staple crop of a country: maize in the USA, wheat in England, oats in Scotland and Ulster; *SND* notes it as referring to bere in Orkney, and this usage is recorded in the rentals of the bishopric of Orkney c. 1500: 'In Sanday etc., malt scat was paid in barley, and called "bere scat, beir scat, bere scat, scat ordeir, and corne scat"' (quoted in *Proceedings of the Society of Antiquaries of Scotland* 1884: 265). Formerly the word had a more general meaning, often referring to a variety of cereal crops, as in Barbour's *Brus* (1375): 'Syndri cornys . . . Wox rype to wyn to mannys fude', or in the Aberdeen burgh records of 1689: 'The corns and other grouth . . . eaten and destroyed by . . . Major Mackay and his forses'. (This refers to the government army of Hugh Mackay of Scourie marching against the rebel army of Viscount Dundee, eating its way across the countryside and destroying as much as possible to prevent its use by the rebels.)

Bere

Bere appears widely in *DOST* in several forms, including *beir*, *bear* and *bair*. Does the last indicate pronunciation? In modern Scots the /e/ pronunciation is found north of the Tay, but some of the *DOST* citations appear to be more southerly. *Bere* often appears in citations along with other cereals, especially *aitis*: 'The Ile called Leuiss . . . [has] plentie of beir and aites' (Dalrymple [1596] in Cody 1885–95: I, 57/27). The form *big(g)* for six- or four-rowed barley (from Old Norse *bygg*) occurs in *SND*, but does not seem to be in the *DOST* record, though it occurs in Northern English. *Barlie/barley* forms are rare in the *DOST* period, though they appear quite early: see the Henryson citation above. 'The five barlie laaues and ij fisches' in Murdoch Nisbet's Gospel of St John of c. 1520 (Chapter vi, verse 9) may be an example of his known tendency to anglicise. 'Barley' also seems to be used to distinguish different kinds of *bere: Edinburgh Burgh Records* in 1600 mention 'barlie beir cum in at Leyth', and in 'An account of Buchan and what is remarkable therein', c. 1680: 'Sometimes they sow bear and reap oats, but it is not every kind of bear that does this, but a peculiar sort which is called barley oats' (Robertson and Grub 1843–69: 95).

Any consideration of *bere/barlie* as a food crop must of course take account of its use in the production of ale and whisky. Since ale was the standard beverage until it was replaced by tea in the late seventeenth and eighteenth centuries, a large proportion of the crop would have gone into its production.

Ait/ate

Ait/ate appears in the earliest records and indeed the Scots forms are found throughout the entire *DOST* and *SND* record. *Ote/oat* forms begin to creep in during the sixteenth century and by the late seventeenth seem to be taking over in formal writing. In the Glasgow University accounts of the provision for the common table, 1639–46 (Glasgow University Archives 2763), *oat bread* appears in 1639 and *ait breid* in 1645, presumably noted by a different and less anglicised officer of the university. *Eit/eat* forms appear from the late sixteenth century (but do not seem to survive into the modern period): 'Eit bread, ill ail, and all things are ane eik' from a sonnet by Alexander Montgomerie in the 1590s. And in 1608 the *Baxter Books of St Andrews* have: 'Quhatsumewir brother . . . sall baik eat bread heireftir, except it be of cleane eat meill, . . . sall pay iiii li. money'. *Ait caikis* appear in the Exchequer Rolls for 1588: 'For broun breid and ait caikes, spendit in his majesties hous'. *Ate brede* is in fact better documented: 'The quhitt breid and aitt breid to be sauld . . . as the prices of quhitt and meill stands for the tyme', from the *Annals of Banff* (1549), and see the Montgomerie citation above. The record may be amplified by a quotation from the diary of Johnston of Warriston for 2 June 1649, quoting the orders for the Covenanting army: '. . . to everie souldier two pund weght of aite bread in the day and twenty eight ounce of wheat bread and ane pynt of aile in the day, . . .' (*Scottish History Society* xxvi 1896: 55). Here the Scots is thinning out, but is still quite strong.

There are rare occurrences in the seventeenth century of *haver* meaning oats, specifically noted as 'bearded wild oats' by Robert Sibbald in his *Scotia Illustrata* (Sibbald 1684: II, 24). From Old Norse or Middle Dutch, the word occurs only in Scots and Northern English dialects. Compare modern Dutch *haver* and German *Hafer* (whence English *haversack*, originally a bag to carry oats for horses). The term continues in Scots into the modern period, as in Thomas Carlyle's *Frederick the Great* (XII, x): 'The hay, straw, barley and haver, were eaten away'. A Dumfriesshire correspondent for *SND* noted in 1925: 'In Canonbie . . . the people always referred to oatmeal as "heffer or hever meal"'.

Mele/meil

Mele/meil, as with *corn* referring to oats, usually refers in Scots to oatmeal, unless qualified by another cereal (*bere-mele*, *ry-mele*). This is quite clear in some citations: 'xxxij bollis of wittell be yeir that is to say twa pairt mele and third pairt beir' from the Boyd Family Papers (1548); 'A boll of oates . . . will give a boll of meal, and a boll of wheat . . . will give a boll of flowr' from the MSS of John Skene of Hallyards in the 1690s. The modern English spelling *meal* (the commonest in modern Scots) appears in 1550 (in the *Breadalbane Collection*): 'Fourtene bollis gud and sufficient meale . . . halfe qhuite meile weill schillit', with clear evidence of the lack of spelling rules in Older Scots. Other forms include *meel*, *meyl*, *mill(e*, *male/mail*. The /e/ pronunciation in modern Scots is recorded mainly north of the Forth (and many of the *DOST* citations are easily identifiable to these areas), but *SND* also records it for Wigtownshire.

Grotis/grottis/groats

Grotis/grottis/groats, meaning hulled oats or barley, occurs from the late fifteenth century. Henryson's Fable 'The Two Mice' has: 'And sekkis full of grotis, meill and malt'. In the *Glasgow Burgh Records* we find in 1649: 'It is thought they wald have kaill, and so for this must have twa peckis of grottis in the monethe . . .'. This is on the setting up of 'Hutchesones Hospitall', an orphanage funded by the brothers George and Thomas Hutcheson (whose trust later also set up the Hutchesons' Grammar Schools in Glasgow). Fergusson's *Scottish Proverbs* in the 1590s has 'Of Weillie persons . . . He kens his groats among other folks kail'; this is repeated in Kelly's *Proverbs* (1721), and in (more) modern Scots: 'There's nae dout he kent his groats in ither folk's kail', found in *Inwick* by J. P. Hunter (1894, p. 9).

Quhete

Quhete appears early in the record, with many variant forms including *quheit*, *quheet*, *qwheyt*: 'Off wyne and wax, oyle and qwheyt . . . sho had copy greyt' from Wyntoun's Chronicle (c. 1420). *Quhite/quit(t)* forms seem to be mainly central and north-eastern, coming in during the sixteenth century, and they can in some citations be confused with *quhite* meaning 'white' (especially as white bread is likely to be made from wheat). In some citations, however, wheat is clearly the meaning: 'Alsweill quhyt breid as aitt breid' in the *Kirkcudbright Burgh Records* in 1657. *Wheat/wheit/white* forms appear in the late sixteenth century. Among the earliest are three from the first two known pieces of lexicography in Scots, Andrew Duncan's *Apologia Etymologiae* of 1595: 'Ador, far, fine wheat', and 'Siligo, fine white', and John Skene's *De Verborum Significatione* (1597): 'The last of wheate' in a list of commodities and their export dues in the entry for 'bullion'.

In the records of the Perth Presbytery of 1605, we find 'Meal, bear and whyt' (Laing MSS I, 103). 'White' forms continue into the modern period and are recorded by *SND* for north-east Scotland c. 1930. The word also appears in the form *fayte* in 1585, a rare early spelling occurrence of the f- for wh- of north-east dialect: 'The thrid of the fayte of the abbasie of Arbrothe', from a list of the payments in kind due to the superintendent of Angus and Mearns.

Ry

Ry seems to have been a common enough grain, often listed with others, as in the 1513 *Treasurer's Accounts*: 'Sour breid furneist be the comptrollar, half qhueit half ry', or in the 1659 *Irvine Muniments*: 'Corne [presumably oats] beir wheit peis ry and uthir stuff grindable'. 'For certane quheit and ry breid' appears in the *Canongate Court Book* in 1569. *Ruggam breid* meaning 'rye bread', in the *Buccleuch Household Book* in 1631, is from Middle Dutch *rogge(n)-, ruggenbroot*; the Dutch influence is explained by the fact that at the time Lord Buccleuch was 'at the leaguer of Bergen op zoom'. Compare modern Dutch *roggebrood*, modern German *Roggenbrot*. Dutch is probably also the origin of the forms *ryne, riens, ryens*, occurring for example in the *Edinburgh Burgh Records* in 1548: '. . . the statutes be kepit in all poynts anent ryne breid oattes hay candill and pultre . . .' and 'Of ryens 2 boll 2 firl left standing in the barne' in the *Diurnals of Sir James Nicholson of Cockburnspath* for 16 March 1666. *Brashloche* appears once in *DOST* in 1638, meaning 'a mixture of rye with oats and barley': 'The sawing of ane boll brashloche estimat to the third corne, extending to thrie bollis brashloche' (*Dumfries Testaments*).

Pese

Pese, collective term for peas, was used in various farinaceous products, as is clear from some of its citations, for instance in 1572 (in a poem in the Bannatyne MS, 'The Lamentatioun of Lady Scotland'): 'And glaid to get Peis breid and watter Caill'. Beans were also used, usually mixed with pease and grains: 'Sum vset breid of ry, sum of qhueit, sum of peise or beanes' (Dalrymple [1596] in Cody 1885–95: I, 89/20). Sir John Foulis of Ravelston notes 'Peasbonocks and turkie eggs' in his accounts for March 1690.

Mastillion and Mashloch

Mastillion and *mashloch* refer to a mixture of grains or to bread made from their flour. The first form is shared with Middle English, deriving from Old French *mesteillon* etc., probably meaning wheat mixed with rye; the latter is an altered Scots form, first appearing, as *maschlache*, in the *Aberdeen Burgh Records* in 1445. It is not possible to tell from the *DOST* quotations what the mixture was, but in the modern period *masloch*, or more commonly *mashlum*, means a mixture of grains or grains and legumes, such as oats and barley, peas and beans, grown together and ground into meal or flour, used to make a coarse bread, and to feed livestock.

Rice

Rice, an upper-class food in the medieval period, imported from southern Europe, appears early in the record, with a vernacular mention in the Latin of the *Exchequer Rolls* for 1343: 'Pro . . . decem libris de ryse'. In 1597 the *Household Books of James VI and Anne* have 'Ane pund ryise' and in 1631 the *Buccleuch Household Book* has the more anglicised 'A pound of ryst'.

Rice apart, what is striking is the wide range of cereals being grown, and the fact that they were sometimes grown together, as part of a farming strategy which encompassed cash as well as subsistence crops. Variety in the latter was of course a partial insurance against the failure of any one cereal crop.

FORMS OF CONSUMPTION: BREAD AND CAKES

The processing of the grain by the miller and the intricate patterns of astriction to the mill have a technical and legal vocabulary which is beyond the scope of this article. But the forms assumed by the processed cereal after baking or other cooking are an essential further chapter in any study of the vocabulary of cereals. Here too the *DOST* record reveals a wide variety of terms in use at the time, many of them surviving to the present.

Brede/breid

Brede/breid in its modern meaning appears in various forms from the fifteenth century, sometimes qualified by the cereal it is made from: *ait breid*, *bere brede*, *quheit breid*. It also means a loaf or roll, as in: 'For ane galloun off aill and twa braid tane up to the stepill to the . . . wrychtis' from the *Edinburgh Dean of Guild Court Revenue Account* of 1590. This usage is noted in Jamieson's *Etymological Dictionary of the Scottish Language* (1825): 'The term is still vulgarly used by bakers in this sense'. In modern, especially north-east, Scots *breid* also means oatcake. While there is no sign of this usage in *DOST*, one or two citations might suggest something other than a yeast-risen dough: 'Thai hed na breyd bot ry caikis and fustean skonnis maid of flour' in *The Complaynte of Scotland* (1549).

Laf/laif

Laf/laif appears in its modern English meaning throughout the *DOST* record, with various forms, including *leif/leaf* as well the more anglicised *lofe/loaf*, etc. In modern Scots it has the additional meaning of 'bread', especially wheat bread, to distinguish it from *breid* meaning 'oatcakes', also in the form *laif bred/loaf bread*. Not so very long ago an elderly (Gaelic-speaking) relative of mine, requesting bread with his soup, said 'Hae ye a bittie loaf?' Again this seems to be a modern development.

Cake/caik

Cake/caik, however, appears early in its modern Scots meaning of 'oatcake': 'The French men . . . learned to eatt . . . caikes, which at thare entrie thei skorned' appears in John Knox's *History of the Reformation in Scotland* in the 1560s. This meaning is the origin of the expression 'land o cakes' to designate Scotland. It first appears (in the *Blairs Papers*) in 1659: 'I am in the land of cayks where all miseryes doe sheem to me mirth and giofulnes'.

Bake/baik

Bake/baik meaning a biscuit is recorded in Scots from the early sixteenth century. *Edinburgh Burgh Records* for 1523 have: 'Anent the flour baiks and fadges that cumes fra landwart into this toune to sell'. 'Ane pynt of aill and ane baick' in the *Irvine Muniments* of 1686 is echoed in *Maybole Past and Present* by R. Lawson (1885): 'with a glass of spirits and a bake' (p. 22). Not recorded in English, the usage survives to the present day in Scotland.

Bannok/bonnok

Bannok/bonnok, meaning a round flattish cake, seems to have been used in Scotland and Northern England for items with various ingredients over the centuries and still has a somewhat vague reference. It usually refers to an unleavened dough, but one of its modern manifestations, the Selkirk bannock, is a yeasted, fairly rich fruit loaf. The Pitcaithly bannock on the other hand is an embellished form of shortbread, with chopped almond and peel. But most of the evidence, old and new, is of a fairly plain cake, baked on a girdle, as with the bere bannocks noted in the Introduction to this chapter. The earliest *DOST* citation, of about 1568, is 'Beir bonnokkis with thame thay tak', from a poem about pedlar rogues in the Bannatyne MS. Two quotations from Pitcairn's *Criminal Trials* suggest different ingredients: 'Quha the samin nycht, buik the meill in bannokis [and] eit thairof' (1596) and 'Scho . . . tuk the blude of it [sc. a red cock], and scho buke a bannok thairof with floure' (1597). Scottish Gaelic *bonnach* has similar meanings and both *DOST* and *SND* derive it as probably from Scots. *OED* however suggests the reverse. There are other theories; Alexander MacBain's *Etymological Dictionary of the Gaelic Language* (1911) suggests a common origin in Latin *pānicum*, *pānis*, 'bread'.

Bap

Bap in modern usage usually refers to a softish floury roll, of different shapes, and this may well have been the meaning in the *DOST* period: 'xj vnce of qhueit bread gaif 8 d, and bappis of nyne for xij d' in the *Diurnal of remarkable occurrents*, dating from the 1570s (Thomson 1833), and 'in beakinge of bunnes . . . oat lowes, kaikis and bappis to the tawernis' in the *Burgh Laws of Dundee* in 1643. In recent decades the bap has reached English bakeries.

Fage/fadge

Fage/fadge is defined by *DOST* simply as 'A flat thick loaf', with the earliest recording in the *Aberdeen Burgh Records* in 1442: 'At the baxtares baake na faiges'. *The Baxter Book of St Andrews* for 1598 has: 'To baike baikes, or faiges, or bread leawes to gang to the sea'. The word, as *fadge*, is recorded in *SND* in south-east Scotland in 1950, and, in the modern period at least, seems to have often meant a loaf of barley meal. In Ulster it means a kind of potato scone.

Fardel(1)

Fardel(1) is defined by *SND* as 'A three-cornered cake, usu. oatcake, gen. the fourth part of a round'; as the word means a quarter, it presumably meant much the same from the start. The *Edinburgh Burgh Records* for 1601 include it in a list of bread commodities: 'becaus the mayneschottis of flour, fadges, fowattis, fardellis, reid bapis, . . . and siclyke breid keipis na pais or wecht'. The reduced form *farl*, much commoner in the modern period, is recorded in the late seventeenth century, for example in the poem 'The Blythsome Bridal' attributed to Francis Semple of Beltrees (Paterson 1849: viii):

> There will be good lapper'd-milk kebucks,
> And sowens, and farles and baps.

The poem has splendid descriptions of the food at the wedding, giving a vivid picture of the diet of ordinary people at the time. *Farl* now refers to different types of baking, including scones and shortbread; Irish soda farls can be bought in some supermarkets, probably an Ulster Scots usage. The *Concise Ulster Dictionary* (1996) lists soda, wheaten and potato farls.

Fowat

DOST's unhelpful definition, 'A cake or bun differing from a fadge', presumably derives from the quotation for *fardel* in the paragraph above and the following (for 1529) from the same source, 'At na hukstar sell nor top ony of the saidis fagis nor fowattis within thar housis'. Indeed the *Edinburgh Burgh Records* are the only source of this word. There is little help from the modern record, except for one reference for Roxburghshire in *Jamieson's Dictionary* (1825): 'FOUAT . . . A cake baked with butter and currants, something like the Scottish *bun* [that is, what we would now call Scotch bun or black bun]'. *DOST* and *SND* derive the word from Old French *fouac(h)e*, 'a cake baked in the ashes on the hearth, erroneously taken as a plural'.

Scone

Scone, a keynote of modern Scottish baking, is but sparsely recorded in *DOST*. 'The flowr sconnys war set in . . . with othir mesis' appears in Gavin Douglas's translation of Virgil's *Aeneid*. *The Complaynt of Scotland* (1549), quoted above under *breid*, mentions 'fustean skonnis'. John Leyden's edition of 1801 notes that 'The phrase [fustian scone] is still current in Angus, and the east coast of Scotland'. It is recorded in *SND* for Angus as *foustie*, meaning a thick floury morning roll. *Fustian* is thought to indicate the inclusion of oatmeal in the dough, giving a coarse appearance.

PORRIDGE

A basic way to eat cereals is of course in boiled form, as in the modern porridge. In medieval times barley or oats were commonly cooked along with meat and/or vegetables to form a kind of thickened hotpot. Such dishes were standard fare for all classes, but they leave little trace in the records since they were domestic and not subject to sales regulations and so on.

Potage/pottage

Potage/pottage from French, literally meaning 'something in a pot', is recorded from the fifteenth century on, and originally seems to have meant some kind of soup or vegetable dish, sometimes with meat, and often with cereal added as a thickener. Subsequently, however, it begins to refer to something like its later altered form *porridge/parritch*: 'The good-wife one morning making pottage for the children's break-fast, had the tree-plate wherein the meal lay, snatched from her quickly' (in George Sinclair's *Satan's Invisible World Discovered* of 1685). Interestingly, the earliest quotation in *SND* for *parridge*, in 1761, is figurative, suggesting its everyday use was much earlier: 'It's as plain as parridge, that he was baith a Romin, and Socinian' (Haliburton and Hepburn 1761: 45). *Porridge* in English began with the same meaning as pottage, but in the seventeenth century it was also used for cereal boiled in water or milk. A quotation in *OED* for 1707, 'Having his belly filled, and his head bedulled, with Scotch porridge', suggests an early association of the dish, if not also the word, with Scotland.

Brose

Brose, oatmeal (or peasemeal) mixed with boiling water or milk, is, or was, one of the most popular ways of eating meal in Scotland. This method of preparation has clearly been used for a very long time but, given its casual nature, it is perhaps not surprising that the word is absent from the *DOST* record. It may well have had many names over the centuries. *SND*'s etymological note still seems to hold: 'Both meaning and form make a connection with *DOST bruis(e)*, broth, doubtful'.

Sowans

Sowans, from Gaelic *súghan* (itself from *súgh* 'juice, sap'), is a more complex preparation. Oat husks and fine meal are steeped for several days in water, then strained; the remaining liquid is left to ferment and then usually boiled like porridge. This was a popular dish until comparatively recently and the word is recorded as far back as 1551 in the *Dundee Burgh and Head Court Books*: 'The said schip ladine with fiftyfoure [lastis] sowyndis beir'. See also the quotation under *fardel(l)* above.

CONCLUSION

A clear picture of the enormous importance of cereals in medieval Scotland emerges from the *DOST* record, even if it is only the tip of the iceberg in terms of the foodlore of ordinary people. Inevitably their eating habits emerge mainly in formal documents indicating quantities. Even for the upper classes we really only get glimpses, though household accounts, from the royal household to those of lairds, do give some information. The problem for the lexicographer is that many of these sources remain in manuscript form and the resources of even the best-funded projects do not allow for the use of other than published, or at least transcribed, material. Some, such as *The Account Book of Sir John Foulis of Ravelston 1671–1707*, have already been published by the Scottish History Society, but there must be a great deal more in the collections of Scottish country houses which could shed further light.

The same applies to recipe collections. The earliest known published recipe book appeared in 1736 (*Mrs. McLintock's Receipts for Cookery and Pastry-Work*) and an earlier MS collection from 1712 was published in 1976 as *Lady Castlehill's Receipt Book*. Are there earlier collections lurking somewhere, waiting to be edited? More collaboration between the historian and the lexicographer could help to expand the record in this way.

NOTE

Unless otherwise stated, quotations are from *DOST*.

CHAPTER 8

The Spread of a Word: *Scail* in Scots and *Sgaoil* in Gaelic

Donald E. Meek, University of Edinburgh

The completion of the *Dictionary of the Older Scottish Tongue* in 2002 was a landmark event in the history of Scottish, and indeed British, lexicography. The finished work provides a splendid picture of the lexis of the Scots language from the twelfth century to the seventeenth. It offers an opportunity for scholars to survey the Scots lexis generally, but it also provides an excellent starting-point for comparing the usages of certain Scots words with those of related words in other languages, notably Scottish Gaelic, which has shared frontiers with Scots for many centuries. Not only has one very important Gaelic manuscript, the Book of the Dean of Lismore (1512–42), been written in an orthography based on that of Middle and Early Modern Scots, but the languages have also been in close contact at various phonological and lexical levels, to the extent of borrowing words from one another. Many fascinating dimensions of language-contact remain to be uncovered when the right tools are in place.*

Unfortunately Gaelic does not yet possess a dictionary comparable to *DOST*. If such existed, it would readily illumine the number and range of usages of words found in Scottish Gaelic and also attested in Scots. The Historical Dictionary of Scottish Gaelic (HDSG) (established 1965) in Glasgow University was intended to fill this gap, but the project – on which the present writer was employed as Assistant Editor from 1973 to 1979 – failed to produce any significant published output. Nevertheless, an archive of paper slips (HDSG-A) was compiled. As it is by no means complete in its citations or exhaustive in its sources, HDSG-A cannot be used as the basis for a dictionary on historical principles. Without significant and time-consuming supplementation, it is often seriously defective in its contextual provision, particularly for the understanding of idioms. Nevertheless, HDSG-A provides a very useful working index to the lexis of Scottish Gaelic (ScG), and it has been used extensively in the making of this chapter.

* For references and sources, see the list at the end of the chapter.

The preliminary steps towards a dictionary of Gaelic, based on historical principles, are now being taken, by transferring skills from *DOST* to Faclair na Gàidhlig. The value of such a dictionary of ScG, when laid alongside *DOST*, can be glimpsed by comparing the usages of the verb *scail* in Scots with those of *sgaoil* in Gaelic, as found mainly in HDSG-A. Such a comparison not only provides an illuminating overview of how, and in what contexts, the two languages employ a similar verb, but it also offers an important insight into their etymological relationship.

It can be assumed fairly readily that the verbs are closely related. Previous lexicographical scholarship has not decided whether they both derive from a common root – and, if so, which root – or whether Scots *scail* is borrowed from ScG *sgaoil*, or from Early Irish *scaílid* (*DIL*, s.v.), the ancestor of the ScG form. *OED* (Si–St 126, s.v. *skail*) concluded that 'the correspondence in form and meaning with O.Ir. *scaílim* . . . is prob. accidental, as the early adoption and extensive use of a Gaelic word of this type would be very remarkable'. *OED* therefore proposed an Old Scandinavian root, **skeila*. *DOST*, on the other hand, edged closer to suggesting an 'Early Irish' origin for the Scots word. It gives ScG *sgaoil* as a comparator on a level with Middle English, Early Modern English, Early Irish and Irish, and concludes: 'The Eng. evidence strongly suggests that the word spread from north to south, perhaps a borrowing from EIr. into Sc. thence into northern Eng.' There are also wider issues of when, and in what contexts, borrowing may have occurred.

This chapter takes the evidence for the use of *scail* mainly from *DOST*, and that for the use of *sgaoil* largely from HDSG-A. The presentation of the Gaelic evidence follows broadly the pattern of the *DOST* entry, and is cross-referred to the relevant sections, but it treats the evidence according to Gaelic sense and idiom. This approach will permit us to reach some broad, but tentative, conclusions. Deficiencies in HDSG-A prevent a properly historical treatment of the verb *sgaoil*, and we cannot yet give definitive answers to key questions about the development of its usages, relative to those set out on historical principles for *scail* in *DOST*. The current ScG sample does not go back beyond the sixteenth century, although it extends to the modern period (within the range of *SND*). In addition, the present chapter employs only a representative selection of those citations in HDSG-A which are sufficiently full to place meanings beyond reasonable doubt. Consequently, it can claim to be no more than a very rudimentary attempt to illustrate the type of comparative analysis which will become possible, on a much larger and more authoritative scale, when Gaelic eventually acquires its own Faclair na Gàidhlig, properly based on historical principles similar to those in *DOST*.

I.   CORRESPONDING GENERAL USAGES OF *SCAIL* AND *SGAOIL*

We may note at the outset that *scail* and *sgaoil*, in their core meanings of 'scatter' and 'spread', represent a very basic concept in human activity. It is hardly surprising therefore that the basic usages of both verbs correspond in general terms. As will become apparent, however, there are some very significant differences between the ScG and Scots applications. The first of *DOST*'s definitions of Scots *scail*, namely 1[a], 'To scatter (things, or the parts or constituents of a person or thing) abroad or in different places; to disperse by separating and scattering', is relatively rare in ScG.

1.1 Flowers or plants are scattered before the wind:

Transitive and figurative

> *Cha do shaoil leam, le m' shùilean,*
> *Gum faicinn gach cùis mar a thà,*
> *Mar spùtadh nam faoilleach*
> *'N am nan [sic] luibhean a sgaoileadh air blàr*
> 'I never thought with my eyes
> that I would see each matter as it is now,
> as if, with the blasting of New Year tempests,
> wild flowers were scattered on the ground'

> (John Roy Stewart [c. 1746]
> in Campbell 1984: 172)

1.2 Bad weather, mist and darkness 'scatter, disperse' or 'are scattered, dispersed':

> *sgap 's a sgaoil, gach dubhradh, 's gach ceothoireachd*
> 'which scattered and dispersed every dark shadow and mistiness'

> (*Ais-eiridh* 1751: 31)

> *'S aoibhin do shiubhal a sholluis aigh,*
> *A sgaoileas le d' dhearsa gach donionn*
> 'Joyful is your journey, splendid light,
> who disperse with your gleam every storm'

> (*GA* 1780: 268)

Intransitive (*DOST* 14; cf. *DOST* 12)

> *mar a sgaoileas an ceo thar aodann an fheoir*
> 'as the mist disperses off the face of the grass'

> (*Ais-eiridh* 1751: 161)

1.3 Materials are spread, scattered or 'distributed' on or over the land:

Transitive

> . . . *bha 22,000 de bharaillean air an sgaoileadh bho'n bhaile* . . . '22,000 barrels were distributed from the town' (*GnaB* VI, 1909: 110)

> *a' sgaoileadh an innearadh* 'spreading the manure' (Oral informant, N. Uist, 1969)

> *sgaoil' na mòin'* 'spreading the peat' (Oral informant, Lawers, Loch Tay, 1975)

The activities in 1.1–1.3 are basic and natural in both languages. In the case of 1.3 it is possible that Gaelic-speakers and Scots-speakers would have co-operated in such labours alongside one another in certain contexts (e.g. seasonal labour on Lowland farms), and they may have shared relevant parts of their vocabulary. The citations in 1.3 are noticeably late, and the record is probably incomplete.

Further ScG examples of *sgaoil* meaning (very broadly) 'scatter' can be found (see 2.7), but, as the remainder of this chapter will show, closer inspection reveals that, in most cases, the nature of the ScG 'scattering' corresponds to 'spreading out' or 'disseminating'. On balance, ScG *sgaoil* seems more controlled and more purposeful in its application than *scail*, even when used of such objects as manure and peat. 'Scattering' (in a more random sense) in ScG is more likely to be expressed by the verb *sgap*, which may be used alongside *sgaoil*, as in 1.2 and 2.7. The *DOST* 1 (a) citations, on the other hand, seem to have a stronger sense of the 'throwing about' of physical materials, while the Scots evidence overall appears to focus more obviously on contexts of 'disbanding, breaking up, dismissing'. Beyond Section 1, ScG *sgaoil* functions within a wider and more complex range of semantic fields, some of which match those of Scots *scail*, as can be seen in Section 2. However, the degree of difference in the usages of the two verbs is probably more noteworthy than the degree of correspondence, as Section 3 demonstrates.

2. CORRESPONDING SPECIFIC USAGES OF *SCAIL* AND *SGAOIL*

The following, more specific, usages appear to be common to both Scots and ScG, although a closer review of the evidence might suggest that some ScG usages (e.g. 2.5, which lacks significant and unequivocal parallels in *DOST*), ought to be reclassified in Section 3 below. In most instances, the semantic concept is comparable. In several instances, however, the ScG noun or noun phrase which is the subject or object of the verb is not attested with the verb *scail* in the samples in *DOST* – a point which may simply underline the capacity of different languages to extend usages without altering the underlying idiom. It may also hint at lost evidence on both sides. The surviving evidence provides a fascinating, but tantalising, picture of idiomatic similarities.

2.1 Rumour, news and fame 'are spread out', or (in the case of 'stories' or 'tales' in ScG, but not in Scots) 'are disseminated':

Transitive (*DOST* 2, *DIL* II (d))

deigheol úaim sgaoileadh a sgél
'for me to spread his history is to impart edification'
(MacMhuirich 1514, Rel. Celt. II, 220)

is searbh an sgéal ré sgaoileadh
'it is a bitter story to spread around'
(BDL/Watson 1937: 166)

Teasda fáidh sgaoilidh a sgéal
'the arch-poet who used to recount their history has died'
(M. D. Ó Muirgheasáin 1642, SGS XII, v. 2a)

sgaoilaibh a chlu a ngcein
'spread his praise far and wide'
(Psalms 1659: 30:4)

do sgaoileadh do chlú fan chruinne
'your renown was spread throughout the globe'
(Eoghan Mac Gilleoin 1661–85, Adv. 72.1.36, fol. 80r. 20)

Anns an t Searmoin a leanas, air tionndadh chum bhur cainnt fein . . . air costas na chuideachd mhòr oirdheirc ann Luinduin, a' ta, chum eòlas an t Soisgeul a sgaoileadh

'In the following Sermon, which has been turned into your own language . . . at the expense of the great, illustrious society in London, which exists in order to spread knowledge of the Gospel'
(Broughton 1797: 3)

Intransitive (*DOST* 13: *DIL* 1 (a))

Scaoil mo Sgial 's gach Sliabh a's Baile
'my story spread in every upland and township'
(MacKenzie 1785: 37)

Cha noimheachd ar fineachaibh treun,
A chogadh 's nach géilleadh beo . . .
Ach noimheachd air soisgeul nan gràs
Bhi sgaoileadh 's gach àird mun cuairt
'It is not a story of brave clans who would fight and not yield while
they lived . . . but a story of the Gospel of grace spreading in every
direction round about'

(MacGrhiogair 1819: 82)

2.2 Emotions, such as horror and sorrow, and sensations such as noise and silence,
likewise 'spread':

Intransitive (*DOST* 13)

Bha mullach nam beann air an òradh le òg-ghathan na gréine; bha 'n
soirbheas a bh' againn ré na h-oidhche, a nis a' failneachadh; bha fèath
nan eun a' teachd air a' chaol, agus sàmhchair maduinn an Tighearn' a'
sgaoileadh ann an àilleachd chiùin air gach taobh.
'The tops of the mountains were gilded with the young shafts of
sunlight; the breeze which we had through the night was now
quietening; the calm of the birds was coming upon the strait [the Sound
of Mull], and the quietness of the Lord's morning was spreading in
calm beauty on every side.'

(Clerk 1910: 487)

Do sgaoil a bhrón fán mBanbha
'Sorrow for him spread throughout Ireland'

(Cathal MacMhuirich 17th c., *FEMN*: 172.26)

'S ma thaisbeanas e ghnùis an gruaim,
Grad sgaoilidh uamhunn feadh nan speur
'If he [sc. God] reveals his countenance in anger,
terror will suddenly spread throughout the skies'

(Bochanan [1767] 1913: 1)

2.3 A plague or illness disperses through the skin (*DOST* 13):

Intransitive

agus gun a' phlàigh bhi sgaoileadh 'sa' chroicionn
'and without the plague spreading in the skin'

(*Lebhiticus* 13:5)

while liquids 'spread' throughout the land or body (*DOST* 13):

> *Tha na sruthanan craobhach*
> *Bha sgaoileadh ad bhallaibh . . .*
> *A nise air traoghadh . . .*
> 'The branching streams [of blood] which [once] were spreading
> throughout your limbs . . . have now dried up . . .'
>
> (Bochanan [1767] 1913: 53)

Figurative

> *Is sgaoilidh 'n tuil ud air gach taobh*
> *A' cur an t-saogh 'l 'na lasair dheirg*
> 'And that torrent [sc. of fire] will spread on every side,
> turning the world into a red flame'
>
> (Bochanan [1767] 1913: 19)

2.4 *Sgaoil*, in the sense of 'spread out, distend, slacken' (*DOST* 5(a)), is well attested in ScG, but with a range of specific applications not found with *scail* in *DOST*.

2.4.1 It is used of the untying of livestock:

Transitive

> *Na ba is na capaill do sgaoilis as do thoigh*
> 'the cows and horses that you untied from your house'
>
> (BDL/Watson 1937: 78)

and the opening of knots (figurative in both citations):

> *agas cred e daingne an t-snaidhm-sa nach bfetar ar en-chor a fhosgladh no*
> *a sgaoileadh*
> 'and what is the strength of this knot that cannot under any
> circumstances be opened or unloosened'
>
> (Carswell [1567] 1970: 71)

> *snaidhm a raith do rosgaoiledh*
> 'the knot of his good fortune has been untied'
>
> (Cathal MacMhuirich 17th c., *FEMN*: 169.1)

2.4.2 It is applied to someone or something in cords or fetters, in the sense of 'being freed, released' (*DIL* II (j)):

Transitive

canamhuin oirdheirc na ntír úd air bhi dhi o shean a mbruid a sgaoileadh
nois o chuibhreach
'the glorious language of those lands, having been of old in captivity, is
now being freed from fetters'

(Robt Campbell 1707, TCD 1392, vol. 2. fol. 8, q. 2)

Past participle

B'fhearr go bithinn sgaoilt as na cordamhsa
'Would that I could be released from these cords'

(*Ais-eiridh* 1751: 18)

Biodh m' anam 's mo chorp gu naomha
O fhuair mi sgàoilte as na glasaibh
'May my soul and my body be holy
since I was released from the locks'

(*E* 1776: 145)

2.4.3 Fetters and locks are themselves opened, untied or unloosened:

Transitive

sgaoil mo ghlasan le t' eochraichin oir
'unfasten my locks with your keys of gold'

(*Ais-eiridh* 1751: 8)

and so too are arteries and veins (cf. *DOST* 4):

mo chuislibh sgaoileadh, iad 's go faodainn snamh
'[that] my arteries be opened up, in such a way that I could swim'
(*Ais-eiridh* 1751: 168 2.7)

Gates, doors or mouths can be spread open:

Transitive

Sgaoilear gu fairsing do d' naimhdibh geatacha do thìre
'The gates of your land will be thrown wide open to your
enemies'

(*Nahum* 3:13 [cf. *DIL* II (j)])

Tha ifrinn agus leir-sgrios a' fosgladh am beoil, agus a' sgaoileadh an
gial gu farsaing as a cheile chum an slugadh a suas
'Hell and destruction are opening their mouth, and spreading their
jaws wide apart in order to swallow them [sc. sinners]'
(MacDiarmaid 1804: 56)

2.5 The planks of boats can 'spread' by 'coming apart at the seams' (cf. *DOST* 16
and *SND* 4, 'To burst (a garment) at a seam'; see 3.12.4 below):

Intransitive

Mu dheireadh sgaoil iad 'nam bordan as a cheile, agus chaidh iad fodha
'Finally they came apart as boards, and they sank'
(*Arabian Nights* 1899, Div 2: 39)

2.6 The hair can spread outwards by being let loose, sometimes in a dishevelled
condition (*DOST* 5(b)):

Verbal noun

B' eibhinn fhaicinn ga sgaoleadh
Is fiamh laista na greina mad chluais
'It was delightful to see it being let loose,
With the shining gleam of the sun about your ear'
(*E* 1776: 221)

Past participle

Agus a falt gun chìreadh sgaoilte sìos m' a sùilean, agus pàirt dheth air a spìonadh
'and her hair uncombed, let loose down about her eyes, and part of it plucked
out'
(*Arabian Knights* 1897, Div. 1: 70)

2.7 Military usages of both *scail* and *sgaoil* are well attested. In ScG usages
corresponding to those of Scots are very evident.

2.7.1 *Sgaoil* can denote the dispersal of an army for tactical reasons (*DOST* 12):

Intransitive

ni fuaradar an riarughadh mar búdh mian leo, ionnus gur sgaoil an tárm
'they did not get satisfaction as they desired, so that the army dispersed'
(*Rel. Celt.* II: 166)

2.7.2 A warrior can 'disengage' his attack (cf. *DOST* 12(b)):

Intransitive

> *Le feadhain daoinigh 'na dhiaidh*
> *ní sgaoiltir go mbearair buaidh*
> 'With a body of men in his pursuit,
> he never disengages until victory is accomplished'
>
> (Eóin Ó Muirgheasáin 1626, *SGS* VIII, 32)

2.7.3 An army or fighting force is 'disbanded' (*DOST* 7(a)):

Transitive

> *Nuair a sgaoileadh am milisi, dh'fhasdadh mi aig tuathanach*
> 'When the militia was disbanded, I was employed by a farmer'
>
> (MacLellan [1960] 1972: 30)

2.7.4 Enemies' armies are scattered by force (*DOST* 8):

Transitive

> *A shaighde leig se chuc' amach,*
> *do sgaoil se iad ar fad*
> 'He let his arrows fly out at them,
> and he scattered them all'
>
> (*Psalms* 1659: 18:14)

(*DIL* II (a), (b))

> *Tha sinn anois air ar sgaoileadh, air feadh ghleann, is fhraoich-beann*
> *ard*
> 'We [sc. Jacobite sympathisers after Culloden] are now scattered,
> throughout glens and high, heather-covered mountains'
>
> (*Ais-eiridh* 1751: 135)

> *Ach thusa, o Thighearna! a 'ta rioghacha thaireis air cumhachd na*
> *mara . . . sgaoil as cheille an sluagh, leis an aill an coga', agus brugh*
> *iad ann do neart.*
> 'But you, O Lord, who reigns over the power of the sea . . . disperse
> the host which is well disposed to war, and crush them in your
> strength.'
>
> (TK 1785: 144)

(Cf. *DOST* 11)

> *Nuair sgaoileadh bhuainn 's gach àite iad,*
> *Mar chaoraich 's gille-màrtainn annt'*
> 'When they [sc. the French army in Egypt] were scattered by us
> everywhere, like sheep with a fox among them'
> > (Alexander MacKinnon [1801] in Meek 2003: 302)

Intransitive (*DOST* 12)

> *Mo chreach, armailt nam breacan*
> *Bhith air sgaoileadh 's air sgapadh 's gach àird,*
> *Aig fior-bhalgairean Shasainn*
> *Nach do ghnàthaich bonn ceartais 'nan dàil*
> 'Alas, that the tartan-clad army
> has scattered and spread everywhere,
> because of the base rascals of England
> who showed not a whit of justice in their encounter'
> > (John Roy Stewart [c. 1746] in Campbell 1984: 168)

> *Chuid tha beò dhiubh an déidh sgaoilidh*
> *'S iad gam fògair le gaothan thar tuinn*
> 'Those of them [sc. Jacobites] who survive have scattered, and are being
> exiled by winds across waves'
> > (John Roy Stewart [c. 1746], ibid.: 170)

2.7.5 People can be dispersed through adverse circumstances, such as clearance:

Transitive (*DOST* 11a)

> *Nan seasadh uaislean na rìoghachd*
> *Cho dìleas ri càirdeas Ailein,*
> *Cha bhiodh an tuath air a sgaoileadh*
> *Gan cur gu aoidheachd a dh 'aindeoin*
> 'If all the nobles of the kingdom
> maintained kinship as faithfully as Alan [sc. Cameron of Erracht],
> the people would not be dispersed
> and made to live on charity, regardless'
> > (Ailean Dall MacDhùghaill [c. 1798] in Meek 1995: 50)

> *Cha till, cha till na daoine*
> *Bha cridheil agus aoibheil –*
> *Mar mholl air latha gaoithe*

Chaidh 'n sgaoileadh gu bràth
'The people will never again return
who were hearty and happy –
like chaff on a day of wind
they have been scattered for ever'

(Whyte 1898: 50)

2.8 *Sgaoil* is regularly used of the dismissal or breaking up of a convivial event, an assembly, commonly a religious gathering, congregation or school, and this ScG usage corresponds particularly closely to that in Scots (*DOST* 12; *SND* 5 (2)):

Intransitive (*DOST* 12)

Agas i ndiaidh na togha marsin moladh an pobal Dia re salm eigin sul sgaoilfeas siad o cheile
'And after making the choice thus, let the people praise God with a certain psalm before they separate from one another'

(Carswell [1567] 1970: 22)

abradh an minisdir an beandachadh so síos, agas sgaoileadh an pobal o sin amach an lá-sin
'let the minister say the blessing below, and let the people disperse thereafter on that day'

(Carswell [1567] 1970: 35)

Sgaoilimit o altair Bhachuis, a chléirich taisg a' chailis uat
'Let us disperse from the altar of Bacchus; cleric, put the chalice away from you'

(Ais-eiridh 1751: 82)

is i chomhairle ar ar chinned(h) leo sgaoiledh o cheile
'the advice which was agreed was to separate from one another'

(Mór mo mholadh 17th c., *SGS* II, 80)

Bha 'sgoil, a rèir choltais, air sgaoileadh tràth, oir bha dròbh mhòr chloinne mun cuairt
'The school, apparently, had broken up early, as there was a big drove of children around'

(MacLean 1967: 9)

2.9 *Sgaoil* is applied to the ending of a close relationship (cf. *DOST* 7d, e):

Transitive

> *Cha mhi fhin a sgaoil an comunn*
> *A bha eadar mi 's creag ghuanach*
> 'It was not I myself who sundered the association
> that existed between me and Creag Ghuanach'

(E 1776: 10)

2.10 Feelings and visions also 'disperse, vanish':

Intransitive

> *Na'n cluinninn féin . . . fear do phearsa thigh 'nn dò 'n fhonn*
> *Gun sgaoileadh mo phramh 's m' airsneal*
> 'If I were to hear of . . . a man of your character coming to the land,
> my gloom and weariness would disperse'

(MacLean 1818: 198)

> *'Nuair a bhios mi leam fhéin,*
> *'S neo-shìtheil bhios mo smuaintean,*
> *A' smaoineachadh air d' aodann,*
> *Gus an sgaoil mo bhruadar.*
> 'When I am alone
> my thoughts are restless,
> thinking about your face,
> until my dream disperses.'

(BL 1916: 135)

The dominant senses of *sgaoil* in the ScG examples in Section 2 seem to be 'setting free, releasing, dismissing, dispersing', often in an orderly way (rather than 'all over the place', a sense which sometimes requires reinforcement with *sgap*), and governed by the subject or object concerned. The Scots and ScG usages which correspond most closely in this section are in violent (and usually disorderly) military contexts (2.7) and in (orderly) 'dismissal, parting, dispersing' (2.8). The military citations in *DOST*, however, represent a greater and more technical range of activity than that found in the ScG examples, including the 'raising' of a siege (*DOST* 9), and the attacking of a town (*DOST* 8 (a) (2)), suggesting that the application of Scots *scail* was developed particularly strongly in a military context. The *DOST* citations for 'dismissing, dispersing' of people are especially close to ScG. If we were to argue for a ScG origin for Scots *scail*, the evidence of this section might suggest that, in the period before 1700, Scots speakers may have borrowed *sgaoil* from Gaelic speakers in the context of fighting and war, and also in the (presumably) less belligerent context of formal meetings, 'moots', or assemblies of other kinds.

3. 'DISTINCTIVE' SCG USAGES OF *SGAOIL*

In some of their more specific applications of *scail* and *sgaoil*, Scots and ScG share common ground, but ScG has a very wide range of usages not found in Scots. In several cases, the 'distinctive' ScG usages can be traced in *DIL*.

3.1 *Sgaoil* is used in the sense of 'separate', sometimes reinforced with *o chèile* ('from one another') (*DIL* I (b)):

Transitive

> *Tha iad a sgaoile' nan nithe sin a chuir DIA cuideachd* 'They are
> separating those things that GOD put together'
> $$(AA \ 1781: \ 55)$$

> *Togamaid duinn féin baile, agus tùr . . . an t-eagal gun sgaoilear o chéile*
> *sinn air aghaidh na talmhainn uile*
> 'Let us build for ourselves a city, and a tower . . . lest we be separated
> from one another on the face of the whole earth'
> $$(Genesis \ 11: \ 4)$$

3.2 It is used of the 'separation' of the sea under certain circumstances, such as the crossing of the Red Sea by Moses and the Israelites in the time of the Exodus (cf. *DOST* 4 (c)):

Transitive

> *'S nuair a chaidh an fhairge sgaoileadh,*
> *Gu 'n robh i aig Maois 'san fhàsach*
> 'And when the sea was dispersed,
> she [sc. the Gaelic language] accompanied Moses in the wilderness'
> (MacCoinnich 1982: 15)

3.3 In military contexts, shields can 'come apart', presumably layer by layer (cf. *DIL* I (a), II (g), and 3.12.4):

Transitive

> *ar chor 's . . . gan lansgaoilid a sgiathan*
> 'in such a way that . . . their shields disintegrate'
>   (Cath Fionntrágha (transcr. Alexander MacDonald) Adv. 72.2.11: 8.25)

3.4 The divesting of clothes can be denoted by *sgaoil* (followed by the preposition *de*):

Transitive

> *Is médach saic, a chean',*
> *Do sgaoileis diom*
> 'and my sackcloth I have already put off'
>
> > (*Psalms* 1659: 30:11)

3.5 *Sgaoil* can be used of the spreading of cloth of any kind, from sackcloth to sails:

Transitive

> *Agus sgaoilidh iad an t-eudach an làthair sheanairean a bhaile*
> 'And they will spread the cloth in the presence of the elders of the town'
>
> > (*Deuteronomi* 22: 17)

3.5.1 It can be applied to the 'unfurling' of banners:

> *'nuair sgaoilte do bhrattach.*
> 'when your banner was unfurled'
>
> > (Donnchadh Bàn 1768: 21)

> *'Nuair a sgaoil iad do bhratach mu'n chrann*
> 'when they unfurled your banner about the mast'
>
> > (Cameron 1785: 54)

and the 'spreading out' of tents:

> *agus sgaoil e mach am bùth os cionn a' phàilliuin*
> 'and he spread out the booth above the tent'
>
> > (*Ecsodus* 40: 19)

3.6 ScG does not appear to attest a usage of *sgaoil* on its own corresponding directly to *DOST* 1b, 'to dispose of one's dwelling, furnishings and belongings'. However, when reinforced by the idiom *ás a chèile* ('from one another, apart') to avoid the sense of 'extend', *sgaoil* can be used of 'taking apart' a tent (cf. *fa/ma sgaoil* below):

> *agus sgaoil e as a chéile a' phàilliun, mar challaid*
> 'and he took apart his tent, as if it were a hedge'
>
> > (*Tuireadh* 2: 6)

3.7 Trees and plants extend their roots and branches:

Transitive and figurative

> *Ga sgaoileadh fein amach mar chraoibh*
> *ag fas gu dosrach ur*
> '[sc. The man under God's curse] spreading himself out like a tree growing luxuriantly and freshly'
>
> *(Psalms* 1659: 37:35)

> *Bha mo fhreumh air a sgaoileadh a mach làimh ris na h-uisgeachaibh, agus luidh an drùchd rè na h-oidhche air mo mheangan*
> 'My root was spread out beside the waters, and the dew lay during the night upon my branch'
>
> *(Iob* 29: 19)

Figurative and intransitive (*DIL* 1 (a))

> *Is geug thorrach Ioseph, geug thorrach làimh re tobar, aig am bheil a meanglain a' sgaoileadh thar a' bhalladh*
> 'Joseph is a fertile branch, a fertile branch beside a well, that has her branches spread over the wall'
>
> *(Genesis* 49: 22)

Birds spread out their wings (*DIL* II (e)):

Transitive

> *Mar a charaicheas iolair suas a nead, a dh'itealaicheas i os cionn a h-àil, a sgaoileas i mach a sgiathan, a ghabhas i iad, a ghiùlaineas i iad air a sgiathaibh*
> 'as an eagle stirs up her nest, flies above her brood, spreads out her wings, takes them [her brood] up, [and] carries them on her wings'
>
> *(Deuteronomi* 32: 11)

Winter, like a large bird, figuratively spreads its wings in Dugald Buchanan's song 'An Geamhradh' ('The Winter'):

> *Sgaoil oirnne a sgiathan*
> *'S chuir e ghrian air a chùlaibh,*

As an nead thug 'e 'n t-àlach
Neo-bhàigheil 'g ar sgiùrsadh
'It spread its wings over us,
and it covered over the sun;
from the nest it brought
the unfriendly brood to scourge us'

(Bochanan [1767] 1913: 51)

The hands are likewise 'spread out':

Agus aig an iobairt fheasgair dh 'éirich mi o m' thùirse . . . agus leag mi
mi féin air mo ghlùinibh, agus sgaoil mi mach mo làmhan a dh' ionnsuidh
an Tighearna mo Dhé
'And at the evening sacrifice I rose from my sorrow . . . and I dropped
myself on to my knees, and I spread out my hands towards the Lord
my God'

(*Esra* 9: 5)

3.8 In the ScG Old Testament, families and kindreds are 'disseminated' or spread
throughout the land purposefully:

Transitive

measg fineach sgaoilidh sinn
'among kindreds we [sc. the Israelites] were dispersed'

(*Psalms* 1659: 44:11)

Roinnidh mi iad ann an Iacob, agus sgaoilidh mi iad ann an Israel
'I will divide them [sc. Simeon and Levi] in Jacob, and I will scatter
them in Israel'

(*Genesis* 49: 7)

Agus na dheigh sin sgaoileadh a mach teaghlaichean nan Canaanach
'and after that the families of the Canaanites were dispersed'

(*Genesis* 10: 18)

Intransitive (*DIL* II (b))

agus sgaoilidh tu mach a dh' ionnsuidh na h-àird an iar agus na h-àird an
ear
'and you [sc. Jacob] will disperse unto the west and unto the east'

(*Genesis* 28: 14)

3.9 Good qualities and vices 'disseminate':

Transitive

> *bha peac agus bas air an tabhairt do'n t-saoghal so, agus air an sgaoileadh*
> *a measg a chloinn uille*
> 'sin and death were brought to this world, and were spread among all
> of his [sc. Adam's] children'
>
> (2 Cat 1774: 42)

and thoughts are 'laid out' or 'arranged' (cf. *DIL* II b):

Past participle

> *tha smuaintibh a chridhe, a bha sgaoilt ann toiseach na h oibreadh*
> 'the thoughts of his heart, which were laid out at the beginning of the
> work'
>
> (Guthrie 1783: 44)

3.10 One of the more sustained and distinctive usages of *sgaoil* is its application
in contexts of hospitality, bounty and reward (though we might compare *DOST*'s
sense 4d '*fig.* to confer; to use wastefully').

3.10.1 The table is 'spread' with food:

Transitive

> *Sgaoil do bhord le fèisd*
> 'Spread your table with a feast'
>
> (*AA* 1781: 89)

> *Sgaoil iad na bùird tharbhach fhial*
> 'They spread the bountiful, generous tables'
>
> (MacLachlan 1937: 23)

3.10.2 Good things and bounty are dispensed (*DIL* II (c)):

Transitive

> *sgaoil é h uile maitheas oirnne*
> 'he bestowed every kind of bounty upon us'
>
> (Donnchadh Bàn 1768: 18)

and cattle are given as rewards to the poets in the Classical period:

> *a gcrodh ar sgolaibh do sgaoil*
> 'he dispensed their cattle to the poet-schools'
> (Eóin Og Ó Muirgheasáin 1626, *SGS* VIII: 42)

3.11 In the late Classical period, Gaelic attests the use of *sgaoil* for the firing of a shot from a weapon, in the sense of 'giving out', 'spreading' or 'releasing' lead from a gun. It is attested in Early Irish (*DIL* II (k)). It is not found in *DOST*, but *scail* meaning 'to discharge a gun' is noted in *SND* 3 (1):

> *Ainnsin do sgaoil Raghnall an t-urch[ar] 7 ni ar fer an bhogha. Tilgis an gunna úagha . . .*
> 'Then Ranald fired the shot, but not at the bowman. He threw the gun away from him . . .'
> (Niall MacMhuirich, *Rel. Celt.* II, 188)

3.12 The past participle of *sgaoil*, namely *sgaoilte*, while mirroring the basic meaning of Scots *scailit*, has a wide range of senses and idiomatic shadings, from the physical to the mental, the great majority of which are not attested in Scots.

3.12.1 It can be applied to mental and physical energy, in the sense of being 'extended beyond the normal':

> *Na h-iuchraichean gaoil sin . . .*
> *Dh 'fhàg aigne nan daoine cho sgaoilt' air an toir*
> 'These keys of love . . . which have caused people's spirits to "go all out" in their pursuit'
> (Stewart 1802: 153)

3.12.2 *Sgaoilte*, followed by different prepositions, can convey aspects of personal 'exposure' to people or things. With the preposition *ri*, it can apparently mean 'open-hearted towards; thus generous, ready to receive friends' and perhaps 'popular':

> *Bha mi uairicin do 'm t-shaoghail* [sic]
> *Bha mi sgailte ris na feara',*
> *Nis fo 'n chinn mi aosda*
> *Cha dig duine an taobh so 'm charradh.*
> 'There was a time in my life
> when I was popular with the lads,
> but now that I have grown old,
> nobody comes near me here.'
> (Cunningham 1806: 76)

With the preposition *do*, it can mean 'exposed to, vulnerable to':

Tha na nithe so ni 'mhàin peacach, ach mar an ceudna gar fàgail sgaoilte
do iomadh peacadh eile
'These things are not only sinful, but make us vulnerable to many
another sin'

(MacDiarmaid 1804: 113)

3.12.3 It is commonly used adjectivally in the Gaelic Old Testament in the sense
of 'smashed to pieces, devastated, ruined, laid waste' (*DIL* II (g) and also s.v.
scaílte, in the sense of 'sundered apart'):

Agus fàsaidh an tìr na làraich sgaoilte
'And the land will become a ruined waste'   (*Isaiah* 17: 9)

Fhuair an fhirinn tuisleadh anns an t-sràid sgaoilte
'Truth received a downfall in the devastated street'

(*Isaiah* 14: 59)

Togaidh iad a rìs na caithrichean a bha sgaoilte
'They will rebuild the cities that were ruined'

(*Isaiah* 61: 4)

ach pillidh sinn is togaidh sinn na h-ionada sgaoilte
'but we will return and we will build the ruined places'

(*Malachi* 1: 4)

3.12.4 It can also be applied to a boat or any wooden vessel which has fallen apart
(cf. Scots *skelt*, 'burst at the seams', *SND* 4, and see also 2.5 above):

Chan fhiach dhomh an lìon a chàradh
A chionn 's gu bheil am bàta sgaoilte
'It is not worth my while to mend the net,
Since the boat has come to pieces'

(Thomson 1951: 47)

3.12.5 *Sgaoilte* can also be applied in contemporary Gaelic to a scatter-
brained, disorganised or dishevelled person, often one who is 'at sixes and
sevens' or the worse for wear through drink (cf. *sgaoilte*, 'dissolute', in *DIL*,
s.v. *scaílte*):

Bha tuataidh an-raoir air a' bhus,
fear sgaoilte gun chuims' gun shnas

ri taobh fir eile
'There was a rustic on the bus last night,
one disorganised, aimless, dishevelled man
by the side of another'

(*SaaC* 1967: 59)

3.13 The verbal noun *sgaoileadh* can be used with most of the meanings identified above, but some specific usages and idioms deserve to be noted.

3.13.1 It is employed in malediction:

Seo a' chomhachag aosmhor
Tha 'n Creag Aodainn seo shìos:
Tha i guidhe 's a' glaodhaich
'Droch sgaoileadh 'nur gnìomh!'
'This is the ancient owl
which lives in Creag Aodainn down here,
cursing and crying,
"May your action come to a bad end!" '

(Meek 1995: 59)

3.13.2 It is used of the 'spreading, shattering, coming apart' of various parts of the body, usually specified after the verbal noun:

. . . air leth truagh is tinn le sgaoileadh-mionaich an deidh an t-uisge sin òl
'very poor and sick with dysentery after drinking that water'

(Dòmhnallach 1974: 20)

Thàinig sgaoiledh 'na chorp
'His bowels loosened'

(FAM 1958, 127)

sgaoileadh cinn
'a head that has been very badly knocked or cracked'

(FAM 1958, VII, 71)

Figurative

Tarraini' miana na feolmhorachd amach thu, ach air do 'n uair dol
seachad, ciod tha thu toirt tachai' ach eullach coguis agus sgaoilea' cridhe [?]
'The desires of the flesh will entice you forth, but when the time has passed, what do you bring home but a burden on the conscience and a distention [i.e. dissipation] of the heart?'

(TK 1785: 32)

3.13.3 Figuratively also, a person can 'spread apart' or 'split his/her sides' with laughter:

> *bha mi gu sgaoileadh le gàireachdaich*
> 'I was on the point of splitting with laughter'
>
> (*Gairm* 4 (1953): 74)

> *theab am bodach sgaoileadh glan a' gàire*
> 'the old man almost came apart completely through laughing'
>
> (MacLellan [1960] 1972: 72)

3.13.4 In a bardic context *sgaoileadh* can be used of the liberality of patrons (cf. 3.10.2):

> *Iain mhic Eachainn, on dh 'eug thu*
> *Càit an teid sinn a dh 'fhaotainn*
> *Duine sheasas nad fhine*
> *An rathad tionail no sgaoilidh?*
> 'Iain son of Hector, since you have died,
> where will we go to find
> another to take your place in your kindred
> in the way of gathering and dispensing?'
>
> (Rob Donn [c. 1759], *BG* 1959: 82)

3.14 Besides distinctive usages of the past participle and the verbal noun, Gaelic deploys a range of closely related prepositional idioms that are not matched in Scots. The noun *sgaoil* ('dispersal, state of being spread'), which can be traced back to Early Irish (see *DIL* s.v. *scaíl*), can be used with a range of auxiliary verbs (such as *cuir* and *leig*), with the preposition *fa/ma* or *air*, to give the sense of 'release, set apart, fall apart', or with *o* in the sense of 'cause to come apart' or 'terminate'. The semantic range of these idioms complements that of the verb *sgaoil* as described above, and, in certain contexts, it may move in roughly the same direction as Scots *scail* in the sense of 'to remove or take away (a responsibility); to annul (a proclamation); to change (a decision)' (*DOST* 10). The use of these idioms avoids any danger of ambiguity that might arise through the application of the verb *sgaoil* on its own in these contexts:

> *Tha obair nan sè là rinn Dia*
> *Le lasair dhian 'ga chur ma sgaoil*
> 'The work done by God in six days
> is being dismantled by means of a fervent flame'
>
> (Bochanan [1767] 1913: 20)

nuair a bha na h abstala air an cur an priosan, bha iad air an cur fa
sgaoil le ainglibh
'when the apostles were put in prison, they were released by angels'
(2 Cat 1774: 56)

Nach fhaodar a chur fa sgaoil a tha eadar Dia agus a phobull
'That [that matter] cannot be taken apart, which is between God and
his people'
(Guthrie 1783: 193)

Ach 'n am measg uile chomharraich mi aon long mhòr a thug bàrr orra air
fad: bha iomadh bàta beag a' gabhail d' a h-ionnsuidh, 'us mhothaich mi
gu-n robh iad a' deanamh deas g'a cur fo sgaoil
'But among them all I picked out one large vessel that surpassed every
one of them; many a small boat was making her way towards her, and I
noticed that they were making ready to unfurl her sails'
(Clerk 1910: 264 (cf. *DOST* 5))

Chaidh an fhàrdach a chur ma sgaoil
'The house was broken up' (*An R.* 1918: 71 (cf. *DOST* 1(b)))

Tha Esan a' siubhal le deifir, a ta teachd a chur a phriosunaich air sgaoil
'He is moving swiftly, who comes to release his prisoners'
(*Isaiah* 51: 14)

Bas Shir Domhnuil bho 'n chaol,
Chuir mo chomhnuidh o sgaoil
'It was the death of Sir Donald from the kyle
Which tore apart my existence'
(*E* 1776: 328)

3.15 *Sgaoil* (vb) also forms a compound with *craobh-* ('tree'-) in the sense of
'proclaim, broadcast, promulgate' (cf. *DIL*, s.v. *cráebscailed*):

'*Craobhsgaoileadh A Bhiobuill agus an t-soisgeil*'
'The promulgation of the Bible and the Gospel'
(MacGrhiogair 1819: 82)

Sin an dà mheadhon leis am bheil fiosrachadh a' chinne-daonna troimh na
linntean air a chraobh-sgaoileadh
'These are the two means by which the information of human kind
throughout the centuries has been broadcast'
(Dòmhnall MacLaomainn *Gairm* 9 (1954): 20)

The examples of ScG *sgaoil* in this section show very precise application of the verb in particular contexts, often with a subject or object which is 'disseminated purposefully', 'extended' or 'distended (to the point of falling apart)'. The idiom *fa sgaoil* and its variants (3.14) delimit such action, and give an unambiguous sense of finality or release, where such is required. It is very noticeable that ScG makes extensive use of the verbal noun *sgaoileadh* and the past participle *sgaoilte* to provide a range of meanings which are particularly sharply focused, and which often relate to individual functions, mental and physical. Such flexibility is not matched in the Scots context, where the use of *scailit* tends to adhere closely to the 'normal' senses of the verb *scail*. The fact that several of these ScG usages can be traced in *DIL* anchors *sgaoil* firmly on the Gaelic side, and suggests strongly that, if we consider direct borrowing to have occurred in this instance, Scots is likely to have borrowed *scail* from Gaelic, in a restricted range of meanings, rather than the other way about.

4. CONCLUSION

This exploratory, and necessarily circumscribed, study of ScG *sgaoil* alongside Scots *scail* demonstrates that, in this instance, the two languages share a comparable range of idioms based on what appears to be (in origin) the same verb. Correspondence in the uses of both verbs is evident in basic discourse, as well as in more specific domains. Most of the sample in *DOST*, insofar as we can judge at present, can be matched within ScG.

Nevertheless, there are very significant differences and distinctive nuances, especially on the ScG side, which will require to be taken into account in a future entry for *sgaoil* in Faclair na Gàidhlig. In the light of such differences, it is understandable that earlier scholars were wary of pressing too strongly a ScG origin for *scail*. It is apparent that, beyond their primary meanings, both languages have developed their respective usages of *scail* and *sgaoil* very extensively for their own specific needs, with different emphases and subtle distinctions in idiom, often heavily dependent on the contexts in which they are used, and/or on the subject or object of the verb. It is clear that *scail* and *sgaoil*, and especially the latter, are forced to work extremely hard for their living – part of the price of being basic, work-a-day verbs naturally applicable to a diversity of contexts.

Overall, the evidence of *DOST* demonstrates that Scots *scail* is semantically the more restricted of the two verbs. It is used predominantly in a physical, non-figurative, manner, of agriculture, the natural elements (including the spilling or pouring of liquid, *DOST* 4 (a), 15), the disposing of houses and personal possessions, the dismissing or parting of people, and (very noticeably) military strategy. Most of these usages are found in ScG also, with the noteworthy exception of the spilling of liquids (for which ScG would normally use *dòirt*).

Military action and formal dismissal are the contexts of closest correspondence, and, if borrowing occurred, these appear to have been the primary points of exchange between the two cultures in this instance. Beyond military engagement or formal dismissal, the application of Scots *scail* to people, individually or collectively, is relatively slight, and the basic meaning inclines towards 'scatter, separate', with a strong sense of energetic, if not violent, physical activity.

While accommodating these meanings, ScG *sgaoil* leans more towards 'disseminate, dissipate, spread out, extend, release' as its primary senses, in many different settings but commonly with an underlying implication of order or purpose (which may explain the absence of ScG *sgaoil* in the sense of 'spill'). It has developed a much wider range of (often) figurative, situation-specific usages, reflecting a much closer association with people, and a deeper, more subjective reach into their psyche. ScG *sgaoil* is commonly applied in a colourfully descriptive way to the 'ordinary' – and even the 'earthy' – aspects of life, such as the weather, the sea, boats, cloth and clothing, plants, animals and bodily functions, human emotions (love, laughter, sorrow), religious beliefs and social customs.

ScG thus appears to have had a more intimate and more creative engagement with *sgaoil* than Scots had with *scail*. Together with the usages of both *scail* and *sgaoil* which can be paralleled in *DIL*, and those usages in Section 3 which can be matched only in *DIL* and later Irish dictionaries, this might suggest that the word is more naturally domiciled in the Gaelic languages. The evidence *prima facie* therefore encourages the conclusion that *scail* may have been borrowed, in very specific contexts, into Scots from one of the major dialects of Gaelic, ScG being the most obvious source. This view would reinforce the thrust of *DOST*'s tentative etymology of *scail*. At the same time we have to bear in mind that the meanings of Scots *scail* match no more than a small proportion of the meanings of ScG *sgaoil*. Consequently, only a properly historical analysis of the entire body of evidence for *sgaoil* in ScG, relative to *scail* and similar verbs in other languages (e.g. Old Norse), will put the matter beyond doubt.

Whatever the answer, words can certainly spread, taking their semantic fields with them. *Scail* and *sgaoil* bear eloquent testimony to their own meanings, since they demonstrate splendidly the remarkable capacity of both Scots and Scottish Gaelic to share parts of their respective lexes, possibly by borrowing. Following the ground-breaking analysis of *scail* provided in *DOST*, we can take the exciting first step in what has been a long-delayed comparison of shared – and potentially borrowed – parts of the lexes in both languages. However, we can see only a fraction of the evidence, and we must guard against precipitate conclusions. The tale of the two languages' lexical relationships will not be told in anything like the detail it deserves until that apocalyptic day when Faclair na Gàidhlig, presently at an embryonic stage, takes its place alongside the mature and venerable *DOST*.

REFERENCES AND SOURCES

The abbreviations are generally those used in HDSG-A, and are based on the lists of works issued and read for HDSG. These lists were made in the 1970s by the present writer (and are thus called the 'Meek Lists').

AA: Joseph Alleine (1781), *Alarm to the Unconverted*, transl. John Smith, Edinburgh.

Adv.: Advocates' Library MSS in the National Library of Scotland, Edinburgh.

Ais-eiridh: Alexander MacDonald (1751), *Ais-Eiridh na Sean-Chanoin Albannaich*, printed for the author, Edinburgh.

An R: *An Ròsarnach* 1–5, Glasgow, 1907–31.

Arabian Nights: Sgeulachdan Arabianach, transl. John Macrury (1897–1900), 3 vols, Inverness.

BG: *Bàrdachd Ghàidhlig*, ed. William J. Watson (1959), Glasgow: An Comunn Gàidhealach.

BL: *Bàrdachd Leòdhais*, ed. John N. MacLeod (1916), Glasgow: Alexander MacLaren.

Bochanan, Dùghall, *Dàin Spioradail*, ed. Donald MacLean (1913), Edinburgh: John Grant.

Broughton, Thomas (1797), *An Saighidear Criosduidh*, Edinburgh: John Moir.

Cameron, Alexander, *Orain agus Rannachd ann Gaidhlig* (1785), Edinburgh: D. Mac-Phatric.

Campbell, John Lorne (ed.) (1984), *Highland Songs of the Forty-five*, Edinburgh: Scottish Gaelic Texts Society.

Carswell, John, *Foirm na n-Urrnuidheadh*, ed. Robert L. Thomson (1970), Edinburgh: Scottish Gaelic Texts Society.

2 Cat 1774: Isaac Watts, *Da Leabhar Chestian agus Urnuighean* (1774), Edinburgh.

Clerk, Archibald (ed.) (1910), *Caraid nan Gaidheal: The Friend of the Gael. A Choice Selection of Gaelic Writings*, Edinburgh: John Grant.

Cunningham, Duncan, *Orain Ghaelich air an nuadh chuir amach* (1806), printed for the author, Glasgow.

Deuteronomi, see *Leabhraichean an t-Seann Tiomnaidh*.

DIL: *Dictionary of the Irish Language, based mainly on Old and Middle Irish materials*, compact edn (1983), Dublin: Royal Irish Academy.

Dòmhnallach, Dòmhnall Iain (1974), *Fo Sgàil a' Swastika*, Inverness.

Donnchadh Bàn: Duncan MacIntyre, *Orain Ghaidhealach* (1786), printed for the author, Edinburgh.

E: *Comh-chruinneachidh Orranaigh Gaidhealach* ['The Eigg Collection'], ed. Ranald MacDonald (1776), Edinburgh: Walter Ruddiman.

Ecsodus, see *Leabhraichean an t-Seann Tiomnaidh*.

Esra, see *Leabhraichean an t-Seann Tiomnaidh*.

FAM: Father Allan McDonald, *Gaelic Words and Expressions from South Uist and Eriskay* (1958), Dublin: Dublin Institute for Advanced Studies.

FEMN: E. Ua Ruain (ed.) (1940), *Féill-sgríbhinn Eóin Mhic Néill*, Dublin.

GA: John Smith (1780), *Galic Antiquities*, Edinburgh.

Gairm 1–200, Glasgow, 1952–2002.

Genesis, see *Leabhraichean an t-Seann Tiomnaidh*.

GnaB: *Guth na Bliadhna* 1–20, Aberdeen, Edinburgh and Glasgow, 1904–25.

Guthrie, William, *Coir Mhor a Chriosduidh*, transl. Patrick MacFarlane (1783), Falkirk.

Iob, see *Leabhraichean an t-Seann Tiomnaidh*.

Isaiah, see *Leabhraichean an t-Seann Tiomnaidh*.

Leabhraichean an t-Seann Tiomnaidh air an tarruing o'n cheud chànain chum Gaelic Albannaich, 4 vols (1783–1801), Edinburgh: A. Smellie.

Lebhiticus, see *Leabhraichean an t-Seann Tiomnaidh*

MacCoinnich, Uilleam (1982), *Cnoc Chusbaig: Orain agus Dàin*, Glasgow: *Gairm*.

MacDiarmaid, Eobhann (1804), *Searmona*, Edinburgh.

MacGrhiogair [sic], Seumas (1819), *Dain a Chomh[n]adh Crabhuidh*, Glasgow.

MacKenzie, Donald (1785), *Oran Gairdeachais*, printed for the author, Glasgow.

MacLachlan: *Ewen MacLachlan's Gaelic Verse*, ed. John MacDonald (1937), Aberdeen: Department of Celtic, University of Aberdeen.

MacLean, Allan Campbell, *Teine Ceann Fòid*, transl. Paul MacInnes (1967), Glasgow: *Gairm*.

MacLean, John (1818), *Orain Nuadh Ghaidhealach*, printed for the author, Edinburgh.

MacLellan, Angus (1972), *Saoghal an Treobhaiche*, *Norwegian Journal of Linguistics*.

Malachi, see *Leabhraichean an t-Seann Tiomnaidh*.

Meek, Donald E. (ed.) (1995), *Tuath is Tighearna: Tenants and Landlords*, Edinburgh: Scottish Gaelic Texts Society.

Meek, Donald E. (ed.) (2003), *Caran an t-Saoghail: The Wiles of the World*, Edinburgh: Birlinn.

OED: Oxford English Dictionary.

Psalms 1659: An ceud chaogad do Shalmaibh Dhaibhidh, Synod of Argyll (1659), Glasgow.

Rel. Celt.: Reliquiae Celticae, ed. Alexander MacBain and John Cameron (1892–4), 2 vols, Inverness.

SaaC: Dòmhnall MacAmhlaidh, *Seobhrach as a' Chlaich*, *Gairm*, 1967.

SGS: Scottish Gaelic Studies, 1–, Aberdeen, 1926–.

SND: Scottish National Dictionary.

Stewart, Robert (1802), *Orain Ghaelach*, Edinburgh: C. Stewart.

TCD: Trinity College Dublin.

Thomson, Derick (1951), *An Dealbh Briste*, Edinburgh: Oliver and Boyd.

TK: Thomas à Kempis, *Imitation of Christ*, transl. Robert Menzies (1785), Edinburgh.

Tuireadh, see *Leabhraichean an t-Seann Tiomnaidh*.

Watson, William J. (ed.) (1937), *Scottish Verse from the Book of the Dean of Lismore*, Edinburgh: Scottish Gaelic Texts Society.

Whyte, Henry (1898), *The Celtic Garland*, Glasgow: Archibald Sinclair.

ACKNOWLEDGEMENTS

Thanks are due to the Department of Celtic, University of Glasgow, for allowing access to HDSG-A. Professor William Gillies kindly read and commented on the first draft of the chapter. My wife, Dr Rachel Meek, read a second draft, and *scail*ed a few errors. I am indebted to Dr Margaret A. Mackay and Professor Christian Kay for their invitation to make a contribution to this volume, and also for their warm exhortations along the way, to say nothing of their patience. I am particularly grateful to Ms Lorna Pike, Co-ordinator of Faclair na Gàidhlig, and formerly an Editor of *DOST*, for making the timely suggestion that, in illustrating lexicographical challenges at the interface of Scottish Gaelic and Scots, *scail/sgaoil* would provide a worthwhile topic for investigation. I am much indebted to her for her detailed commentary on successive drafts of this chapter, and for her calm and measured advice at all stages. She has been remarkably tolerant of a 'lapsed lexicographer' to whom the term *sgaoilte* (in the possible sense of 'spreading oneself too thinly', if not in several others listed above) could well be applied.

CHAPTER 9

Place Names as Evidence in the History of Scots

W. F. H. Nicolaisen, University of Aberdeen

My interest in the topic to which this brief essay will be devoted goes back several decades, finding an early, and still somewhat tangential, written expression in a detailed exploration of the complex linguistic history of the name *Falkirk* (Nicolaisen 1969). More recent relevant studies have been concerned with the contrasting development of the place names *Stirling* and *Dunfermline* (Nicolaisen 1989) and, in a somewhat wider perspective, with 'Scottish place names as Evidence for Language Change' (Nicolaisen 1993). In 1996, I presented a paper with the same title as this essay to the Eighth International Conference on Medieval and Renaissance Scottish Language and Literature at St Hilda's College, Oxford. This paper has never been published and it seemed appropriate to offer a much revised and updated version for inclusion in a volume celebrating the completion of the *Dictionary of the Older Scottish Tongue*.

It may appear strange to put the emphasis in this examination on the ways in which toponymic evidence can assist the historian of the lexicon and, by implication, phonology of Scots rather than on the reverse process by which lexical material, that is, a dictionary like *DOST*, can be helpful in establishing a history of Scottish place names. Naturally, the place-name scholar turns repeatedly to the lexicographer as part of the latter quest, which, to a considerable degree, consists of an attempt to convert retrospectively the names under scrutiny into the words they once were; but whether one looks at the criss-crossing relationships between words and names from one direction or the other, either exercise requires an awareness of the differences, as well as the similarities, of the characteristics inherent in a lexicon and an onomasticon.

It is a truism in the profession that place names have a particularly effective role to play in the elucidation of language history. Indeed, many, if not most, students of toponymy, like the present writer, used to come to this field of study because they were linguistic historians, and the stress on the historical facets of place-name research has been so strong that, for example, the English Place-Name Survey, in the county volumes it produced, for many years insisted on a cut-off date of 1500. In what follows, we will examine whether the place-name evidence contemporary with the lexical materials contained in *DOST* confirms this assumption, always bearing in mind that the dictionaries' fundamental quest for meaning is not shared by the corresponding toponymicon since names can and do function very well without semantic transparency.

Let me begin by looking once again at a name which has been of considerable interest to me for many years, the name *Falkirk*, and spread out from there. In my 1969 article, the substance of which was included in my book (Nicolaisen 2001: 9–21), I traced the history of this name in great detail, from its twelfth-century forms, *egglesbreth, Eiglesbrec* and the like, the Latinised *Varia Capella*, and the Frenchified *la Veire Chapelle*, to the Scots *Faukirk* of 1298 and beyond, and ultimately to our modern *Falkirk*, which first occurs in 1458. This is neither the place nor the time to reiterate the intricate and complex arguments concerning the sequence and inter-relationship of these recorded forms except to draw attention again to the conclusions which I reached in my original discussion.

'Our name', I said in 1969, supported by a diagram,

> can therefore demonstrably be shown to have started out as a Gaelic *Eaglais B(h)rec* before 1080 (with a reasonable possibility of an earlier Cumbric name) and to have been translated into English by 1166 although there is initially only indirect evidence for this in the Latin *Varia Capella* and the Norman French *la Veire Chapelle*. This new name is *Faw Kirk* which like the Gaelic and the Latin names means '(the) speckled church'. By false analogy, a new spelling *Falkirk* is produced from the middle of the fifteenth century onwards which in turn has given rise to a new pronunciation ['fɔlkɛrk] although this is hardly used in Falkirk itself.

I still stand by the validity of this conclusion although it hardly does justice to the more than ten closely argued pages which preceded it in the original publication. From a toponymic point of view, that is when regarding the evolution of the *name* Falkirk as a *name*, it is, I feel, highly satisfactory, and there are unfortunately not many other Scottish place names which have been subjected to, or which one can subject to, the same detailed scrutiny, because the documentary evidence is simply not available. Are we, however, entitled to display the same kind of smugness when it comes to reconstructing and dissecting the name as the lexical compound it once was? This relocation of an item which has been part of an onomasticon from at least the eleventh century onwards in an earlier lexicon which required semantic transparency demands different questions, especially in view of the fact that for many centuries, as the Celtic, Latin, French and Middle English or Older Scots forms demonstrate, this semantic accessibility had obviously never been lost sight of without apparently interfering with the function of the name. This parallel existence in both lexicon and onomasticon allowed our name to be translated several times on the lexical level while gradually approaching the degree of semantic opacity, at least in its first element or specific, which is frequently and typically associated with onomastic items. There can be little doubt that *Faw-*, or the Northern Middle English *fawe* or *faȝe* from which it derives, must have been a productive adjective not only in 1298 when *Faukirk* was first recorded, preceded by the French feminine definite article *la* in continuation of an earlier *Chapelle* or Latin *capella*, but probably even as early as 1166 when we first come across the Latinised *Varia Capella* in the slot normally reserved for the vernacular form. It is also more than likely that the unusual aspect of the actual structure it must have first designated continued a recognisable reinforcement of *faw* in its basic meaning of 'speckled, variegated', perhaps in reference to brickwork or a painted wooden church. Whether this visual confirmation disappeared first or the loss of meaning of *faw* preceded it, is difficult to say, but the fifteenth-century spelling *Falkirk* and the sixteenth-century *Fauskirk* are persuasive indicators that *faw* was no longer part of the active Scots vocabulary of the area. The hypercorrect form *Fal*-kirk presumes both that the final *-l* in words like *wall* or *ball* had already been lost in Scots and that the pronunciation *wa'* and *ba'* was regarded as uneducated and therefore undesirable, so much so that the *-l* was restored in words in which it had never existed before. The spelling *Fauskirk* implies misinterpretation of the specific as a personal name.

So far so good because there is much here to conjure with onomastically, and the name *Falkirk*, in these and other respects, certainly repays the attention it has received. But how valuable is this information with regard to Scottish language history, particularly the history of Scots? Does our toponymic evidence, for example, have anything to say about the presence of *fawe* in the Scottish variety of Northern English? A brief glimpse at *DOST* shows that the thirteenth-century *Faukirk*, like the name *Fausyde*, considerably predates the first recorded lexical usage of *faw* in Henryson's *Fables* (approx. 1460–88). As we have already seen, the Latin *Varia Capella* is evidence that *faw* was present even a century earlier, although a precise spelling as guide to its twelfth-century pronunciation is, of course, not available. It must, however, be noted that this earlier record points to toponymic usage *only* and does not permit any inference as to the frequency of its corresponding lexical application. In addition, as I have shown elsewhere (Nicolaisen 1993), we must take into account a certain lag factor since the earliest record of a place name is only under exceptional circumstances co-eval with the creation of that name, or any linguistic changes which have produced it, and does not allow any precise dating of its coining or, most importantly, of its first usage by others than the name givers. Paradoxical as it may sound, the use of something named is much more important than the process by which it initially received its name; not the etymology of a name but the changing contents which it acquires over the years, decades, centuries, sometimes even millennia of usage, is what really matters here.

How typical or exceptional is the fact that the earliest mention of names like

Faukirk and *Fauside* predates the earliest recorded reference to the lexical usage of *faw*, in this case by about a century? A spot check in *DOST* provides the following information regarding the chronological relationship of a handful of common Scots place-name generics to their counterparts in the topographical sector of the lexicon:

1. *cleuch, clewch* 'a ravine or gorge'. First toponymic references: *Edwardescloch, -clouch* c. 1190, *Meldrescloes-heued* c. 1240, *Ernesclucht* c. 1350; earliest lexical reference in Barbour's *Bruce* (1370s).
2. *dene* 'a hollow where the ground slopes on both sides, generally with a rivulet running through it; a small valley'. First toponymic references: *Lummesdene, Fugeldene* c. 1100, *Ravedene* c. 1150, *Botheldene* 1159, *Ernbrandesdene* c. 1190, *Ellesdene* 1218; earliest lexical record: 1509 in the Acts of Parliament.
3. *hauch, hawch* 'a haugh'. First toponymic references: *de le Quenys Hauche* 1457 ER, *the Quhyt Auche* 1464 Peebles Bur. Recs.; earliest lexical record *cum pratis, pasturis et hawkes*, c. 1240 Kelso Liber.
4. *heuch, hewch* 'a precipice'. First toponymic reference *Our Ladie Kirk of the Hewch, in Sanctandrois* 1497 TA; earliest lexical record in Henryson and Wyntoun (1420s).
5. *hope, hoip* 'a small enclosed valley'. First toponymic reference: *Ruhope, Berhope* c. 1190, *Elrehope* c. 1200, *Hollehope* 1200–2; earliest lexical record Wyntoun (1420s).

Without wishing to claim any statistical validity which this small sample cannot possibly command, it is perhaps not without significance that in three out of the five randomly chosen examples quoted (*cleuch, dene* and *hauch*) the toponymic references are earlier than the lexical record whereas in the other two they are later. The *faw* of Falkirk would, of course, also fit into the former category but is not quite comparable since it is a specific and not a generic. What has further to be borne in mind is the fact that all the examples cited are from the south of Scotland, especially the Borders, and therefore come from a privileged documentary environment which cannot usually be matched further north (Nicolaisen 1999). Even taking into account these restrictions and disclaimers, however, it cannot be denied that, as far as the medieval background of Scots is concerned, place-name evidence for certain lexical items is often of value because it is recorded earlier than any non-toponymic references, therefore extending their historical record backwards by a century or more. In many instances therefore the linguistic historian may look with legitimate expectation to the evidence place names may afford when it comes to establishing a chronological record of certain word usage in Scotland. The dates involved – twelfth, thirteenth, or even early fourteenth century – do not, however, in their medieval ambience, guarantee that the claims made for the Middle Ages are equally applicable to what one might call the history of Scots proper, since non-toponymic textual evidence becomes much more commonly available, and therefore access to lexical usage much easier or, to put it the other way round, place names lose their special advantages over words.

Not unrelated to this last point is the question of meaning. In this connection it is again important to remember that the reason why place names have a much greater power of survival than their lexical counterparts lies in the fact that, as we stressed above, they can and do function independent of any lexical meaning. This frequent semantic opacity makes them poor candidates for throwing light on a quest for meaning in a historical context. As has already become obvious, the name *Falkirk* is, in fact, an exception in that respect, as the Gaelic predecessor which it translates, as well as its Latinisations and Frenchifications, provide unequivocal lexical pointers as to what *fau-* meant. This is not the case with *Fausyde* or the instances of *cleuch, dene, hauch, heuch,* and *hope* cited, but rather the opposite applies: any hint that we may have as to the lexical meaning of a toponymic element comes from the lexicon itself. It is probably fair to say that in this respect the majority of place names are not very useful to the linguistic historian, including the historian of Scots. As usual, exceptions prove the rule, especially when an inspection of the ground in an atypical continuity of contents provides clues as to the nature of the topographical feature originally designated.

Perhaps the one facet of language history on which place names can be expected to throw light with some success is the history of pronunciation. This claim is again based on the major difference between words and names, that is that words must have lexical meaning in order to function whereas names do not. For this reason, medieval and post-medieval spellings of Scottish place names of whatever origin might be expected to be virtually free from semantic interference or motivation, the kind of influence which in Modern English, for example, demands four different spellings of the sound sequences [raɪt] or [ro:z] depending on the word meaning in question. That is not to say that name spellings are purely arbitrary within the framework of the orthographic conventions of the day, but one might think that as visual representations of the pronunciations they reflect or are intended to convey, their links with their audible counterpart, might, in many instances, be closer. We have already seen that the spellings of the name Falkirk became of real interest to us in the middle of the fifteenth century when the meaning of the first element is no longer understood and *Fal-* spellings begin to appear. What these -*l*- spellings do for us is not so much of benefit to our examination of the history of the name Falkirk itself as to the implications it has for our understanding of the phonological development of words like *wall > wa'* or *ball > ba'*, without which the hypercorrect spelling of *Falkirk* is unlikely to have come about. Now it would be wonderful if we could brag that this is a very real contribution that the spelling history of the name *Falkirk* and of some other names containing *Faw* has made to our ability to date this particular phenomenon. Unfortunately, the best we can say is that the 1458 spelling of the name *Falkirk* confirms our knowledge in this respect, derived from non-toponymic sources, and if we were completely honest, as all scholars are supposed to be, we would have to admit that it is our previous knowledge from lexical evidence which allows us to recognise the *-l-* spelling of *Falkirk* for what it is, and not the other way round. This is, of course, an argument which we also advanced earlier with regard to the meaning of *Faw* – in place names.

In order to meet the accusation of underselling the importance of place names for the history of Scots pronunciation and spelling, a sideward glance away from an individual name is called for, such as the alternating or parallel occurrence of *-n-* and *-ng-* spellings which I have discussed elsewhere in the contrasting cases of such names as *Dunfermline* and *Stirling*, and the cluster of names associated with them (Nicolaisen 1989). In both these names, the syllable *-line* or *-ling* appears to have been meaningless ever since the beginning of their documented history. For that reason, whatever spellings we encounter for it, even within the scribal conventions of a single source, are likely to have been intended as an acceptable orthographic representation of its pronunciation. One further advantage is that we have a very large number of recorded spellings for both these names and are therefore not restricted in our evidence. Taking *-y-* as an allograph of *-i-*, broadly speaking, the picture which emerges is this: almost from the very beginning of the recorded history of *Stirling* in the first half of the twelfth century, *-lin* (with its variant spellings *-lyn*, *-line* and *-lyne*) and *-ling* (with its variant *-lyng*) occur side by side, although *until* the fifteenth century the former are much more common than the latter. From the fifteenth century onwards, *-ling* spellings predominate and take over completely from the second half of the sixteenth century on. A potted history of the spelling of the whole name *Stirling* would read like: Strivelin > Striveling > Strivling (or Stirveling) > Stirvling > Stirling, though in reality the picture is, of course, much more complex.

In comparison, for Dunfermline, *-lin/-lyn* spellings are by far the most common in the initial three centuries of its recorded history, with two thirteenth-century spellings being rare, almost inexplicable, forerunners of *-ling*, which does not occur again until the beginning of the fifteenth century but then predominates until the middle of the seventeenth century, with the original *-lin* ending petering out by the middle of the sixteenth century. Up to this point, the history of *-fermline* does not differ substantially from that of Stirling, but about the middle of the seventeenth century *-lin(e)* spellings are beginning to replace *-ling* spellings again after a break in continuity of about a hundred years; the chronological sequence is therefore *-ferm(e)lin* > *-ferm(e)ling* > *-fermlin(e)*. The *-ling* forms dominate at the same time as those of *Stirling* (fifteenth-sixteenth century) and then also take over at the same time (mid-sixteenth century) but, unlike *Stirling*, are completely replaced a century later by a *-lin(e)* ending which does not represent the original *-lin* suffix.

Basing my argumentation on the somewhat puzzling spelling history of these two names as well as on dozens of others displaying *-ing-* or *-in-*, I concluded in my original paper that all the spellings encountered were intended to represent the same pronunciation of the final nasal consonant and that -*lin* and -*ling* and their variations have therefore to be seen as variant spellings or allographs of the same pronunciation and not as visual reflexes of two different sounds. This would explain the apparent instability of the spellings encountered, the dominating choices displayed at certain times, and the divergence of the spellings for the two names in recent centuries. What an examination of literally hundreds of place-name spellings does not produce, however, is a provision of illuminating insights into the history of the pronunciation of the sound sequence in question, unless the conclusion that there was no change is acceptable as such an initial insight. The underlying sound may well have been on the border of [n] and [ŋ].

The emerging picture with regard to the value of place-name evidence for the history of Scots is, consequently, as I hinted at the beginning of this essay, not a very encouraging one, despite some bright spots. Place names are apparently of greatest value when their earliest spellings predate any other references to a particular Middle Scots lexical item, thus recording its presence in Scotland, and particularly its spelling, at an earlier date than would otherwise have been possible. The scribal environment in which these appear, let us say between the twelfth and the fourteenth century, is, however, usually Latin, and the names form a kind of interspersed vernacular toponymic text within a non-vernacular lexical text. In some instances – I have often quoted *Hawick* as an example (Nicolaisen 2001) – they preserve lexical items for us which have otherwise become obsolete. The toponymic contribution to the history of phonology in Scotland is, again with certain exceptions, minimal, and when it comes to their semantic aspects, the traffic is, as one would expect, normally in the opposite direction, that is occurrences in other sources deepen our knowledge or make possible our quest for the lexical meaning of names. In all instances, it is therefore appropriate and helpful for *DOST* to list the place name evidence separately or at least to draw attention to an item's predominant toponymic usage.

For these reasons it is, one would have thought, wise not to expect from place names what they cannot give while, on the other hand, exploring their real potential to the full. Among their strengths is, of course, the fact that they are anchored to the ground and are therefore excellent source material for distribu-tion maps, thus creating the possibility of establishing toponymic dialects which may or may not coincide with their equivalent lexical dialects (Nicolaisen 1980). Sometimes it is possible to translate these spatial maps into maps of time and to utilise them in the construction of chronological strata although this has to be done with great caution (Nicolaisen 1984; 1991). In this respect, place-name evidence is much more effective inter-linguistically than intra-linguistically, and it probably has its greatest potential at the interface or margins of languages and in the recording of language change (Nicolaisen 1993; 1996).

It is probably in these areas and in linguistic contact situations that lexical compendia like *DOST* and a Scottish place-name dictionary are likely to be of the most effective use to each other.

CHAPTER 10

DOST and *MED* and the Virtues of Sibling Rivalry

Paul Schaffner, University of Michigan

THE TWO DICTIONARIES

Viewed from the offices of the *Middle English Dictionary* (*MED*),[1] the *Dictionary of the Older Scottish Tongue*, more than any comparable project, always seemed a lexicographic brother-in-arms, even if one kept at arm's length. The language it aspired to document was divided, at least in its early and transitional stages, from the northern dialects of our own Middle English (ME) by criteria that seemed at best artificial and at worst arbitrary; and even the fully formed and independent language of Middle Scots proper declared its kinship with Middle English at many points, not only in what it preserved of the earlier language (or borrowed from it), but in its characteristic openness to external borrowing and neologism. Like any pair of brothers sharing a common space, our activities were governed by careful respect for territory – the *Pistil of Susan* was ours, *Golagros* theirs; *Awntyrs* ours, *Lancelot* theirs – with small commons (*Kingis Quair*) and rare early incursions (Wyntoun, the *Bruce*, Scottish documents and saints' lives) by one side or the other, dwindling away in maturer years.

   MED and *DOST* were not only siblings but virtual twins, both born of Craigie's vision, first publicly enunciated in 1919, of a series of period and regional dictionaries springing from and advancing the work done in *OED*. *DOST* was begun earlier, in 1921, *MED* not till 1928, and began publication much earlier, in 1931, *MED* not till more than twenty years later. This meant that, with the vicissitudes of publication schedules, *DOST* more often than not did not have *MED* to consult, but had to rely on *OED* for Middle English coverage; whereas *MED* frequently was in a position to consult *DOST*, and often did, a fact of importance to readers who need to consult the dictionaries now. Both dictionaries inherited the appropriate slips from the *OED* collection; both dictionaries went through some very dry years of uncertain funding and limited staffing; both were consistent in insisting on the intellectually labour-intensive character of lexicography; both grew enormously larger and more expensive than first predicted, bloated by 'sent-on' slips and a continued reading programme, and suffered consequent major changes of editorial policy and purpose during the course of preparation and publication. Both, moreover, were attached to, but not exactly of, the university at which they were housed; both fought for and retained editorial control of their content, independent of financial considerations, regarded themselves throughout their history as heirs to the Murray tradition of meticulous historical lexicography, and needed constantly to fight the temptation to perfectionism that that tradition entailed; and both were finally completed within a few months of each other under a rigorously enforced production schedule that required unprecedented efficiencies. At *MED*, these included eliminating the citation of most phrases and the consistent checking of source words in translation texts; at *DOST*, the abandonment of many niceties of etymology.

Like *MED*, *DOST* departed in many ways, large and small, from the *OED* model. Most are merely formal and likely to be apparent, or important, only to fellow lexicographers, for example the curiously arbitrary distinction between large and small entries. Others have been rendered harmless by the development of an electronic version of *DOST*, for example the variety of places and ways in which variant spellings are cross-referenced to headwords. But some affect the usefulness of the dictionary, even in electronic form. The following are among the most important.

Spelling

DOST is very concerned with spelling, even to the point of preserving a distinction between < y > and < i > (*MED* does not); *DOST* 'exemplifies the earliest example of every variant spelling' (*MED* troubles only to exemplify every listed spelling, not necessarily the earliest example). More importantly, multiple spellings generated multiple headwords and (in volumes I–VI) often multiple entries, even when the meaning and etymology did not differ substantially from one entry to the next. *MED*, on the other hand, is much more likely to split an entry on the basis of etymology, especially if reinforced by a semantic split and by real differences in phonetic realisation. This means that a user of *DOST* seeking a comprehensive view of a particular word often needs to assemble two, three or more entries, following the cross-references from entry to entry. And even within entries, groups of quotations employing different spellings are often separated out into separate lettered paragraphs.

Etymology

In general, *DOST* seems to have been more interested in presenting complete information from which the reader can construct an etymology, rather than a historical statement about the word's development, as suggested by the term

DOST uses to describe the listed forms: 'comparators'. Policy changed over time, but *DOST* often lists comparators, often in a fixed order without relevance to the likelihood of actual influence, and chooses to be agnostic about the route by which a given word actually entered the language, a practice that can be quite misleading if not prepared for. On the other hand, when words are especially problematic, *DOST* etymologies are at their clearest, since *DOST* is willing to be quite discursive, discuss alternative etymologies, and cite specific forms listed in specific dictionaries as possible sources for forms. Unlike *MED*, *DOST* routinely follows etymologies back to ulterior, if not ultimate stages. On the other hand, *MED* tends to be more exact in stating what it thinks to be the most likely immediate source(s), and to distinguish those from sources about which it prefers to make fewer claims. Furthermore, as usual, some caution is called for when reviewing the lists of comparators, since some of them are taken over from *OED* without checking; and some of them (especially the Middle English) were compiled without reference to sources available only more recently, such as the *MED*, the *Anglo-Norman Dictionary* (*AND*), and the *Dictionary of Medieval Latin from British Sources* (*DML*(*BS*)).

Illustration

Perhaps the most confusing *DOST* practice is the 'paragraphing' of illustrative quotations. Though some words (more in some parts of the dictionary than in others) follow the *MED* practice of providing a one-to-one link between every numbered or lettered subsense and the quotations that illustrate it, many words 'paragraph' the quotations into blocks with only implicit connections to the definition that they illustrate. Numbered paragraphing of quoted material, especially common in O–S, may be on the basis of either syntactic or semantic criteria, and may or may not be signalled by something in the definition. Such paragraphs may, and often do, co-exist with paragraphs of quotations divided by inflection (e.g. singular and plural), either so labelled, labelled with italic letters, or left unlabelled and implicit. Reading a *DOST* entry with full attention can involve a lot of work. Equally confusing is the opposite practice of creating subsenses (say a, b and c), but presenting the quotations as an undivided block, on the grounds that the quotations are difficult to assign unambiguously to particular senses: a very handy liberty for a lexicographer, albeit one that makes greater than usual demands of the reader. Finally, literary (as opposed to documentary) citations are generally given without date, on the assumption that the date is well known or is available in the bibliography; no attempt is made (so far as I know) to distinguish composition date from manuscript or publication date; and many references are supplied as bare citations, without accompanying quotation. In each case, the working philosophy seems to have been that the most important function of the dictionary was the assembling of information rather than its synthesis into a definitive account, the latter being left to the reader.

Definition

So far as my small reading extends, both *MED* and *DOST* moved during the course of their history from a concern chiefly with registering the presence and form of words, to a concern with exploring the details of their usage, but it is only at the end of the dictionary, and in words of particular importance to the Scottish language or nation (e.g. *Scot* n.!), that *DOST* approaches the *MED*'s devotion to hair-splitting refinement of definition. The use of 'umbrella definitions' (said to be favoured especially in volumes V and VI), its willingness to define a word chiefly as 'patience in the usual senses', stands in sharp contrast to *MED*'s perhaps excessive reluctance even to use the modern cognate in a definition. *MED*'s first definition for the same word (*pacience* n.) is: 'the calm endurance of misfortune, suffering, etc.; a willingness to bear adversities, wrongs, etc.; steadfastness against temptation; also *fig.* a mantle of patience'. And that is just sense 1(a). *MED* is much more concerned than is *DOST* with delineating nuance, and with providing both a comprehensive definition and (where possible) a substitutable gloss for every occurrence in the corpus. On the other hand, *DOST* does a great deal of implicit defining by means of 'paragraphing' (as above); and *DOST* is generally more willing than *MED* to comment on the word's generic distribution ('only in verse, including alliterative') and linguistic distribution ('sense 2 only in Sc.'). Both dictionaries note proverbial uses and phrases (the *MED* perhaps more so, and sometimes more needlessly so). And *DOST* is much more prone than *MED* to allow subsenses to inherit the value of their parent, especially in a cascade from vague and general to more specific. For the lexicographer, this provides an easy way to place the vaguer quotations, at the higher and vaguer level; for the reader, it is rather more intuitive than the verbose lists contained in the *MED*, and truer to the realities of natural language.

Relation to English

In the vast majority of entries, *MED* could safely pay Older Scots little or no attention, or so it seemed: the chief contexts for understanding Middle English were English itself, from earlier and later periods; French (especially Anglo-French); Latin (in some cases Anglo–Latin); and the North Sea routes of influence of various periods, from Norse through Frisian and Dutch. The same cannot be said of *DOST*: it demonstrates an awareness of Middle and Early Modern English in virtually every entry, indicating routinely both where Scots paralleled English developments (whether that be by analogous or common development, or by borrowing from one to the other), and where Scots departed from them and struck out on its own.

Now that these sibling dictionaries have finally grown up and moved out into the world, what should their relationship be? So far as is technically feasible, they should be made to converse, if not embrace. In the meantime, every student of the medieval and early modern vernacular needs to consult them both. If one thing has become clear in the study of the vernacular in medieval and early modern Britain, it is that borders are permeable and categories misleading. *DOST, MED*, and alongside them, as appropriate, *GPC (Geiriadur Prifysgol Cymru* = University of Wales Dictionary), *OED, AND, DOE (Dictionary of Old English)*, and *DML(BS)*, though created piecemeal and to some extent in false isolation, must be used jointly, as if they were a single description of a single complex linguistic situation, for that is what in effect they are.

MED and *DOST* work best together most commonly when the words or works in question occupy the debatable ground betwixt languages, or when the true home of a given word is in the unified literature artificially divided by the *MED/ DOST* split: to name only my own interests, in the alliterative tradition generally, or the tradition of rhymed alliterative stanzas particularly; in heroic verse; northern regional *fachliteratur*; and even (because of the presence of Gilbert Hay's translations, the *Buke of the Chess*, and *Ratis Raving*, among others) in the secular literature of political morality and the profession of chivalry. In such cases, the two dictionaries need really to be used as one, not only so that their stocks of quotations can supplement each other, but so that the conclusions drawn by one dictionary from one set of partial information can be corrected from those drawn by the other. Two lexicographic heads are frequently better than one, if only because they are good at undermining each other's authority.

MED PROVIDES A LARGER CONTEXT

Perhaps the most obvious cases calling for co-operation between the lexicons, because of the larger ME corpus, are those in which rare Scots words find a fuller context and history within English. Scots *berslete, barslet* n. ('a hunting dog') is a oncer in *DOST*, where it is quoted from Wyntoun; *DOST* notes that it appears in ME with various spellings, but even so the one example in Wyntoun is effectively stranded without recourse to the *MED*. *MED* provides two contexts in which the word is likely to appear: the French-derived technical cynegetic literature on the one hand (Gaston Phoebus and Master Twiti), and the alliterative tradition on the other (*Awntyrs, Wars of Alexander, Parliament of the Three Ages, An a byrchyn bonke*, etc.). Wyntoun's alliterative collocation 'with bow and wyth berslete' in fact appears verbatim in the Thornton manuscript version of *Awntyrs* ('with bowe and with barcelett').

Another *DOST* oncer, *sil(e* v. 3 'to sink', found only in *Golagros* 524 ('the seymly sone silit to the rest') is another of many words in the category of Anglo-Scottish, chiefly alliterative, poetic vocabulary. Its meaning in ME is somewhat broader ('sink, fall, drop, flow; proceed, go'), though in ME too it is collocated with 'sun': 'the sone was sett and syled full loughe' (*Parliament of the Three Ages* 658); 'the sunne siled west' (*Asneth* 274). Its English attestation is considerably broader, though largely confined to verse, and chiefly confined to northern or alliterative verse. *Schalk*, found only in *Golagros* (many times) and Dunbar, belongs to the same category, and is likewise found widely distributed throughout ME northern and alliterative verse, as well as in a few personal names, as *MED* attests. *Unquart* n. (*MED unquert* n.) 'distress, disquiet', also a *Golagros* oncer, is another. And the *-e-* form of *lere* n. 'complexion, countenance' is yet another, alongside the more common Scots form in < y > ('luflyis of lyre'; 'lufly of lyere'), in the ubiquitous alliterative pairing with 'lufsum': 'ladis lufsum to lere' (1253); compare ME 'Þei . . . lede forþ þat ladi louesum of lere' (*Pistil of Susan* 275). *Torfeir* n. 'hardship; harm' may be taken as typical of such hapax legomena: in Scots it appears again only in *Golagros* ('Ye sall nane torfeir betyde' 875). It is Norse in origin, and found in ME with the same collocation as in the Scots example, which is thereby established as conventional: 'Thow betydes tourfere' (*Morte Arthure* 4280); 'Som torfoyr is be-tidde vs' (*York Plays* 431/160); 'na torfar him tid' (*Wars of Alexander* 1193); and 'Sall no torfure þe be tyde' (*Metrical Old Testament* 16400). The distribution in ME is generically confined to verse, and geographically largely but not exclusively to northern and north Midland texts, in this case including the Vespasian manuscript of *Cursor Mundi*, the Northern Homily Cycle and the *Destruction of Troy*, as well as the works listed above.

Even when the word is perfectly well attested on both sides of the border, particular senses, or particular collocations, may not be, and may be illuminated by cross-border comparison. *Lance* v. 'to bound, spring, leap' is seen by comparison to *MED* (s.v. *launcen* v., sense 2) to have specialised a single intransitive sense of the ME verb, confined in ME as in Scots to poetry (much of it, though not all, northern). The transitive sense of *shaw* v. 'to look at, gaze upon', which *DOST* notes is found 'only in alliterative verse', is in fact again found only in *Golagros*, and only in alliterative tags such as 'seymly to schaw' and the like. The comparable sense in ME *sheuen* v.1 is much larger and longer-lived, and the formulaic collocations, though naturally confined largely to alliterative verse (*Gawain*, *Morte*, *Wars of Alexander*), also appear in Chaucer (*House of Fame*), suggesting that this sense is much more active in English than in Scots, where it is a mere alliterative fossil.

Similarly, the absolute use of *stern* adj. ('fierce', etc.) to refer to a bold man appears only in *Golagros*, which in common with much alliterative poetry is given to turning adjectives into nouns (or vice versa) when necessary to the metre. Consulting *MED*, s.v. *stern(e* adj. sense 2 (f), makes it clear that this habit is not peculiar to *Golagros*: *Gawain*, the alliterative *Morte*, *Destruction of Troy* and *Awntyrs* all do the same, the last, unsurprisingly given the thematic connections between the poems, in a manner most like that of *Golagros*. *DOST* leaves the application of *stern* to combat as rare; *MED*, having at its disposal a much larger corpus, is able to rectify that impression, associate the tumult of battle with other terrifyingly tumultuous events (storms, for example), and, typically, to make finer distinctions than *DOST* is interested in, and separate out, however dubiously, a sense 'alarming, dreadful' from the sense 'violent'. In each case, the combination of *MED* and *DOST* provides a larger corpus, a variety of nuance in interpretation, and above all a larger set of associations and collocations than either dictionary could provide alone, or than even a single comprehensive dictionary could provide.

The special connection of *Golagros* with *Awntyrs* appears again when one considers another sense unique to *Golagros*: *royal(l* adj. used absolutely in the singular: 'Thus the royale can remove with his Round Tabill' (*Golagros* 14). Though absolute uses appear in the *MED*, s.v. *roial* n., only *Awntyrs* has a comparable singular use: 'Scho rydes vp . . . by-fore the royalle' (Thornton MS, line 345). *Golagros* does appear to push this habit further than most, but one can confirm that it outdoes *Awntyrs* in this regard only by tracing similar absolute adjectives – *lordly* (1276), *myghty* (1012), etc., many of which are found nowhere else in Scots and scarcely in English. The number of *Golagros* compounds in *un-* (*unmarrid, unrude, unmaglit, unstonayt, unlufsum, unlamit, unfair, unfane*, etc.), some with and some without ME analogues, suggests another stylistic peculiarity of the poem that could usefully be explored through comparison of *DOST* and *MED* entries.

Similarly the common Scots verb *merk* contains a relatively rare transitive sense of 'strike, hit' in *DOST* (sense 9), along with scarcely less rare related senses ('aim a blow', etc.), all of which are far more common and well supported in ME (*MED* s.v. *merken* v.2 sense 10), not only in the alliterative poems, but also and especially in Lydgate, of all people, and (in a transferred sense 'to afflict') in the mystery plays. To read *Golagros*, for example, which contains both the intransitive and the transitive variants of this sense of *merk*, by the aid of *DOST* alone is to see it as an innovator at the source of a tradition followed soon by Douglas's *Aeneid*, among others; to read it by *MED* alone is to see it as participating in a nationwide poetic vocabulary: both views are partly true; neither alone is sufficient.

While we are attending to *merk*, note that sense 11 of the Scots verb (refl. and intr. 'to go'; tr. 'to cause to go') is treated by *DOST* as a regular and well attested sense, with the comment that it was originally 'as apparently in ME' confined to verse, especially alliterative verse. Virtually the identical sense does indeed exist in ME, with essentially the same restriction to verse, especially alliterative verse, and a comparable set of collocations ('mark forth'; 'mark hir to/till', etc.). But *MED* has enough doubts about the sense that it accords it a separate entry, as a possible blend, possibly influenced by *marchen* v.2 and the 'track, trace' sense of *mark(e* n. Here too readers will be repaid by considering both treatments: *MED* supplies a much longer prehistory for the sense (or word), back to Layamon's *Brut*; *DOST* a longer and later development into the prosaic; *MED* and *DOST* taken together provide not only alternative views of the etymology, but a much larger view of the place of the word in Anglo-Scottish poetic diction. Conversely, when *MED* is silent, though that silence cannot be definitive, it is indicative; 'trew vndre tyld', for example, another nonce collocation in *Golagros*, finds no match under either *MED teld(e* n. or *treue* adj., suggesting oh so faintly that it is an original creation, albeit on a very traditional frame.

Moving a little away from the vocabulary of the alliterative romances, *solance* n. ('recreation, pleasure'), another oncer in *DOST*, where it is quoted from the Scottish lives of saints, produces entirely typical results. *MED*'s quotations (s.v. *solaunce* n.) place the word firmly in the north, and especially in the output of Robert Thornton, with appearances in *Awntyrs*, the alliterative *Morte*, and (from Thornton's BL Add. MS 31042) the *Siege of Milan* and the *Infancy of Christ*.

Comparable examples include *wirling* n. (*DOST* 'a wretch', found only in Dunbar), exemplified also in several ME texts of mixed provenance, beginning with the Vernon manuscript of the Northern Homily cycle, the *Wars of Alexander* (Ashmole), and the *Libel of English Policy*. *MED*'s gloss, 'a deformed creature, monster – used as term of abuse', seems inspired more by *warlou* than *wirling* and unjustified by any of the examples, English or Scots; *DOST*'s more modest gloss is perhaps to be preferred. *Sayndis-man* n. (*MED sondes-man*), another oncer in *Golagros*, is likewise revealed by *MED* to be a widely distributed ME word appearing as early as the Peterborough Chronicle in 1123 and as late as Malory in 1470 and the *Destruction of Troy* in 1540, far from exclusively northern or even exclusively poetic. The example in *Golagros* is simply a northern outlier of an old and common compound. The same is true of *menskful* adj. 'proud', *mene* v.4 '(mal)treat', and *lusch* v. 'to rush', three more *Golagros* oncers, all of them at least moderately well distributed in ME, albeit with a bias toward poetic, alliterative and northern texts; and *unsaucht* adj. 'hostile', another peculiarly *Golagros* word (or rather sense), which is fairly common in ME without noticeably distinctive distribution.

A rather different case is represented by *DOST to-turve* v., glossed as 'tr. absol. to dash to pieces . . ., wreak havoc' and found only in *Golagros* 704 'in that hailsing hynt grete harmys and here / All to-turuit thair entyre'. This is reasonable, and supported to some extent by the rare and early ME transitive verb *to-torfian* 'to pelt', which *DOST* cites as etymon or (as *DOST* would say) 'comparator'. But the form in *Golagros* is in fact an emendation of *to-turnit*, based on Skeat's conviction (followed by Amours 1897: 274, note on 1. 704) that the French root *turnen* could never be prefixed by the native form *to-*. Unfortunately for Skeat's conviction, *MED* preserves two or perhaps three clear examples of *to-turnen* v. in ME, one of which, from the earlier Wycliffite version of the Bible, translates Latin *subvertere* and is rendered *distrie* in the later Wycliffite version. This is not enough to overturn Skeat's (and *DOST*'s) interpretation, but it is perhaps enough to render it unnecessary.

Not dissimilar is the uncommon Scots adj. *schirely*, which *DOST* appears to derive from the equally uncommon ME *shirliche, schyrly* (*MED* s.v. *shirli* adv.). Only by pursuing the matter in the *MED* does one learn that the Scots examples are all chivalric (*Golagros, Alexander Buik*), are all collocated with 'shining', and are all readily glossed as 'brightly' in the physical sense; the Middle English examples by contrast, though occurring partly in alliterative works, appear exclusively in religious contexts, collocate with 'shrive', and mean something like 'completely, without reservation or qualification'. On the other hand, the Scots represents exactly the predominant sense of the underlying ME adjective. It is quite possible that the English and Scots words are independent formations on a common (English) adjective.

Finally, note that cross-dictionary comparisons can be worthwhile even when *DOST* assures us that the word, or the sense, is found only in Scots. For example, *lyke* n. 'body; corpse' putatively enjoys an exclusively Scottish sense 2 (doubtless a shortened form of *lyke-wake* or similar compound) that means either (a) funeral rites (pl.) or (b) in the north-east only, a wake (sg.). But sense 2 (b) is in fact attested in ME as *MED lich* n. sense 1 (c) 'a wake'. Some of the quotations in that sense are dubious (the very early Lambeth Homily quotation, I am sure, belongs to the simple sense 'corpse'), but others are quite clear:

> c1450(?c1425) *St. Christina Mirab.* (Dc 114) 120/14: Þen þe deed body was leyde forþe and þe lyche doon of hir sistres and frendes.
> c1450(?c1425) *St.Mary Oign.* (Dc 114) 182/2: Whan sche come to vs, þe belles were rungen for þe liche; and þen she was present while þe body was wasshen and buryed. a1475 *Form Excom. (2)* (Rwl B.408) 2/24: Alle þo þat customably come to lyches and occupy hem with vanytees and rybawdry, wher þei shuld pray for þe sowle.

DOST PROVIDES A LARGER CONTEXT

If *MED* can extend the range of *DOST*, *DOST* can do the same in turn for *MED*. *MED biclagged* ppl. ('bedaubed') is a oncer in *MED*, quoted from the *Awntyrs off Arthure*; *MED* obligingly notes the existence of a similar word in Older Scots. *DOST* provides (s.v. *clag* v.) enough information in the form of quotations both in verse (Wallace) and in prose (Hay) to make it clear that the word is a workaday piece of Scots, doubtless borrowed just this once, perhaps for alliterative convenience or perhaps as a piece of anti-heroic tone-setting. *Anerli* adv. (for 'only') similarly appears just once in ME, in the Vespasian manuscript of *Cursor Mundi*, where, *DOST* makes clear, it is only an outlier of a common Scots word that occurs in the *Brus*, the saints' lives, Hay, *Rauf Coilzear*, and many other works. The formation, however, is not of a particularly common type in either branch of the language, and both dictionaries are tentative in assigning sources for the analogous insertion of '-er-' (*DOST*: ?modelled on *enkerly*; *MED*: ?modelled on *utterli, formerli*). The common Scots adverb and preposition *atour* similarly appears only three times in ME, twice in the northern *Life of Cuthbert* and once in the dubiously English *Kingis Quair*, curiously in each case in the sense of 'all over', a rare sense in Scots itself, where the main development comprises the senses of 'above, across, beyond, besides'. Other cases of Scots words in English include *flipen* v. 'to fold back', found only in the late and archaising alliterative *Destruction of Troy*, and explicable only on the basis of sixteenth-century Scots *flype*; *flouht* n. 'flutter, perturbation', found only in the Northern Homily cycle, but comparable to *flocht* in Henryson, Douglas and others; *glotheren* v. 'to flatter', found in English only in the Vespasian manuscript of *Cursor* but in Scots (as *gluther* or *gluder*) in the Scottish saints' lives; *tratelinge* verbal n., found in a number of northern ME texts but having a verb only north of the border in the common Scots verb *trattill*, *tratel* 'to prattle, chatter', found in Wyntoun, Hay, Kennedy, and the *Thewis of Wysmen*, among others; and *furlenth* n. 'furlong' found only in *Wars of Alexander* in ME, but in *Golagros* (*DOST* s.v. *fur* n.) and *King Hart* (*DOST* s.v. *fure, feure* n.) in Scots, alongside *fur breid* in Douglas, all of which suggest that such compounds with *fur* (ME *fore*) continued to be 'live', at least in the north – perhaps even *furlong* itself. *Falset* n. 'falsehood', found in ME only in the Northumbrian MS Add 25719 of the *Alphabet of Tales*, is common in Scots, including the *Brus*, the *Buke of the Chess*, Wyntoun, the saints' lives, Hay and Dunbar. Though the word is a direct French loan, the northern distribution indicates that the ME and Scots examples should be taken as representing a single history. *MED* at this point had not learned its bounds and quoted Barbour, as it did elsewhere, for example s.v. *forci* adj. 'powerful', which appears in ME again only in the Thornton copy of the alliterative *Morte*, but commonly in Scots (*DOST* s.v. *forsy* and *forcy*). ME *mithen* v.2 'to see, observe' is a straggler in ME, found only in the Auchinleck manuscript of *Guy of Warwick*, but fairly common in Scots, which helps elucidate both its phonology (with an unexpected long vowel) and its sense, if not its hidden history between *Guy* in 1300 and Gavin Douglas in the early sixteenth century. *Brank(en* v. (*DOST*: 'to behave violently . . .; to bear oneself proudly . . .; to prance') appears once in ME as a participial adjective *brankkand* in the alliterative *Morte*, more illuminatingly thereafter in Dunbar, Wyntoun and Gavin Douglas. As often, each dictionary refers to the other in seeking an etymology; the Scots examples are all later than the ME; but the early history of the word is almost certainly northern, if not exclusively Scottish, and hidden only by the lack of extant texts from the right period. Reconstructing vernacular terms for vernacular pursuits is similarly vexed by scattered and missing evidence. *Dinmont(h(e* appears frequently in Scots from 1306 onward ('a wether between the first and second shearing'), and is thus in a position to illuminate the obscure terms that appear in fourteenth- and fifteenth-century Yorkshire and Northumbrian English, if it is that, or rather in the linguistically non-specific superficially Latin language of monastic documents, as *dinmo(u)th*, *?dinmou*.

BINOCULAR VISION

Especially when it comes to more obscure vocabulary, or vocabulary of more obscure history, or vocabulary even partly confined to the dialects of the North, each dictionary finds an essential supplement in the other. Take the noun known to *MED* as *trail* n. 1, which it derives from the equally difficult *trailen* v. 1. It is not clear even that either entry has the integrity befitting a single lexeme. The predominant sense of the noun is 'foliate ornament', perhaps especially the branch of a vine; less common is sense 2, 'the train of a gown'; and there is a slightly attested sense 3 comprising a harrow and maybe a sledge. The verb, which *MED* takes as the etymon of the noun, is even worse. The predominant sense is 'to hang down loosely so as to be dragged along the ground' or 'to walk with trailing garments'; a less common transitive sense 'to tow (sth.), drag' with extensions to 'to tarry', and a variety of miscellaneous senses including 'to flow, trickle'; 'to lie extended' (as a vine); 'to follow an animal's trail'; and 'to decorate with foliate ornament'. There is also a dubiously distinguished verb (2), 'to support on a trellis'. *MED* warns that sense 1 of the noun may instead belong to *trail* n. 2 ('a trellis' < OF *treille*) or perhaps to an entirely different word related to AF *traille* ('spray, tendril'); it certainly finds little and confusing support in the verb: a sensible approach might be to regard the group of senses related to vines and flowers as a separate entity in which the noun ('a vine') is primary and the verb ('to decorate with vines') denominative.

With that group removed, the noun consists of things that are drawn or dragged, and the verb (primarily) of the action of drawing or dragging. Turning to *DOST*, we find exactly this group represented neatly in Scots. The less common English sense of the verb ('to drag something', transitive) is the more common Scottish sense, from as early as the Scottish saints' lives, including examples that support specific meanings related to punishment of the drawing and quartering variety, and including *nomen agentis* and gerund variants. The more common English sense (to hang down and be dragged, as the train of a gown) is also clearly present in the Scots from Gilbert Hay's *Alexander* on, as is the rare English sense found in the Northern Homily cycle, 'to walk with trailing garments'. Above all, there is a oncer noun in Scots that provides vital support to the English noun's dubious sense 3: 'a harrow, ?a sledge': Hay's *Alexander* (again) contains a noun that must refer to a sledge or hurdle. Though they do not solve all the problems, *DOST* and *MED* taken together present a much clearer view of the 'trail' group than either dictionary alone. The intransitive sense of the verb, associated especially with the trains of gowns in the noun, has no particular geographic associations; the transitive 'drag' sense of the verb, predominant in Scots, and associated with the 'thing dragged' sense of the noun, has a clear northern bias: the English verb occurs in the alliterative *Morte*, the *Pistil of Susan*, and the *Destruction of Troy*, and the noun in the northern life of *Robert of Knaresborough*. Scots knows nothing of the vinous and floral senses, which apparently travel as a group and perhaps represent a different word altogether.

Similar benefits accrue from considering other words in the *trai-* group through a kind of *MED/DOST* binocular. *Train*, for example (*DOST trane*), overlaps with *trail* to the extent that in rare cases the two words can appear as manuscript variants for each other. Once again, the semantic variety in the English examples has led *MED* to multiply entries, centred respectively on seduction and trickery, and on things that drag: retinues, the trains of gowns, protracted tarryings, strings of events, drawstrings (traces), and strings of morsels, and inevitably vines and branches again, whereas *DOST*, following the French dictionaries, is content with one verb and one noun.

Finally ME *traisen* v. (ppl. *trased*) is saved by the *DOST* oncer entry *trase*. *Traisen* is an entry created on the theory that putting two obscure cruces in a common entry creates a legitimate word. *Arthur and Merlin* contains a verb 'trayse' that seems most naturally interpreted as 'tie or attach with traces (reins, etc.)'; the York Plays contain an obscure participle 'trased' that means something amounting to 'stopped' or 'hindered', but which could be regarded as a figurative use of 'put in traces, harness; hence leash, restrain'. These would be speculation if it were not for a single occurrence in *Golagros* of *trasit* ppl., at least plausibly with the meaning 'reined in': 'thair hors . . . trasit in vnquart quakand thai stand'.

Comparison of course does not necessarily clarify mysterious connections, like that presumably underlying ME *badde*, and Scots *baudrins* as the name of a cat. In some cases the two dictionaries seem to walk together propping each other up, whilst neither really has a clue, as in the case of *DOST ousett* n. and *MED osete* n. ('a kind of cloth').

Nor does comparison always yield a common history; where the Scottish texts are late, and the source Latin or French, independent borrowing is always a likelihood. Scots *astrolog* bears comparison to English *astrologer*, both from Latin *astrologus* or F *astrologue*, largely because the clipped form is the Scots one. *MED compair* n. is probably independent of *DOST compare, compair* adj. *Altitude* is more common in ME than *DOST* knew, but Scots *altitude* n. (a oncer in *Buke of the Chess*) is still likely to derive directly from the Latin, as perhaps are *crudelite, ingenious* and *pulchritude*, all from the *Buke of the Chess* and otherwise represented chiefly in translation texts in both languages.

In some cases, the language of the word in question is in a real sense not English or Scots at all. ME *ponde* n. 'a pledge', found once in a late ME poem, is comparable to but likely independent of the common Scots *pand, paund* n. 2, probably an international and 'interlingual' commercial word extant also in Anglo-Latin, Dutch and (rarely) Old French. The same is probably true of *verdyt* n. (ME *verdit* n.), in the distinctive insular sense of a judge's or jury's decision, which, though appearing in English and Scots dress, is 'really' an Anglo-French legal term. *Warrop(e* n. 'a rope [of a certain sort]' (ME *war-rop*) is doubtless a northern nautical term. The word appears only once in ME, in a fourteenth-century Yorkshire will, alongside many Scots examples from the sixteenth century, but, as *MED* makes clear, it is also part of a large group of mysterious nautical terms in *war-* (*war-pin*, *war-shete*, *war-take*, *war-withe*, *war-wrethe*, *war-line*) that show cognates around the North Sea. *MED* and *DOST* together, though better than either separately, show only part of the picture.

Finally, and to me most interestingly, there is a large common abstract vocabulary of social, ethical and political virtue and vice that differs only in the most subtle ways from nation to nation or from language to language. When the Scots translator of Alain Chartier's 'Breviaire des Nobles'[2] describes the twelve qualities belonging to 'nobilnes' as 'faith (foy), lawte or treuth (loyaulté), honoure (honneur), ressoun (droitture), worthynes (proesce), luf (amour), curtasy (courtoisie), deligence (diligence), clenlynes (netteté), larges (largesce), sobernes (sobresse), and perseuerance (perseverance)', he poses a challenge to any lexicographer to capture exactly what flavour of large fundamental value he is trying to express, much less to relate that flavour to the complex mix of meanings thrown up by legal, popular and theological works employing the same words. There may be something distinctively Scottish or English in the usage of these words, but any difference is in practice probably overwhelmed by differences of interpretation introduced by the individual lexicographers; to set the dictionaries side by side is to set them talking to each other and learn from the conversation. *Faith* in this work (173/24), for example, seems to represent a blend of fidelity to God and faithfulness in the performance of obligation – moral life regarded as service to a divine liege – a sense not perfectly represented in either dictionary, but perhaps best in *MED*'s sense 5, which combines faithfulness to a trust with loyalty to a person. *Resoun* (176/3), equated with equity and 'mesure', is represented by *DOST*'s sense 7 'a view of things . . . in conformity with reason or what is good or right', combined with 8 'treatment which accords with . . . right or reason, justice', and *DOST* comments that there is perhaps overlap between 7 and 8. *MED* is a little less apt, since it is more rigorous in separating the reasonable from the just. *Luf*, in the sense of 'generosity of affection; ability to love', is unusual enough that it is not quite captured by either dictionary, though touched on by *DOST*'s 'love as a . . . disposition'. And *clenlynes* – well, cleanliness, which appears in both languages, is apparently omitted by both dictionaries!

NOTES

1. *DOST* and *MED* are cited without distinction from the print and the electronic editions. *MED* = *The Middle English Dictionary*, republished electronically as part of the *Middle English Compendium* at URL http://ets.umdl.umich.edu/m/mec. Quotations from primary sources, except as noted, are taken from the dictionaries, not from the editions on which they draw.
2. *The Porteous of Noblenes*, in *The Asloan Manuscript: a Miscellany in Prose and Verse*, ed. W. A. Craigie, vol. 1, pp. 171–84, is a paraphrase of Alain Chartier, 'Le Breviaire des Nobles', in *The Poetical Works of Alain Chartier*, ed. J. C. Laidlaw, pp. 393–409.

CHAPTER 11

Was it Murder? John Comyn of Badenoch and William, Earl of Douglas

W. D. H. Sellar

The following passage occurs in Sir Gilbert Hay's *Buke of the Law of Armys* written in 1456, a translation, albeit a rather free one, of Honoré Bonet's *L'Arbre des Batailles*, completed in 1387. In it Hay discusses the legality and morality of a challenge to combat, and concludes that it transgresses all laws, both God's and man's:

> Bot before or I schaw thir casis [some exceptional cases], I will first prove opynly that gage of bataille be all lawis is forbedyn expressly, bathe in Goddis law and mannis law, in commoun lawe and canoune lawe, and als, be gude resoun naturale, quhilk is callit lawe of nature, and als, be the law civile to geve gage of bataill or to tak. And for sik querele, to fecht is a thing condampnyt bathe and reprovit be all lawis. *And first and formast, I preve it be resoun naturale. For gage of batail cummys ay of forethocht felony. Bot naturally all maner of creature naturale has a passioun of nature that is callit the first movement; that is, quhen a man or beste is sudaynly stert, thair naturale inclinacioun gevis thame of thair complexioun to a brethe, and a sudayn hete of ire of vengeance quhilk efterwart stanchis efter that hete. Bot bataill taking cumis of lang forset and forethocht purpos of malice that is nocht naturale to man.* Item it is a thing reprovit of God and his lawis, and condamnyt. (Stevenson 1901: iv, c. 110; present writer's italics)

The standard modern French edition of *L'Arbre des Batailles* is that of Ernest Nys in 1883, and the standard modern English translation that of G. W. Coopland in 1949 (Nys 1883; Coopland 1949). Although *L'Arbre* was translated many times into various romance languages, Hay's remained the only translation into English until Coopland almost 500 years later. Sir Gilbert Hay, as he informs us himself, completed his translation in the year 1456, at the castle of Roslin, near Edinburgh, at the command of William Sinclair, earl of Orkney and lord of Roslin. It is not known, I believe, what manuscript of Bonet's work Hay used, nor whether that manuscript still survives. Coopland pays generous tribute to Hay's spirited, if rather free, rendering, saying, 'No modern translator can hope to equal this in life and dignity' (Coopland 1949: 11).

There are a number of points of interest to the legal historian in the passage from Hay. One is Hay's listing of various types of law: *Goddis law*, *mannis law*, *commoun lawe*, *canoune lawe*, *the lawe of nature* and *the law civile*. It is worth noting that Coopland's translation of Bonet's original, following the original text more closely, is rather different here:

> But before I name them I wish to show plainly how, according to
> divine law (*droit divin*), the law of nations (*droit des gens*), the law of
> decretals (*droit des decrets*), and civil law (*droit civil*), to give wager of
> battle and to receive it for the purpose of combat is a thing reproved,
> and is condemned by reason. (Coopland 1949: iv, c. 111; original
> French from Nys 1883)

However, the focus of this article is on the second part of Hay's text, italicised above, which draws a contrast between 'forethocht felony', that is, acting 'of lang forset and forethocht purpos of malice', and 'a sudayn hete of ire of vengeance'. Had it not been for the *Dictionary of the Older Scottish Tongue*, which I consulted when researching the terminology and classification of homicide in older Scots law, I should probably never have come across this highly significant passage, referred to there under *For(e)thocht*.

A short excursus into the classification of homicide in Scots law in the later Middle Ages should help to highlight the significance of the passage.[1] The main distinction in Scots law (and, I believe, in English law also) was between killing or slaughter with forethocht felony, that is, with malice aforethought or premeditation, and slaughter in the heat of the moment, alias chaude-melle, sometimes referred to as slaughter 'on a suddenty'. The term 'murder' applied only to the first of these.[2] The distinction appears clearly from three entries in that earlier dictionary of the older Scottish tongue, Sir John Skene's *De Verborum Significatione* of 1597 (subtitled *The exposition of the termes and difficill wordes, conteined in the foure buikes of Regiam Majestatem, and uthers . . .*) under Forthocht felony, Chaude-melle and Melletum:

> FORTHOCHT felony, *praecogitata malitia*, quhilk is don and
> committed wittinglie and willinglie, after deliberation and set purpose,
> and is different from *chaudmelle*.

> CHAUDE-MELLE, In latin *Rixa*, an hoat suddaine tuilzie, or debaite,
> quhilk is opponed as contrar to forthoucht fellonie . . . *vid. Melletum*,
> vid. Forthoucht fellonie.

MELLETUM . . . Ane French word, *Melle*, dissension, strife, debate, as we saye, that ane hes melled or tuilzied with ane uther. And in the actes of Parliament, and practique of this realme, *Chaud-mella* is ane faulte or trespasse, quhilk is committed be ane hoate suddaintie, and nocht of set purpose or *praecogitata malitia*.

The first Act of Parliament to note the distinction was a statute of David II passed over two hundred years earlier, in 1369/70, which stated that no remission or pardon should be given for homicide until an inquest had determined whether the killing had been committed *per murthyr vel per praecogitatam maliciam*, the word *vel* here clearly being intended conjunctively (*APS*: I, 509). Two years later a statute of Robert II of 1371/2 set out that when homicide had been committed an inquest should decide whether killing was *ex certo et deliberato proposito vel per forthouch-felony sive murthir vel ex calore iracundiae viz. chaudemellee*. Here, confusingly, the first *vel* is conjunctive but the second disjunctive. The statute continues that if it was found to be forethocht felony or murder, sentence was to be carried out without delay; but if it was found to be chaude-melle the accused was to have all customary exceptions and defences. Full benefit of sanctuary was to be allowed in the latter case only (*APS*: I, 547–8).

Some Formularies show this legislation in practice. For example, a style in both *Formulary E* and the Bute manuscript is headed *Inquisitio si talis interfecit talem per forthought felony vel non* (Duncan 1976: no. 14).[3] Two later statutes, now expressed in Scots rather than in Latin, use the concept of acting on a suddenty as a synonym for *chaude-melle*: an Act of 1425 which concerns the breaking of the king's peace distinguishes between acts committed upon 'forthocht felony' and those committed 'throw suddande chaudemellay' (*APS*: II, 9); while an Act of 1469 complains of 'gret slachteris . . . baith of forthocht felony and of suddante'. Only the latter category was to have benefit of sanctuary (*APS*: II, 95–6).

Pitcairn's *Criminal Trials* provides a useful guide to the terms of art used in practice in prosecutions for homicide from the end of the fifteenth century, as evidenced by the following examples (Pitcairn 1833):

1493 'art and part of the forethought felony done . . . by way of Murder' (*William Tayt*) (Pitcairn, I, pt. 1, 17*);

1497 'art and part of the Murther and Slauchter of . . .' (*Patrik McKowloche*) (Pitcairn, I, pt. 1, 99*);

1509 'Convicted of art and part of the cruel Slaughter . . . committed upon forethought felony' (*Alexander Lecprevik*) (Pitcairn, I, pt. 1, 62*);

1512 'art and pairt of the Slauchtir and Murthure' (*William Douglas of Drumlanrig*) (Pitcairn, I, pt. 1, 79*);

1530 Accused of 'Cruel slaughter . . . acquitted of forethought felony . . . Wherefore they were restored to the sanctuary of Torphichen' (*Robert Manderstoune*) (Pitcairn, I, pt. 1, 151*).

By the middle of the sixteenth century the indictments become more formulaic, usually combining the elements of old feud, provision, set purpose and forethocht felony:

1539 'indict and accusit for art and pairt of the felloune and cruell Slauchter . . . apoun auld feid and forthocht felony . . . comitit the said Slauchtir upon provisioune and foirthocht fellony' (*James Reid*) (Pitcairn, I, pt. 1, 220*);

1562 Convicted of 'the crewell and unmercyfull Slauchter . . . upone ald ffeid, sett purpois, provisione and foirthoicht fellonye' (*William Fergusone*) (Pitcairn, I, pt. 1, 425*);

1581 Accused of slaughter 'upoune sett purpois, provision, auld feid and foirthocht fellonie'; defence claims that it was 'done on suddantie . . . and denyis foirthocht fellonie' (*William Bikartoune*) (Pitcairn, I, pt. 2, 98–9).

The passage from Hay's *Buke of the Law of Armys* is of interest in its use of these terms of art. Hay writes of 'forethocht felony', of 'lang forset and forethocht purpos of malice', of 'a sudayn hete of ire of vengeance', and of being 'sudaynly stert'. But the greater value of the passage lies in its disclosure of the way of thinking which lay behind these legal distinctions. The division into slaughter by forethought felony and slaughter chaude-melle reflects a very real difference in the way men thought about these two types of killing. Killing by forethought felony was unnatural, against the law of nature. Killing chaude-melle, on the other hand, although clearly sinful, was the result of natural passion. The first deserved the description of 'murder', a term, then as now, reserved for the type of killing deemed most reprehensible by society. The second did not. One might compare the distinction in Scots law today between murder and culpable homicide, or murder and man-slaughter in England. If, therefore, we describe killing in hot blood as 'murder' at this period, we are not only guilty of an anachronism, but are also in some danger of misunderstanding and misjudging the reaction of contemporaries.

With this in mind, it is worth revisiting two of the most famous killings in later medieval Scotland, almost invariably referred to by historians as 'murder', to see how they are described by contemporaries: the killing of John Comyn of Badenoch by Robert Bruce and others in the Church of the Greyfriars in Dumfries in February 1305–6; and the killing of William 8th earl of Douglas by James II and others in Stirling Castle in February 1451–2. Did these killings amount to murder in the eyes of contemporaries? The context of both these killings is well known and is taken for granted here.

Was Bruce's killing of Comyn premeditated? Early Scottish sources suggest that it was not. English sources, however, such as the Chronicle of Walter of Guisborough and Sir Thomas Gray's *Scalacronica*, antagonistic towards Bruce, suggest that it was. The very earliest accounts are both English. The first, a newsletter written within weeks of the killing, gives a detailed account of Bruce's recent movements, but has only a glancing and neutral reference to the killing of John Comyn (*la mort le dit monsire Johan*) (Stones 1970: no. 34, 266–7). However, in the 'confession' of Bishop Lamberton recorded only a few months later in August 1306, Robert de Cottingham, an English royal clerk, uses the term *murdrum* to describe the killing of Comyn (*tam de murdro et interfectione quondam domini Johannis Comyn*), and refers to the 'premeditated iniquity' (*excogitata nequicia*) of Robert Bruce (Stones 1970, no. 35, 274–5). The considered view of modern historians appears to be that Bruce's killing of Comyn was not premeditated. This is the view taken by Geoffrey Barrow in his biography of Bruce: 'It is contrary to everything we know about Bruce's character that he should have called Comyn to the Greyfriars' church with the secret intention of killing him' (Barrow 1988: 146). The historian of the Comyns, Alan Young, is of the same mind: 'It is unlikely that the murder was premeditated' (Young 1997: 198). Archie Duncan too believes that there was no premeditation: 'It is surely clear that the murder was unpremeditated, but there must be a suspicion that Comyn, who had shown himself a violent man, was provocative' (Duncan 1997: 80n.). Edward I's biographer Michael Prestwich agrees: 'Comyn's death was not premeditated, but was the result of a quarrel over Bruce's plans' (Prestwich 1997: 505). Historians, I think, have sometimes found it difficult to explain why Bishop Wishart of Glasgow and Bishop Lamberton of St Andrews, among others, continued to give Bruce their full support apparently undeterred by the murder of Comyn, Wishart absolving Bruce from his sin shortly after the event, and Lamberton saying pontifical high mass at Bruce's inauguration as king later in 1306. The answer is clear. It was not murder.

It is worth noting at this point that the medieval Church was capable of a far more advanced analysis of homicide than the rough distinction between forethought felony and chaude-melle under review. The Canon law, as set out in a chapter headed *De Homicidio Voluntario vel Casuali* in the *Decretals* had elaborated a theory of culpability of considerable sophistication, elucidated on the basis of actual examples, the immediate concern being whether a priest who had been in some way the cause of another's death could be permitted to continue to celebrate mass.[4] In the long run the Canon law analysis was to be very influential in the later classification of homicide in many European jurisdictions, including Scotland. But its impact on secular mores in the fourteenth and fifteenth centuries was limited.

The only detailed contemporary account of the killing of William, earl of Douglas, by King James II in February 1452, despite the king's special assurance and respite, is given in the *Auchinleck Chronicle*'s distinctly breathless prose:

> That samyn zer Erll William of Douglas wes slane in the castell of
> striuling be king James the second that had the fyre mark in his face
> . . . and this samyn Monday [Douglas] passit to the castell and spak
> with the king that tuke richt wele with him be apperans and callit him

on the morne to the dynere and to the supper and he come and dynit
and sowpit and thai said thair was a band betuix the said erll of
Douglas and the erll of Ross and the erll of Crawford and efter supper
at sevyne houris the king then beand in the Inner chalmer and the said
erll he chargit him to breke the forsaid band he said he mycht nocht
nor wald nocht/ Than the king said fals tratour sen yow wil nocht I
sall/ and stert sodanely till him with ane knyf and straik him at the
colere and down in the body and thai sayd that Patrick Gray straik him
nixt the king with ane poll ax on the hed and strak out his braines and
syne the gentills that war with the king gaf thaim Ilkane a straik or twa
with knyffis . . .[5] (McGladdery 1990: 165)

Was this killing done with forethocht felony? Most modern historians, although
referring to the deed as 'murder', have concluded that it was not. Christine
McGladdery writes of 'the hot-blooded stabbing of the earl by the king', and
concludes that 'the murder of Douglas is unlikely to have been premeditated'
(McGladdery 1990: 69). Annie I. Dunlop takes the same view in her biography of
Bishop Kennedy: 'No doubt James was carried away by a sudden outburst of
unbridled fury' (Dunlop 1950: 133). In fact, the language of the *Auchinleck
Chronicle* is that of suddenty or chaud-melle. The *Chronicle* is clear that the
slaughter of Douglas was not premeditated, using the words 'the king . . . stert
sodanely till him with ane knyf'. This statement should be compared with the
passage from Sir Gilbert Hay already given, written less than five years after the
killing of Douglas, which contrasts killing by forthocht felony with killing 'quhen a
man or beste is sudaynly sterte' and experiences 'a sudayn hete of ire of vengeance'.

Douglas's killing, therefore, was not murder. It was right, however, that the king
should make amends, so far as possible, to the kindred of the man he had slain. He
should not profit from his misdeed. This is why, I would suggest, King James
entered into a bond of manrent with William Douglas's brother and successor,
James 9th earl of Douglas, in January 1453, and personally petitioned the Pope to
grant the necessary dispensation to allow the new earl to marry William's widow,
the heiress Margaret of Galloway, and thereby acquire control over her lands
(Nicholson 1974: 365; McGladdery 1990: 82). This behaviour has surprised
historians. Ranald Nicholson comments, 'Even more astonishingly James bound
himself to aid the earl to consolidate his territorial power by furthering a marriage
betwixt Earl James and the latter's sister-in-law'; while McGladdery follows
Dunlop in considering that James's promotion of the marriage is proof of his
impotence and the insecurity of his position (Nicholson 1974: 365; McGladdery
1990: 83; Dunlop 1950: 43). On the contrary, the king's promotion of the marriage
should be seen above all as a fitting act of expiation, a just and necessary assythment
for the slaughter of Earl William in hot blood, done to prevent further feud.[6]

What of the terms of art used in the passage from Hay which conform so closely
to those used in Scots law? What terms do they translate or mirror in the original

French of Honoré Bonet, composed some seventy years before? Might the original and the translation, taken together, throw some light on the comparative legal history of homicide? The answer to these questions came as a surprise. There is no parallel passage in Honoré Bonet.[7] The entire passage given in italics at the beginning of this paper is an interpolation. Why?

One can only speculate. Hay's patron, as he tells us, was that great survivor of Scottish fifteenth-century politics, William Sinclair, earl of Orkney (later earl of Caithness) and lord of Roslin. The interpolated passage which echoes so closely the words of the *Auchinleck Chronicle* was written within five years of the slaughter of the earl of Douglas by the king, and must, at the very least, have stirred memories of that death in Hay's patron. Is there any reason to suppose that William Sinclair, earl of Orkney, had a particular interest in the fate of the Douglases? Every reason, it transpires. His relationship to the Douglas kin could not have been closer: his mother was a Black Douglas; his first wife was a Black Douglas; and his sister was married to a Black Douglas. Through his first wife, Elizabeth, the earl of Orkney was the uncle of William 6th earl of Douglas and of David his brother, who were both executed judicially after 'the Black Dinner' at Edinburgh Castle in 1440. He was uncle also, through his sister Beatrice, of William 8th earl of Douglas, killed by King James at Stirling.[8] The earl of Orkney was also, like most of the higher nobility, a close cousin of the king, being a great grandson of Robert II. He is likely to have reflected more than most on the events of that February day in 1452 when the king stert sodaynly towards the earl of Douglas with a knife. Is it not likely that William earl of Orkney may have had a hand in this interpolation?

NOTES

1. This section of the paper draws on my 'Forethocht Felony and Malice Aforethought' (Sellar 1991).
2. The term 'murder' had earlier been restricted to killing by night or secret killing.
3. Compare Bute Manuscript no. 68 (Cooper 1946).
4. *X 5.12. Liber extra (Decretales Gregorii IX)* in *Corpus Iuris Canonici.*
5. The *Auchinleck Chronicle* is transcribed from the Asloan MS (NLS MS Acc. 4233) in McGladdery 1990: Appendix 2.
6. It does not appear that this precedent for marrying a brother's widow was cited in the case of Henry VIII and Catherine of Aragon.
7. There is no parallel in Nys's standard edition, nor, I suspect, in any manuscript of the original. I am assured by Sally Mapstone, who has made a close study of Hay's work, that this is far from the only occasion on which Hay departs from Bonet's original text.
8. For these relationships, which are uncontroversial, see Balfour Paul, *Scots Peerage.*

CHAPTER 12

Interpreting Scots Measurement Terms: a Cautionary Tale

A. D. C. Simpson, University of Edinburgh

INTRODUCTION

Weights and measures were as much a part of the social fabric in medieval times as they are today. Then as now, measurement units were used in the trade of foodstuffs, raw materials and many finished goods. In addition, Scottish units have also been used for centuries in land contracts, as the basis for taxation, and in rental and tenancy agreements, and notably in circumstances where payments of all sorts were made in kind. To understand these activities we require a knowledge of the sizes of these units and an appreciation of the way in which they were used. Taking the broad perspective, Professor Christopher Smout has recently posed the question: 'If we do not know the true volumes of trade, the movement of prices or the worth of goods, how can the history of a nation be properly known? Whole areas of economic experience will be a closed book.'[1]

In common with other mercantile nations, Scotland had its own well-defined systems of weights and measures for external and internal trade, and the legal and administrative structures for enforcing their use. The sizes of certain measurement units, and the relationships between them, were principally controlled through periodic acts of the Scottish Parliament known as assizes of weights and measures. The Scottish units almost certainly had their origins in the early English system in the twelfth century, imported into Scotland by David I and his largely Anglo-Norman followers. However, the Scottish system evolved along a separate path, and so the units came to be of different sizes. Subsequently, Scottish units were more strongly influenced by trading contacts with the Low Countries (particularly Flanders) and France. A number of Scottish units have familiar names (for example, pound, stone, pint and gallon) which are also found in England, but others are distinctly or predominantly Scottish, such as the grain firlot and boll. Some betray Continental origins, such as the chopin or half-pint (French) and the mutchkin or quarter-pint (low German).

The administration also held physical standards, which were accurately made and adjusted vessels and weights, designed to be the principal authorised reference standards for the kingdom. At times of major assizes, the principal burghs were required to purchase authenticated copies of these weights and measures, and they could then issue verified duplicates to neighbouring burghs. In due course, four particular burghs were identified as holding one each of the four key standards, and they were authorised to make more accessible copies for all the other burghs. Thus, Stirling held the commercial pint standard (the Stirling Jug or Stoup), Linlithgow held the firlot (for dry measure), Edinburgh had the ell (linear measure) and Lanark had the stone (of weight).

A typical weights and measures assize would provide a series of definitions of key measurement terms. These definitions name the units and explain numerical relationships to one another. They also describe how one type of unit is defined in terms of another. Thus, the pint is defined as a vessel which contains a particular number of ounces of water, and the dry measures contain a set number of pints and may have particular dimensions in inches. These helpful and descriptive assize definitions should form a natural source for the dictionary definitions in the *Dictionary of the Older Scottish Tongue*.

The problem is that assize texts turn out to be quite complex, and whereas they are strictly correct when understood in context, they often cannot now be interpreted at face value. It has long been appreciated that these assizes show internal inconsistencies and contradictions, and that they appear to describe runaway growth in the size of the dry measures. It has only recently become clear that the surviving texts incorporate early revisions, and that assizes are in their nature very selective in their scope. We now know, for example, how to relate the pounds of the assizes to the various other types of pound, which are not distinguished from them but are used for different purposes. We also now understand that the volumes of the capacity measures described in the assizes were not generally used: the trading measures were larger and incorporated a series of fixed customary allowances on the basic or legal sizes.

All this formed part of the 'tacit knowledge' of the market-place, known to everyone at the time, but almost never recorded. The effect of taking aspects like this into consideration is to allow a self-consistent interpretation to emerge, but it also emphasises the difference between these less familiar medieval customary practices and modern concepts of fairness and equality.

MEASUREMENT TERMS IN *DOST*

Since the late 1980s, Robin Connor and I have been working on a history of Scottish weights and measures, with the support of the National Museums of Scotland. As part of this we have been trying to locate and catalogue as many of the surviving early burgh standards as possible, and this information has been crucial to resolving some of the central problems of Scottish metrology and the testing of our conclusions.

During this time, I was fortunate to be able to spend part of 1991–2 as a visiting fellow at the School of Scottish Studies at Edinburgh University, and I was able to establish links with the staff of *DOST* and work with some of their source material. It was at about this time that we were completing and publishing our explanation for the progressive enlargement of the dry measures (Simpson 1992), and we were also pleased to have the chance to discuss our emerging conclusions with two groups of economic historians who had been considering the evolution of Scots weights and measures in the course of preparing histories of prices and wages in Scotland. Both studies, by Elizabeth Gemmill and Nicholas Mayhew for the period to about 1540, and by Alex Gibson and Christopher Smout for the subsequent period, were published in 1995.

The editing of *DOST* had reached the point when the Editorial Director, Marace Dareau, was tackling the entry for 'Stane' and we had the opportunity to incorporate some idea of the historical development of the stone of weight.[2] It was hoped that this would make the entry more useful and informative, and would reflect an understanding of the weight series that had improved significantly since the entries for 'Ounce' and 'Pound', published in 1983 and 1986 respectively, which had contained no early quantitative detail.

In a recent discussion of the development of editorial policy and methodology for *DOST*, Marace Dareau has examined the changing perceptions of successive editors from *DOST*'s inception in the 1920s to the completion in 2002 (see also Chapter 3). She has stressed the progressive shift from a more limiting linguistic analysis in the early years towards a broader view of the cultural and social context of language; and she describes the settled view of the editors of the past twenty years that 'the job of historical lexicography is to provide the most useful tool possible for all those likely to be users of the Dictionary, historians as much as linguists' (Dareau 2002a: 83).

This approach, in which there is a greater emphasis on defining the things and concepts denoted by words, can be described as 'encyclopaedic'. William Craigie, who edited the first two volumes, covering the letters A–C (1937) and D–G (1951), is characterised by Dareau as a 'closet encyclopaedist' who had restricted his work in the volumes very largely to linguistic analysis (Dareau 2002a: 81). Jack Aitken, his colleague and successor (in 1955), broke with Craigie's conservative approach and broadened the scope of entries to provide more emphasis on usage, but also the definition of technical terms. Aitken's co-editor and (briefly) successor, James Stevenson, extended this approach, describing *DOST* as 'an attempt to provide a key to the whole range of Scottish culture' (Dareau 2002a: 80). The need to retain this valued encyclopaedic aspect of *DOST* was recognised at reviews in 1981 and 1994 which were prompted by funding crises: at both it was agreed that the quality of subsequently published parts of *DOST* should not be compromised. Pressure from users of the dictionary was effective in 1981, and meeting the expectations of the user community has remained a major consideration.

The experience of involvement in the entry for 'Stane' has led me to look more closely at the other entries for measurement terms. It is perhaps unfortunate that the initial letters of so many of the key terms of Scots metrology occur in the early part of the alphabet, and therefore appear in Craigie's initial two volumes. These include not only the firlot, boll and chalder of the dry measures, and the gallon of the liquid series, but also the principal linear units of the ell and fall. Here, by intention or mischance, there is little to suggest that Craigie felt impelled to provide more than linguistic definitions.

The great majority of entries for measurement terms, particularly in Craigie's volumes, merely record the use of these terms by quoting phrases from lists of merchandise or produce (so many ells of cloth, or bolls and firlots of barley). From these we can certainly extract linguistic information about variant spellings or plural forms. It is more difficult to find sources that can illuminate the practical contexts in which measurements were made or which reveal useful quantitative detail.

There are a few valuable sources of this type, which Craigie did use. For example, Alexander Huntar's quasi-official text of 1624 on weights and measures provides a late and brief overview of Scots weights and measures: Craigie cited it to show an important point (the significance of which may not have been fully recognised): that the trading divisions of the ell were sixteenths. Another is a fragmentary merchant's handbook of c. 1400, cited as *Scots Merchandise*, which gives a rare early view of the relationship of trading quantities at Bruges (although there is residual ambiguity about whether some of the names are Scots or Flemish).[3] Similarly, material extracted from the records of the Scottish Mint, and published by R. W. Cochran-Patrick, provides valuable comparisons between the various weight series, particularly in the mid-seventeenth century (Cochran-Patrick 1876).

However, the most useful (but slippery) sources of information about measurement terms are the periodic parliamentary assizes of weights and measures, which set the legal sizes of the measurement units, and authorised changes or revisions to these. Strangely, Craigie made little use of these measurement term definitions; but where he did include quotations from assizes, for example for the boll and the related firlot and chalder, he seems to have had little sense of the confusion caused by selective use of partial and incomplete descriptions. One can extract little more than the theoretical relationships of four firlots to the boll and sixteen bolls to the chalder, even though in practice the use of customary allowances disguises these simple equivalences.

Craigie may on occasion have felt that a definition term was well enough known for numerical definition to be in some way superfluous; but it is extraordinary that he did not give clues as to the length of the ell, even though every weights and measures assize repeats the liturgy of the ell being 37 inches long, and thus being an inch longer than the equivalent English yard.

Although Aitken and Stevenson undoubtedly adopted a broader and more informative stance in most instances, they nonetheless appeared reluctant to engage in the more technically loaded detail necessary to flesh out the use of measurement terms. Yet from the user's perspective, we naturally assume that these terms must have had distinct and mutually understood contemporary meanings. We instinctively feel that they should be amenable to accurate quantitative explanation, and even at a qualitative level we appreciate a need to convey an adequate context for their practical application. In the internet age there is an increasing expectation that answers to such questions can be found.

Because the current phase of work on *DOST* involves digitising the text and making it freely available on-line, the disparity between these early entries and the ones produced towards the end of the work will become more noticeable, particularly by comparison with, for example, Elizabeth Gemmill's 1995 glossary of Scots measurement terms to 1540 (Gemmill and Mayhew 1995: 382–409). Although I am dealing here with only a small group of words, it is likely that there are a number of other such groups in equally restricted technical areas where it will also be apparent that there is scope for revision. However, the transfer of the paper *DOST* to a digitised form presents the ready opportunity (which the strictures of the printed edition always denied) for progressive improvement to selected earlier entries in *DOST*, providing that the new Scottish Language Dictionaries (SLD) can retain a critical revision facility and the ability to respond to new research.

To take this suggestion further, firstly I will discuss some of the features of assize texts that provide cautions about their interpretation, and secondly I want to look at the layers of meaning that need to be considered to approach an understanding of the 'pint'. The *DOST* entry for this crucial weight-based unit, on which the capacity series depended, appeared in Part XXXI in 1983. Greater reliance was placed here on official and semi-official sources, but some of the quotations are not self-explanatory and contain evident contradictions. Although we know much more about this term now, there are still large gaps in our knowledge of its historical evolution that raise interesting problems about the contemporary naming of the unit.

INTERPRETING ASSIZE TEXTS

The first weights and measures assize is a text attributed to the legislative vigour of David I; but, although some parts are certainly very early, the text survives in a form that has clearly been subject to amendments in the fourteenth century. It is included in the collections of statutes and regulations traditionally known as 'the Auld Lawes', some of which depend on earlier English legal sources. However, much now has no secure history, principally because of the confiscation and loss of the original parliamentary records during periods of foreign military occupation. Something like a full account of parliamentary acts is available in official records only from the 1420s, and there were subsequently half-a-dozen major assizes of weights and measures, the last of which took place in 1618.

These assizes tend to come near the beginning of reigns (or at least the start of majorities or periods of personal rule) and they can perhaps be interpreted as efforts to maximise aspects of royal revenues, presumably with similarly beneficial effects for the landed elite. A principal feature of these assizes is a progressive increase in the volumes of the crucial measures for grain and meal, and the interpretation of this rise is the main battleground in Scots historical metrology.

Perhaps the most interesting of these is a complex and frequently misunderstood Assize of 1426, dating from near the start of James I's personal rule after his ransomed return from a period of eighteen years' exposure to the English court and administration. The assize is remarkable for two reasons. Firstly, it provides a rare comparison of newly defined units with the earlier units (inevitably ascribed to David I) which were in force before the Act; and secondly, it includes the single recorded example of a permitted heaping allowance, introduced as an apparent compromise gambit to restrict a larger customary allowance.

Revision of Assize texts

These definitions provide much of the information that is necessary to determine the sizes and relationships of the Scottish measurement terms, but for a number of reasons, assize texts are difficult to use and contain traps for the unwary.

There are several distinct reasons for this. The first is that there are some apparent internal inconsistencies and contradictions in assize texts. Although a fairly full record of the parliamentary Acts exists from the start of James I's direct rule in 1424, there is no single authorised text for legislation before the 1460s. What we know of the period before this has to be pieced together from a range of sources. The most important for the old laws are the small number of extant manuscript digests and early legal compendia, which are necessarily selective in their coverage and are the products normally of several stages of copying from earlier manuscripts. Not only do these texts vary between themselves, they also tend to introduce and perpetuate occasional transcription errors, which may sensibly alter the meaning. Additionally, since the purpose of making a compilation is to extract a legal record that has current relevance, alterations and revisions may be included, and it is clear that this might affect metrological Acts where legal definitions had been changed.

The first collected edition of the parliamentary Acts, Henryson's *Actis and Constitutionis*, covering the period from 1424, was published in 1566. It was the outcome of the latest of several commissions to produce a revision of the statutes in force and was the work of James Balfour of Pittendreich, the Clerk Register for the time. It can be shown that Balfour modified some numerical data to bring the text more into line with the situation in the mid-sixteenth century, and subsequent sixteenth- and seventeenth-century editors were satisfied to accept this modified version of the 1426 Assize, which also appears in Balfour's influential *Practicks* (McNeill 1962–3: I, 90).

In contrast, Thomas Thomson, the editor of the vast nineteenth-century 'Record Edition' of the *Acts of the Parliaments of Scotland* (*APS*), was not trying to provide a revision of the statutes but a unified chronological edition of the original text of the statutes. Because the authenticated parliamentary record begins in the 1460s, Thomson was obliged to rely on early printings of the 1426 Assize, supplemented by any manuscript copies of the lost record. His version of the 1426 Assize was published in 1814 and it incorporates significant changes from Balfour's version (*APS*: II, 12). Thomson has recognised some difficulty with the figures for the weights and dry measures given by Balfour (but did not appreciate that they had been modified to account for over a century of change before Balfour's time) and he has uncritically incorporated information from Balfour's *Practicks* and two fifteenth-century manuscript copies to produce a new version. The earlier of these manuscripts (which are still at the National Archives of Scotland), a near contemporary copy from the 1450s, contains an accurate reflection of the original text; the second dates from the 1470s, after another revision of the statutes, and is already to some extent modified and perhaps corrupted by transcription errors.

Thomson's attention was drawn to these manuscripts by a scrupulously accurate transcription printed for publication by William Robertson of the Record Office in the first volume of a projected series of *The Parliamentary Records of Scotland*, which Thomson successfully advised the Record Commission to suppress at its publication in 1804. However, a few copies of Robertson's volume survived, and so when the general introduction to *APS* was written, Thomson's successor Cosmo Innes felt obliged to mention the suppressed volume. Thomson himself never referred to Robertson's work, nor provided more than a cursory description of the two manuscript sources. Instead he felt constrained by the nature of his criticism of Robertson's volume to provide a single and supposedly definitive text avoiding any potential textual ambiguity.

As a result, no information is given about the choices he made between the various texts. Inevitably some of these choices were incorrect: they seem almost arbitrary and they betray a lack of understanding of the statute itself. Far from providing a definitive text for the Assize, Thomson created a version which has confused subsequent commentators, including, it has to be said, William Craigie. Perhaps uncharacteristically, Craigie gave the dimensions of the boll defined in the 1426 Assize, but these are the corrupt dimensions from *APS*.

The scope of Assize legislation

Secondly, assize legislation is selective in scope and it normally provides information only on some aspects relevant to merchant activity. It is not intended to illuminate other issues such as the nature of the units of internal market trade. There may, for example, be several types of pounds in use at any given time, appropriate for different goods and in different circumstances, but most go unrecorded in the assizes. Only the context of a particular reference may allow the pound type to be identified.

At the 1426 Assize a new ounce type is introduced, with a descriptive name of 'trois' or 'troyis', and this is a weight series restricted to bullion operations. It turns out to be the same as the English 'troy' ounce (about 31g), which had recently been incorporated into formal English metrology. However, a subsidiary Scots Act of 1426 allows us to see that this trois pound was different from the current merchant or 'Scottis' pound, although they shared the same stone (*APS*: II, 10: Act 14).

Perhaps more significantly, the assizes tell us nothing at all about the 'trone' weight series, which was described in 1613 as 'the ordinair and proper weght of the kingdome' (Burton, *RPCS*: series 2, VIII, 333), and which dominated the burgh markets. It is mentioned only once in the legislative record, when an unsuccessful attempt was made to abolish it in the final major Assize in 1618. So entrenched was trone weight in market practice that it continued in everyday use until at least the mid-nineteenth century. It has only been by locating and measuring surviving sixteenth–century trone standard weights that we have been able to confirm much later statements that trone weight was maintained at 1¼ times the size of the merchant weights.

But there are other instances in this vein. Wool, for example, was a major export for Scotland. Perhaps it should not be unexpected, but Scottish wool was reckoned in the particular Flemish pound of the wool market in Bruges where most of it was sold.

Change in the Assize units

A third problem with assize definitions is that they describe situations which are clearly not static, and in which changes are introduced by the legislation. This is made quite explicit in the 1426 Assize, which compares the original with the new units. This reveals, amongst other changes, that the gallon has been doubled in size. As a general rule the market resists change that disrupts trade. We must ask therefore whether this is a case of the legislation catching up with changing practice, or whether perhaps the change does not affect the operation of trade and is in some way specific to the process of formulating definitions. Clearly this has an impact on any attempt to quantify the trading gallon's size. We will return to this issue in the discussion of the pint.

Customary allowances

A final problem with interpreting assize texts is that they provide only the theoretical relationships between the capacity units, and this masks the traditional practice of taking various levels of heaping allowances or 'charities' in the course of transactions. These form part of the tacit knowledge of the market and are almost never explicitly mentioned. As an example of this, a tenant who paid his rental in grain might expect to pay a set number of firlots measured to the flat brim of his superior's capacity measure, the surface being 'struck' level with a rod. Instead, he would in effect face a demand that the measure should be 'heaped'. Because the permitted size of the heap was strictly controlled, the capacity measure was constructed with a larger volume in order to incorporate the heaping enlargement so that the measure could again be struck with a level surface.

Merchants who traded by the larger boll would be allowed an additional charity, ostensibly to compensate for loss or spillage in the course of dividing goods for resale in smaller quantities. Similar additional allowances applied when trading at the level of chalders and when shipping material by the so-called water metts used only at ports. In practice, therefore, the quantities traded were often significantly larger than would have been the case if measured by the units described in the assizes.

Throughout the sixteenth century the acceptance of heaping allowances in the burghs meant that the customary firlot was up to an eighth larger than the 'legal' firlot, and was increased by this amount at each assize. To take a greatly simplified view, the process involved Parliament calling for the standard to be produced by the official cooper of Linlithgow. It was measured and found to be larger than authorised at the last assize, perhaps forty or fifty years before, but the cooper would swear that it was the original, true and just measure. With a show of reluctance, the parliamentary commissioners would accept and legalise this larger size. But, recognising that the burghs would insist on having the full advantage built into their measures, the cooper would make them one eighth bigger. It would be this larger size that would be presented at the next assize – when the cycle of enlargement would be repeated.

It is quite clear that everyone knew what was happening, and although there were safeguards incorporated for re-calculating existing contracts, these must have been widely disregarded. And again it was the tenants who bore the brunt of the increase.

When we add in further refinements – reflecting, for example, that the size of the defining pints changed subtly during periods when French and then Flemish troy weight was the official standard in Scotland – the progression of firlot sizes that can be deduced from the assizes matches intervals of one eighth. We can accurately recreate the firlot sizes of the 1618 Assize, but only by using the appropriate dry fill to raise the firlot from the pint, and we can confirm the permitted customary size in 1500 from a rare surviving burgh firlot gauge.

In theory, the Scottish units were abolished in favour of the existing English weights and measures at the Union of the Parliaments in 1707, and new sets of English standards were issued to the main Scottish burghs. In practice, Scottish units continued in widespread use, particularly in country markets, until the mid-nineteenth century, when they were progressively replaced by the new British 'Imperial' system. However, in the absence of centralised control, the sizes of units began to diverge, and different patterns of use developed. People had also forgotten just how the definition system operated, and in trying to re-interpret the old legislation a number of unfortunate errors and wrong assumptions were made. Much of the received view of Scots metrology is based on somewhat naïve comparisons made at the time between the new Imperial standards and the traditional units, and on earlier antiquarian enquiries. It is these figures from the 1820s (which were gathered together more accessibly by George Buchanan and published in 1829) that form the basis of the measurement entries in the *Scottish National Dictionary (SND)*.

THE SCOTS PINTS

The word 'pint' brings together at least two separate functions that were arguably central to burgh life. Not only was it the retail unit for drink throughout the kingdom, it was also the principal intermediary in defining the firlot, which was clearly a crucial measure in trade and the payment of rentals. But was the name applied in a similar fashion in both contexts? What was understood at the time by the word 'pint'?

James Stevenson's 1983 *DOST* entry on the pint, initially edited in 1973, slides over quantitative meanings by describing it merely as 'a pint in the general senses and collocations . . . varying in capacity according to time and locality'. His reference to the firlot being 21¼ pints is from a late seventeenth-century source and gives no indication of the evolution of this final (legal) definition, nor indeed that the more significant barley and malt firlot of 1618 was 31 pints. The pint's size is given as 41 ounces from the 1426 Assize, and then 55 ounces (or 3 pounds 7 ounces) in Huntar's description, taken from the 1618 Assize. In addition, however, Stevenson repeats the anomalous description as 41 trois ounces from the 1587 Assize (where the legislators were merely covering their backs because the texts of the earlier definitions at 55 ounces had not survived). The main thrust of his definition is hardly supported by quotations that pass the test of being self-explanatory, and even his subsidiary point about geographical variation does not apply in the period covered by *DOST*.

In fact the pint, as defined in the assizes, changed its size twice. At the 1426 Assize the gallon is doubled in size, but the definition also shows that it moves from being a 6-pint gallon to becoming an 8-pint gallon. The pint, therefore, was increased by a half in 1426. A further enlargement, in which its volume is increased by a third, occurs in about 1500. (The parliamentary record of this last Assize is lost.)

A number of surviving standards of this last period are known; indeed Stevenson himself referred to the standard retained at Stirling, the so-called

Stirling Jug, as David Murison had earlier done in *SND*. On the face of it, it seems unlikely that Stevenson was unaware that the Stirling Jug survives, because it has been reproduced so many times and was indeed discussed by Lawrence Burrell, a former senior weights and measures inspector, in a 1961 article. Such was the paucity of secondary literature in this area in the 1980s that almost any enquiry would have led quickly to a reference to Burrell's analysis. Burrell argued (incorrectly, as we now know) from his inspection of several sixteenth- and seventeenth-century standards available to him, that the size of the pint had not sensibly altered from the 1450s until the mid-nineteenth century. It was this size of about 104 cubic inches (1.70 litres), based on Buchanan's published results of the inquiries of the 1820s, that was reproduced in the table of 'Scottish Currency, Weights and Measures' in the Volume 10 *Supplement* to *SND*.[4]

Although the 1426 Assize tells us that the pint had increased in size, in fact this did not represent a disruptive change because there was a constant underlying unit. Whereas the pre-1425 pint comprised two chopins, the 1426 pint contained exactly three such units, and indeed the larger pint of about 1500 contains exactly four. It is therefore quite possible that the popular names for the vessels for drink and other trade and domestic uses did not change, or at least were transferred to the larger sizes only gradually.

Several other aspects of the 1426 Assize appear to show similar changes which would be disruptive to trade, but when we examine the reconstructed original text we find that in every instance the Assize shows continuity in the trading units, and in this sense it is a declaratory Act.

The occurrence of sharp increases in the defined size of the measurement terms themselves poses a problem, because it implies that the name is being applied in a very specific and more limited sense as part of a metrological definition. In the 1426 Assize the pint and the gallon are used, through their weight equivalence, to define the (theoretical) sizes of the large grain measures, the firlot and boll. However, enough evidence is provided to show that these dry units do not exhibit jumps in size – indeed we can demonstrate continuity in the size of a customary boll which is considerably bigger than the legal boll. This must be the real boll of the market. But might the legislators merely be telling us that the proper *administrative* units for the purpose of defining the boll are a 'pint' and a 'gallon', which are respectively half as big again and twice as large as the old units? This is an important issue if our purpose is to provide data useful for the description of market practice.

In fact, a number of features of the 1426 Assize suggest that its form may consciously have mirrored the evolving metrology to the south of the border, which was familiar to James and his advisers. Firstly, there is the unexpected introduction of a troy weight that matches the new English troy series, for which the proper areas of application were bullion, pharmaceuticals and 'measure' – meaning use in metrological definitions. There is also the 8-pint gallon, at 8 gallons to the boll, which can therefore be seen to mirror the 8-gallon English grain bushel. To some extent, such relationships represent ideal situations which take no account of traditional allowances, and at least in the case of the 1426 boll it is clear that the administration ultimately failed to contain the growth of the customary size. Perhaps for this reason, this was the last time that the Scots gallon figured in the dry measure definitions, and in subsequent assizes the only intermediary was the pint.

But when we look for evidence that an 8-pint gallon replaced the older 6-pint gallon in trade, this is more difficult to find. Elizabeth Gemmill has recorded a specific example in the early sixteenth century, and another (which indicates only that there were 16 chopins to the gallon) in the Aberdeen records for 1458–9 (Gemmill and Mayhew 1995: 394). An attempt to justify a consistent volume for the salmon barrel, which was given in terms of gallons, suggested that the 8-pint gallon was in use before the 1470s. It is perfectly possible, therefore, that the 1426 gallon was introduced initially only as a dry definition gallon, intended to form part of the dry capacity series, acting as a mirror of the English corn gallon, which was the only statute form of gallon in England, differing from the separate wine and ale gallons.

We can now appreciate that we are indeed in deep water, because there were also separate wine and ale gallons in Scotland, at least before the 1426 Assize. The *DOST* entry for 'Gallon' is in Craigie's section of the dictionary; and in it he cites the portion of the early David Assize of Weights and Measures that described the boll as a sexterne or 12 gallons of ale, but not the parallel definition of the wine gallon in the undatable David Assize of Wine (*APS*: I, 676: *Assisa de Vino*). From these we can deduce that the ale gallon was the same size as the statutory gallon before 1426, whereas the wine gallon was half as big again and matched a 6-pint gallon with the larger 1426 pint. Perhaps the implication of this is that the change in 1426 was simply an administrative decision to base the dry series on the wine rather than the ale pint. (Each pint had its own chopin; so the Aberdeen reference of 1458–9, which was specific to the import of wine, tells us nothing about the ale units, or about the underlying relationship of the ale chopin to the statutory pint.)

There is a further level of complication. Although these pints have been equated to two levels of the basic statutory pint, drink was always sold in vessels that were a sixteenth larger. The origin of this tradition is unknown, but it may perhaps have been because part of the volume was considered tainted by residue and therefore an allowance was given so that tax was paid only on the drinkable portion, namely the basic pint. This allowance is seen in wine calculations in the Scots merchant handbook of c. 1400 discussed earlier, although to interpret it we must consider that two wine pints were the same as a 'stope' (Hanham 1971: 119); however, the allowance is first explicitly described in the eighteenth and nineteenth centuries.

In England, separate wine and ale gallons continued in use for centuries; indeed the English standards sent in 1707 included wine gallons and the pints and quarts of the ale gallon (in addition to copies of the dry gallon). But in Scotland we have no clear evidence of the use of separate gallons after 1426 – but probably only because we don't yet recognise it. It remains possible that the old ale pint remained the normal size for retail use, emerging as the half of the large sixteenth-century pint. Thus, conceivably, the alternative name for the Stirling pint – the Stirling Stoup – may refer to its being twice the usual (old) pint, as in the early merchant handbook. There is some indirect evidence for the overlapping use of different pint sizes: Shetland rentals were rendered in kind in Edinburgh using a unit directly related to the Scots pint, but it was only in the 1560s that these rentals were increased by a third to reflect the change in the statutory pint that had been introduced in about 1500.

By the third quarter of the sixteenth century, drink was certainly being sold in the large pints of 104 cubic inches (or over three present-day pints). We know this because there are two surviving burgh standards, of 1563 and 1574, which are made a sixteenth larger than the basic size; both are self-levelling vessels with spouts, and therefore eminently suitable for the rapid testing of large numbers of retail vessels.[5] One is specifically named as a 'pint' in an inscription ('PINTA SANCTI ANDREAE' – the St Andrews pint). Reliable early eighteenth-century references describe this enhanced size as the 'pewtherers' pint, and so clearly identify it with the usual vessels for retail sales (Grabiner 1996: 236).

But if the bulk of burgh standards of the 'basic' size are not involved with liquid sale, what is their purpose? We are almost obliged to conclude that they exist to provide a back-up route to the defining or testing of a standard firlot, which contains a set number of pints. It is certainly the case that in the 1770s the official cooper at Linlithgow was using the town's pint to gauge firlots, because we know that his work came under the critical eye of the Court of Session, which was being advised in such practical matters by the Professor of Natural Philosophy at Edinburgh University. His slap-dash procedure gave results which help explain some of the variation in dry measure noted at the time; and his use of water as the measuring medium, rather than grain, gave an enlarged size which only approximately matched the single stage of enlargement allowed on the old 1618 measures.

Knowing more about the greater variety in size and purpose of the pint takes us further down the road to understanding its use. But this only poses more questions, and there are still strict limits to our knowledge.

CONCLUSION

It is inevitable that in the editing of *DOST*, spread as it was over such a substantial period of time, there would be some unevenness in the presentation of any group of associated words. To a great extent this has necessarily been conditioned by the evolving scope and editorial policy of the dictionary. In the particular case of measurement terms, which are tightly related in an adminis-trative sense, there has been the additional constraint of a developing understanding of the subject matter and its social and economic context. However, earlier editors of *DOST* did not engage in the technical detail of these terms, and so the entries do not exemplify the clear encyclopaedic approach which has become such a valued feature of *DOST*.

This approach contrasts with that of *SND*, where measurement terms are assigned clear values at the start of the entries, reinforced by presenting the information again in tabular form in the *Supplement*. There is, unfortunately, great danger in presenting seemingly exact detail in this way, even in the somewhat different circumstances of the eighteenth and nineteenth centuries, and much of the detail of this tabulation is now appreciated to be incorrect or inappropriate.

However, the tabulation was undoubtedly found to be useful, and its perceived value to users led to its later incorporation in the *Concise Scots Dictionary* (*CSD*). A revised analysis, which presents a more balanced view of the historical development and operation of Scots metrology, is likely to replace the earlier table in the planned new edition of *CSD*. As well as the need for revision, this acknowledges the established benefits of having such information available in a digested form.

The ability to consult *DOST* and *SND* on the web will inevitably expose SLD to a new type of dictionary user, indeed to a user community which is sophisticated in the use of on-line resources. This is not only an issue of freely providing public access to its database; SLD will also be in a position to demonstrate its responsiveness to user expectations for limited and targeted electronic revision programmes, following the editorial standards which have been tuned so effectively to the need of the existing user community in Scotland and abroad. Perhaps through the proposed Institute for the Languages of Scotland, SLD can retain the necessary editorial expertise and capacity to maximise the potential of the early volumes and the revision materials already gathered.

NOTES

1. Connor and Simpson 2004, Foreword, p. ix. Unless otherwise noted, the issues discussed in the present article are drawn from this volume.
2. *DOST*, s.v. *stane* n.III. I am grateful to Marace Dareau for her advice and comments in the preparation of the present article. Eileen Finlayson kindly provided additional details.
3. Hanham 1971. The manuscript is in the National Library of Scotland, Adv. MS 34.7.6. Alison Hanham was Assistant Editor at *DOST* from 1965 till 1968.
4. For a corrective see Pryde 1996: 104–5.
5. The Jedburgh and St Andrews pints are discussed in Connor and Simpson 2004: Inventory, numbers 110 and 111.

CHAPTER 13

The Use of the Scottish National Dictionaries in the Study of Traditional Construction

Bruce Walker, Formerly of University of Dundee and Historic Scotland

Language is used to describe every facet of human activity. The wider the range of terms used by a society to describe a particular activity the more important is that activity to the society as a whole.

Previous studies of aspects of building construction using the national dictionaries have shown that traditional forms of building construction using turf and earth have a much wider range of terms than does masonry (Walker and McGregor 1996; Walker, McGregor and Stark 1996a, 1996b and forthcoming). It was also discovered that although the same or similar terms were used in Ireland the meanings were often quite different. The Scots, for example, burn 'peat' while the Irish burn 'turf'; the Scots build with 'turf', the Irish with 'sods', whilst the Scots use a 'sod', in this case a piece of sandy turf, to bank the fire at night to prevent the peats from burning away before morning. Similarly the *Oxford English Dictionary* gives *divot* as '(1) (Sc) piece of turf, sod; (2) (Golf) piece of turf cut out by club-head in making a stroke [sixteenth century: orig. unkn.]', whilst in Scottish building terms a *divot* is a large flat piece of turf used for roofing or as a bonding course in a 'fale and divot' wall (Figs 13.1 and 13.2). The *SND* gives *divot* 'n.1 A turf, sod; n.2 Turf or peat regarded as a material; v.1 To thatch with turf; v.2 To cast or cut *divots*'.

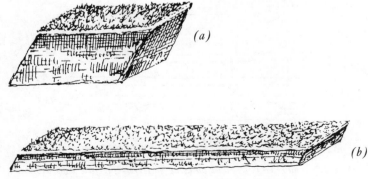

Figure 13.1 (a) A fale (b) A divot

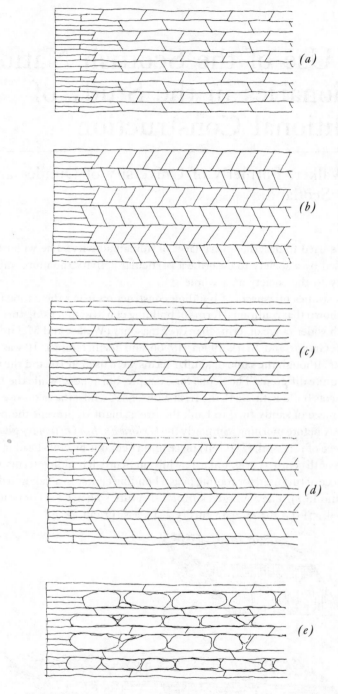

Figure 13.2 (a)–(d) Typical bonding patterns for fale and divot walls.
(e) Divot used with boulders in an alternating stone and turf wall.

A study of the use of *skailie* in medieval and post-medieval Scotland (Bruce Walker 2001) shows that the word was applied to any scale-like roofing material or wall cladding, including timber shingles, small lead plates, roofing tiles, grey slate and blue slate. These are listed in chronological order as found in excavations in all parts of Scotland. The use of shingles starts in the Dark Ages and remains popular until the seventeenth century (Fig. 13.3); small lead shingles were used

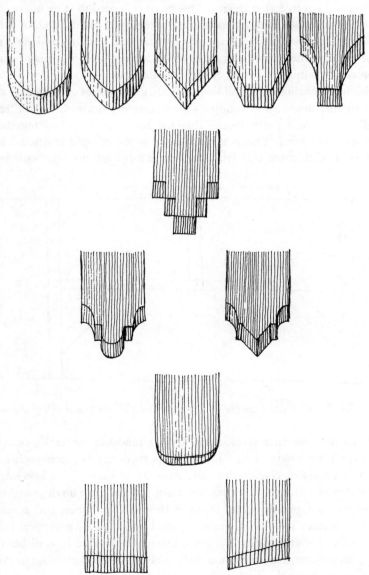

Figure 13.3 Typical timber shingle tails.
The top row are all commonly depicted on Scottish hog-backed tombstones.

until the development of the technology to produce sheet lead in the fifteenth century; tiles appear from the fourteenth century onwards; grey slate first appears in the archaeology of the royal castles and palaces about 1600 but is used earlier in the grey-slate producing areas of Angus and Caithness; and blue slate does not appear until about 1700. In this instance the *DOST* entry for *scailȝe* n. 'slate, the material, blue roofing slate' is far too restrictive, referring only to its later application and not to earlier usages. This point is argued in 'The use of "skaile" in medieval and post-medieval Scotland' (Walker 2001) but the *DOST* definition is not surprising given the emphasis put on masonry building and slate roofing from the nineteenth century onwards, which has resulted in a major misinterpretation of the nature of earlier Scottish buildings.

Traditionally smaller rural buildings were largely built of earth or turf round a timber structure made up of couples with connecting timbers but not 'framed'. 'Framed' in technical usage means that the structure is locked together in a three-dimensional form. This is achieved by the use of rigid joints and bracing (Fig. 13.4). The Scottish and Irish rural structures are not 'framed' since the

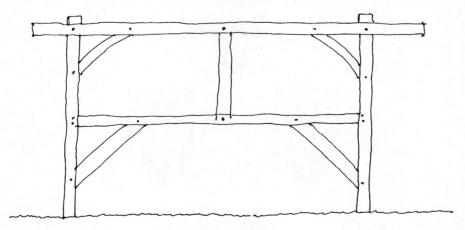

Figure 13.4 Small framed timber structure with rigid joints and integral bracing.

basic structure when first erected will have a tendency to 'rack', that is lean sideways along its length (Fig. 13.5) and this tendency is counteracted by the secondary structure or cladding of turf, mudwall or masonry. The tendency to 'rack' can also be reduced by setting the main couples at an angle, resulting in a structure that is a parallelogram on plan (Fig. 13.6). Urban and upper class buildings appear to have been timber-framed and clad with vertical boarding (Fig. 13.7) (Walker and McGregor 2001; Davies, Walker and Pendlebury 2002: 18–23). This statement is based on a wide range of evidence, set out in the cited papers, none of which is conclusive in itself.

The opportunity to produce this paper formed an ideal vehicle to test the theory that for the greater part of Scottish history, timber was the basic building

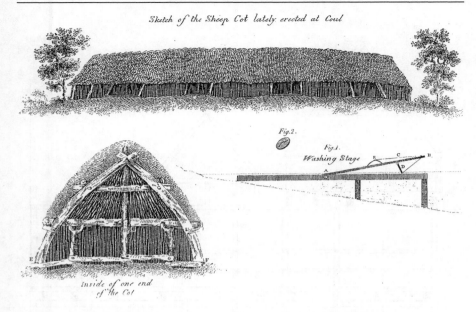

Figure 13.5 Sheep cot at Coul. Small timber structure
with flexible joints and no bracing (Mackenzie 1809: frontispiece).

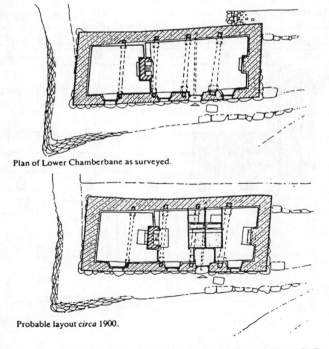

Figure 13.6 Plan of house at Lower Chamberbane, Strathtummel, Perthshire,
where the cruck couples are set at an angle to produce a parallelogram on plan.

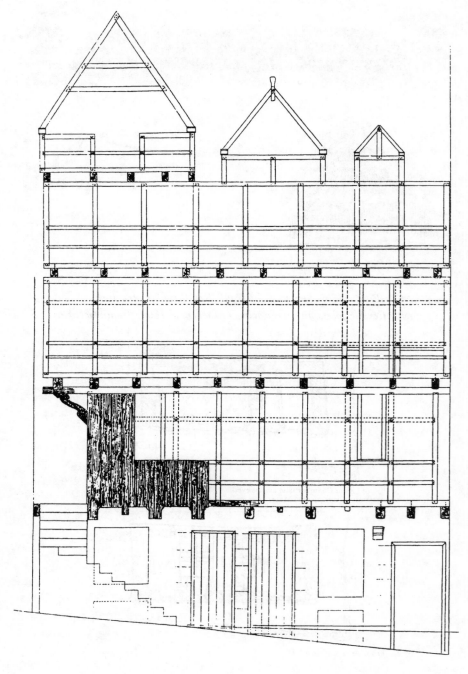

Figure 13.7 Elevation of house in the Lawnmarket, Edinburgh, as surveyed by John Dick Peddie (Proceedings of the Society of Antiquaries of Scotland, XVIII, Plate I).

material, and that in most classes of building, masonry construction developed in parallel with other northern European countries rather than with the nearest neighbour, England.

A search of the Scottish dictionaries for the French carpentry items introduced into England about a hundred years after the Norman Conquest (Goodburn: personal communication) and adopted by the English language drew a complete blank. It was decided at this stage that a much more basic approach had to be taken and the Scottish words for tree, timber and wood, that is *tre*, *tym(m)er* and *wod(e*, should be investigated.

All these terms provided a number of definitions, references to cuts of timber and uses of wood. *Tre* has a number of contradictory meanings, as the *DOST* definitions show:

> n.1 A tree, chiefly a growing tree, also fallen or uprooted by natural agencies; n.2 A part of a tree broken or cut off and used (1) in some celebratory fashion esp. as a crown (2) as kindling wood; n.3 A tree felled for timber, the trunk of a tree used as timber, passing into a balk or beam of wood put to various uses; passing into next n.4 A balk or beam of wood supplying a major element of a structure, a rafter, post, stake, mast etc. along with a range of specific elements such as Bere-tre, Double-tre, Kill-tre, Litsta-tre, Palʒo(u)n(e-tre, Pan-tre, Perch-tre, Ruf(e)-tre and Tym(m)er; n.5 (1) The cross on which Christ was crucified; (2) A gallows; n.6 A pole, shaft or staff; n.7 (1) The wooden part of an object or structure; (2) A block on which a boot is shaped or stretched; n.8 A barrel; n.9 Wood, the substance; n.10 Wooden objects of little value; n.11 A representation of a tree; n.12 A family or genealogical tree; n.13 (1) Made of wood, wooden; (2) Of or belonging to a tree.

All these terms must be borne in mind when reading texts but it is those under definition 4 that are most relevant in the study of buildings.

The terms *tym(m)er* and *wod(e* also present a number of problems. In general terms 'timber' and 'wood' are interchangeable but in forestry and building the technical uses of the terms 'timber' and 'wood' refer to very different parts of a tree and very different products. 'Timber' is that part of a tree that is capable of conversion for building purposes and also the various pieces of converted material. 'Wood' is the lighter branches and twigs used to make charcoal, hurdles, poles and wattle and as fuel. Basically *DOST* agrees with the above but it uses the term 'wood' to describe the whole tree. The definitions for *tym(m)er* read:

> n.1 (1) Wood used in construction, the building of houses, ships etc.;
> (2) Wood as a substance, the material of which objects are made; n.2
> Applied to the wood of growing or newly felled (large) trees, chiefly

viewed as a resource, trees collectively; n.3 The wooden parts of a building . . . the wood of which parts of a building are constructed; n.4 Wood used as a fuel.

The last definition is a complete contradiction of the normally accepted technical definition. This is to be expected, as *DOST* has to cover general uses of the word as well as technical uses, but may refer to the use of timber offcuts or the burning of old timbers removed from a disused structure. Similarly *DOST* defines *wod(e* as 'n.1.1a An area of trees, smaller than a forest, a stretch or piece of woodland; n.2 Trees collectively, woodland, wooded land; n.5 Wood as a substance, material or commodity'. From these descriptions it can be seen that the Scottish building industry is accepting the normal usage of 'timber' as a constructional and structural material and 'wood' as being either the growing raw material or the smaller branches and brushwood used for lesser purposes. In estate papers, valuations and sales notices, a 'mature wood' is usually referred to as 'a stand of timber', confirming that those selling and buying fully recognise the distinction between the terms.

The quoted passages from the dictionaries or the original source books provided a further range of technical terms for cuts of timber, uses of these cuts, and other timber-working terms. On checking the meaning in the Scottish dictionaries it was found that many terms involved in the timber trade were international and are still used today. The British Standards Institute gives cross-sectional dimensions for the cuts of timber as follows:

'Batten' 50 to 100mm by 100 to 200mm; 'Baulk' approximately square, not less than 100mm by 125mm; 'Board', softwood less than 50mm by 100mm, hardwood less than 50mm by 150mm; 'Deal' 50 to 100mm by 225 to 300mm; 'Half-timber', greater than 125mm by 250mm cut through the pith; 'Lath' 6 to 17mm by 22 to 36mm; 'Plank' 50 to 100mm by more than 250mm; 'Slatings', less than 25mm by less than 100mm; 'Scantling', softwood 50 to 100mm by 50 to 125mm, hardwood timber converted to agreed specifications, otherwise square edged timber of dimensions not conforming to other standard terms; 'Strip', softwood less than 50mm by less than 100mm, hardwood less than 50mm by less than 140mm; 'Log' round timber.

The weakness in the Scottish dictionaries' definitions comes when they use common technical terms erroneously to describe other technical terms. For example *bauk* (*balk* or *baulk*) is defined as 'A beam of wood, a plank, a tie-beam or cross-beam connecting the rafters of a house' (*SND*). It is in fact a squared log, not a plank and has a wide range of purposes. It would assist researchers in the future if technical terms were dealt with in a similar way to that used in the technical dictionaries. Care would have to be taken to ensure that Scottish usage was not diffused in the resulting definition. On the other hand the technical dictionaries would benefit from the inclusion of particular Scottish usages of common terms.

The dictionaries often cite the Dundee Shipping Lists regarding the cuts and quantities of timber being imported. In these lists the terms 'fathom', 'square' and 'standard' are associated with quantity. These are not given in the Scottish dictionaries. The 'fathom' is a cubic measure based on a fathom, that is 6 feet by 6 feet by 6 feet, and is an approximate measure for round or cleft timber where the solid contact varies with the straightness of the timber and equals 6.2 stacked cubic metres or between 3.9 and 4.3 cubic metres of timber. A 'square' of timber is 100 square feet or 9.29 square metres irrespective of thickness. A 'standard', or more correctly a 'Petrograd standard', is 165 cubic feet or 4.67 cubic metres. There were other 'standards' in use but the Scots seemed to use the Petrograd standard for most transactions. The other standards are shown in the Table below.

Table 13.1 Standards used for cubic measures of timber

Standard	Measure (cubic feet)
Christiana	$103\frac{1}{8}$
Durammen	$121\frac{7}{8}$
London	270
Quebec	$229\frac{1}{8}$

(Boulton and Jay 1945: 9)

A 'load' is 1.41 cubic metres of timber and 'a bundle of laths' is 150 metres run of sawn laths. These help considerably in calculating the quantity of timber being handled.

One surprising discovery was the amount of evidence for timber building in Scotland to be found in *The History of the King's Works* (Brown, Colvin and Taylor 1963) for England. These start about the date of the Norman Conquest and continue beyond the Union of the Parliaments.

The Scots have no early castles such as the Tower of London or the large English-built castles in Wales. There are no descriptions of the early castles occupied by Edward I in 1296 and recovered by William Wallace in 1297. A campaign in 1298 saw the recapture of a number of the Scottish castles by Edward I, and Sir Robert de Clifford was set the task of building a 'peel' or fortified enclosure (Figs 13.8 and 13.9) round the existing Bruce castle at Lochmaben. '8 carpenters, 4 sawyers, 48 workmen were sent there from Carlisle to set out the timber palisade from which the peel derived its name while 26 crossbow men kept guard over their labour' (Brown, Colvin and Taylor 1963: 409–11). The new peel was successfully defended in August 1299 but orders were given about three months later for it to be further strengthened.

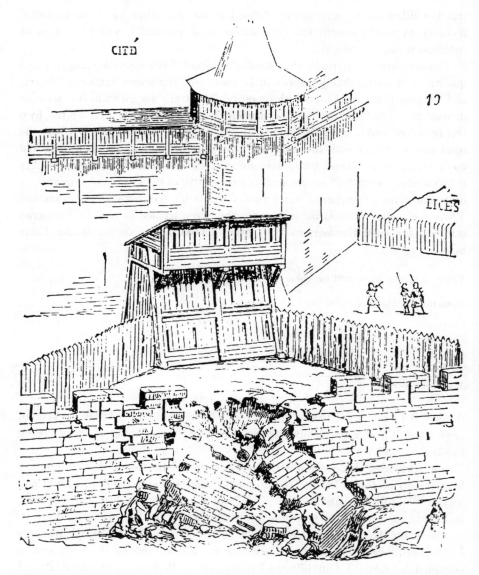

Figure 13.8 Palisade construction similar to that used to construct peels, used here to form an inner defence to a breached masonry wall (Viollet-le-Duc 1854–61: 1, 348).

The Royal Castle of Dumfries was also being strengthened by a peel. The workers comprised 200 ditchers, 80 carpenters and 15 masons with a further 76 ditchers arriving about a month later. In addition to digging new ditches and enlarging those already existing, it was decided to 'make joists for the "alures" on parapet walks round the palisade, and steps up to the brattices . . . a new gate and drawbridge . . . and to construct a strong timber building covered with boards

LEPROSEN-HUIS tot Amsterdam 1608.

Figure 13.9 Leprosen-huis, Amsterdam, 1608, showing palisade construction still in use at the beginning of the seventeenth century (Rademaker 1725: 1, 13).

and flat on top to serve as a gatehouse commanding the bridge . . .' (Brown, Colvin and Taylor 1963: 411). An outer peel was also constructed.

Brattices were constructed at Edinburgh in the winter of 1300 (Brown, Colvin and Taylor 1963: 412). The text continues to refer to a peel and palisades at Hermitage Castle, Roxburghshire, and a wooden tower called a 'belfrey' being constructed in Glasgow for the siege of Bothwell. One of the largest projects was carried out at Linlithgow in 1301:

> The King's chamber was repaired or rebuilt, and a peel was constructed by the labours of 80 ditchers and 100 carpenters . . . The palisade was to be constructed of whole logs (fustӡ) or of 'great logs not split too small' . . . A wooden brattice 'at the gate' is also referred to. (Brown, Colvin and Taylor 1963: 412–14)

Similar work was carried out at Selkirk where a timber tower was built. This peel was captured by the Scots in 1303 and the newly completed defences were destroyed. Orders were then issued in 1304 for its rebuilding and the work took place in 1306–7 (Brown, Colvin and Taylor 1963: 415).

The story continues with similar works at Dunfermline, Kirkintilloch, Stirling and Perth. Colvin notes that after the War of Independence, Robert the Bruce systematically destroyed all the Scottish castles 'lest the English should ever again be able to lord it over the land by holding the castles' (Brown, Colvin and Taylor 1963: 419–20). Whether all the Scottish castles were constructed of timber in 1314 or whether the replacement of timber with masonry in castle building had been progressing in parallel with England since the eleventh century is difficult to establish but it seems unlikely that the Scots built many masonry castles before the fifteenth century.

The dictionaries do not help with the history from the twelfth to the end of the fifteenth century since the next set of timber building terms tends to be taken from *The Accounts of the Masters of Works* (Imrie and Dunbar 1982) and various sets of Burgh Records all starting in the early sixteenth century. This is unfortunate as all the countries with significant fleets of ships, improving agriculture, increasing populations and the beginnings of industrial development faced a shortage of timber from their respective traditional sources around 1500. The situation is not the fault of the dictionaries but a reflection of either the poor record-keeping or poor survival rates of building records for this period. Building records do exist for various monastic settlements but these tend to be written in Latin and, since the monastic settlements were amongst the earliest utilisers of masonry, are less valuable to this particular study. However, on-site evidence of masonry structures in Scotland from this period is much scarcer than one would expect and the follow-up research to the peel or palisade construction cited by Colvin (Brown, Colvin and Taylor 1963) led to various descriptions of crannogs in *Ancient Scottish Lake Dwellings* (Munro 1882), which show that timber buildings were possibly the norm until the great tower-house building period of the fifteenth and sixteenth centuries, and that some timber structures were still in use later than that.

The crannog in Loch Connor or Kinord, Aberdeenshire, is first mentioned in 1335. King James IV visited it in 1506 and it continued to be a place of strength until 1648 when 'the estates of Parliament ordered its fortifications to be destroyed' (Munro 1882: 21).

> Before the level of Loch Connor was reduced in 1858, it appears that it contained four islands – only one of which was found to be artificial. Of the three natural islands, the largest has an area of about an acre (Scotch) and is known as the Castle Island, because the traditional castle of Malcolm Canmore was placed on it. It is supposed, from the occasional fishing up of large oak beams between it and the shore, that it was connected with the mainland by two projecting piers and a draw bridge . . . the artificial island . . . Prison Island, is about the middle of the loch . . . It is something of an oval shape . . . 25 yards long and 21 yards broad. It is evidently artificial and seems to have been formed of oak piles driven into the loch, the space within the piling being filled up with stones, and crossed with horizontal beams or pieces of wood to keep all secure. The piles seem to have been driven or ranged in a rectangular form. They are quite distinct and apart from one another. The upright ones are generally round, though some of them have been splitted. The

horizontal beams are mostly arms from trees from 4 to 6 inches thick, but there is one horizontal beam, squared evidently by an iron tool, about 8 inches on the side. There are not many horizontal beams now to be seen. I remember having seen more . . . a good many years ago. My recollection of them is that they had been splitted. There seems to have been upright piles on all sides of the island, but least distinct at the east end and most numerous at the west . . . On the south side, outside the regular row of piles, is a kind of out-fencing of upright and horizontal beams . . . At the west end are two rectangular corners, and there may have been the same at the east, though now overgrown with grass. Outside the piles is what may be called a rough loose causewaying of stones sloping outwards into the water . . .

The description continues with the other islands and the various finds including a dug-out canoe. It is not backed up by excavation, but in other crannogs where excavation did take place the remains of timber buildings were found on the decks (Munro 1882: 21–2n.).

A similar crannog on the Loch of the Leys near Banchory, Kincardineshire, was roughly 200 feet by 100 feet (Fig. 13.10). It was drained in July 1850. Traditionally it was known as Castle of Leys and was the seat of the Burnetts of Leys until the middle of the sixteenth century when they built the present Castle of Crathes. The earliest reference is in a grant by Robert I and there are three seventeenth-century references under the name 'The Isle of the Loch of Banchory' (Munro 1882: 25–7).

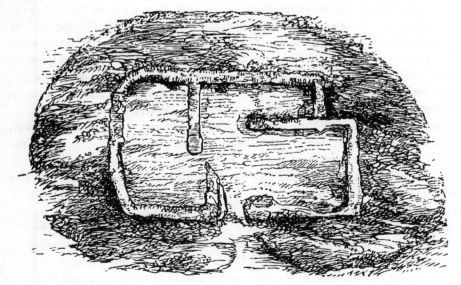

Figure 13.10 Plan of crannog known as Castle of Leys on the Isle of the Loch of Banchory (Munro 1882: 27, Fig. 9).

In some cases the ruins on the artificial island are of masonry. Lochindorb Castle, Moray, is such a crannog. The castle was visited by Edward I of England in 1303 and was possibly strengthened by him. Edward III of England led an army of relief to the castle in 1336. The island on which the castle stands is, at least in part, artificial as 'great rafts or planks of oak' are occasionally to be seen when the loch is low (*Old Statistical Account* 1794: VII, 259).

Mr Chalmers, writing to Mr Knox in 1813 regarding the report on the Dhu-loch crannog, Bute, says: 'It goes directly to illustrate some of the obscurest antiquities of Scotland – I mean the wooden castles – which belong to the Scottish period when stone and lime were not much used in building' (Munro 1882: 18; Mackay-Mackenzie 1934: 117–24). The *Master of Works Accounts* for 28 July 1617 confirm that timber buildings had been erected for the king during the period not covered by either the dictionaries or the surviving records. The entry reads: 'To thrie wrichtis fur downtaking of the twa tymber houses quihilk served his majestie in Glasgow and laying yp the tymber thair to keep . . .' (Imrie and Dunbar 1982: II, 42). This timber was sent to Dumbarton Castle. Other timber was also being shipped to Dumbarton Castle and an entry for 27 August 1617 states: 'Item to the carters for 22 cartfull of tymber and dailles dune to the Brumlaw at 2s 8d ilk cartful . . . lvii s. vii d. Fur fraucht of the said tymber to twa boittis fra Glasgow to Dumbartane xii lib. v s. vii d' (Imrie and Dunbar 1982: II, 42–3). It is not certain what this timber was used for when it reached Dumbarton, perhaps for conversion to roofing timbers, temporary buildings, scaffolding or some other utilitarian purpose, but all the accounts tend to indicate that the walls of the new buildings were of masonry construction.

Returning to the theme of timber buildings, one of the dictionary references to *tym(m)er* led to a series of references to crannogs in the western Highlands. The original quotation referred to stands of trees in Glenmoriston, Invernessshire: '. . . great and long woods of firr trees doeth grow in that countrey and the river doeth transport big Jests and Cutts of timber to the fresh water Loghnes . . .' (Macfarlane in Mitchell 1907: II, 171). 'And there is ane litle parish Church of timber in this countrey called Millergheard . . .' (Mitchell 1907: II, 171). The reporter talks about oak trees on the north side of Locheil (Loch3eld); he then states: 'In this Logh there is little Illands and the Laird and Superiours of the countrey doeth dwell in one of them haveing but timber houses builded thereintill . . .' (Mitchell 1907: II, 159). These are obviously references to crannogs. The report continues:

> Lord Cumming . . . of Loquhaber . . . builded ane Illand or ane house on the southeast head of Loghloghie with four bigg oak Jests that were below in the water. And he builded ane house thereupone and ane devyce at the entrance of the said house That whaire anie did goe into the house ane table did lye by the way, that when anie man did stand upon the end theroff going fordward that end wold doune and the other

goe up and then the man woman or dog would fall below in the water
and perish . . . And when summer is, certaine yeares or dayes, one of
the bigg timber Jests the quantitie of ane ell theroff, will be seen above
the water. (Macfarlane in Mitchell 1907: II, 162)

Another report tells a similar story but refers to a trapdoor rather than a table:

The Cumings were of old lords of this country of Lochabyr. After it
fell out that one of them was mislykead be the people who thereupon
be a devyce of a house built upon the waters and a trap in the floor
thereof destroyed manie of the people, whereof they relate a long storie,
but it succeeded so evill, that he left the countrey and never dwelt anie
more therein . . . (Macfarlane in Mitchell 1907: II, 519)

That a variety of other timber structures existed can not be disputed since
evidence is available from a wide range of sources (Walker and McGregor 2001:
10–17 and Davies, Walker and Pendlebury 2002: 14–30) but what is interesting is
that Scotland and the northern English counties of Cumbria, Northumberland
and Durham have a different tradition and range of linguistic terms from the rest
of England and Wales. As late as the beginning of the eighteenth century Edmund
Burt (1754: I, 104) commented on the complete lack of carpenters and joiners in
Scotland and that he had to employ a wright to make a small timber chest. This is
confirmed when one compares *The History of the King's Works*, referring to the
activities of the English Crown, with the *Accounts of the Masters of Works*
referring to the Scottish Crown. In England timber workers were 'carpenters', in
Scotland they were 'wrichts'. *Tymmermen* are also to be found, the earliest
reference being 1429. *DOST* gives the meanings: (1) 'a person who works with
timber; a woodman or woodcutter, a carpenter or joiner (esp. on a ship)'. That
this is too vague may be suggested by a quotation from 1643 (Banff) defining a
number of specific crafts: 'any . . . wright, aixman or eichman (adze-man) or
timberman for working of any sort of timber work'. Many of the references
quoted are very vague, such as: 'Wat Blak, timmerman' in Dundee in 1521, or
'with tymmermen gar hew the wod away' (1693) and 'timbermen travelling and
carrying their timber from the Highlands to the low country mercats' (Alford
Records: 1663). The impression given is that these are lumberjacks rather than
timber merchants.

Numerous terms were found by following up the references given in the
Scottish dictionaries, but not all of them appear in both *DOST* and *SND*. There
were too many to deal with comprehensively in this article and it was decided to
deal with a representative selection under the general headings of Conversion of
logs into timber, Cuts of timber and building with timber, and Timber finishes.

CONVERSION OF LOGS INTO TIMBER

There are three main methods of converting round logs into building timber: cleaving, hewing and sawing.

Cleaving is the oldest of these techniques and some of the terminology ends up being transferred to the newest technique, that is, sawing. Timber wedges or a *cleaving iron* (*DOST*) are inserted into the *awte* or *aat* (*SND*), the natural plane of cleavage. When the log is split there are two *clift* timbers (*DOST*); when these are split again they are *quarter clift* (*DOST*), and so on. These sorts of timber continue to be known as *clefts* even when the timber is sawn (*DOST*).

Hewing was one method of converting a log into a *balk*. Imported balks were large enough to be further converted into joists or rafters but there is ambiguity since *SND* states: '1. the lower beam (in a roof) is called a "jest" or "joist"; the one above that a "bauk" and sometimes a third is added called a "wee-bauk"'. These terms tie in with the modern usage of *baulk*, which is a hewn or sawn softwood timber not less than 100mm by 125mm (BS 565; no upper size is given). Imported bauks or balks are often referred to as being capable of being sawn to produce six or twelve rafters or joists. More work has to be done on sawyers' accounts to establish a more accurate definition. Scottish carpenters and joiners of the twentieth century tend to use 'baulk' as a large square-section timber. 'Hewing' refers to the use of an axe in preference to a saw and can be used to convert a round 'log' to a square 'baulk'. When these baulks were sawn the number of axe-marked faces in relation to sawn faces indicated the original size of the baulk. A number of roofs along the main street of South Queensferry, West Lothian, show this very clearly. These tend to date from the seventeenth or eighteenth century. 'Sawyers' are referred to from 1350 onwards. The process was originally hand sawing. 'Sawmilns' are referred to in a number of seventeenth-century documents.

CUTS OF TIMBER AND BUILDING WITH TIMBER

The production of building timber inevitably produces a considerable quantity of *wode*, in the form of branches less than 150mm in diameter, *backs*, the curved sections removed when squaring a log, and *cabers* (also *kabers*), 'a pole or spar, a long slender tree trunk' (*DOST*). The terms *back-tree* and *bauk-tree* are defined in *SND* as 'the joists in a cot house' and may refer to the common practice of using backs on edge as joists in poorer class houses. A *bauk-tree* is defined as 'a tie-beam stretching from wall to wall' or 'a joist' (*SND*). This may be a timber rather than wood. *Quhitce-werk* is given as 'wicker or basket work' in 1664 (*DOST*; in the etymology with reference to English usage). This is more commonly referred to in *DOST* as *wattelling*, 'The action of Wattill; b. Poles, small timber for use in building', equivalent to *wattillis*, 'A structure built of wattles, wattlework'. The material was used both as a walling material and for the floors of lofts in the sixteenth and seventeenth centuries. Some of the entries are for high status buildings such as the tolbooth of Edinburgh, where an entry in an account for 1561–2 reads: 'for deichting of the filth of the wattelling of the awld Tolbuith . . . ij s'. A more common expression is 'rice, rise' in combination with a word for 'stake', for example 'stake and rice', 'stab and rys'. The earliest recorded use in *DOST* is 'That na man mak ʒardis nor heggis of dry staikis na rys or stylas . . . but allanerly of lyff and wode' (1657).

The various cuts of timber have distinctive names as one would expect in a country with a strong timber building tradition. Again there is a distinction between the self-build cottars' and farmers' houses and those of the upper classes who used tradesmen to carry out the work. Such a distinction may well blur or disappear between clan chiefs and their followers but this requires a more detailed study.

The self-build houses comprise a series of 'cuppills' made up of two 'siles' linked by a 'jest', 'bauk' and 'wee-bauk' (Fig. 13.11). The sets of 'cuppills' span the width of the house and are joined lengthwise with a 'ruf-tre' or 'first' and 'pans'. These in turn support 'cabers' forming the 'pitch' of the roof.

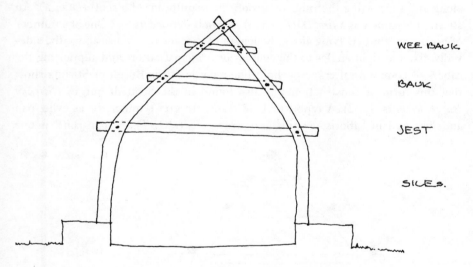

Figure 13.11 Elevation of a typical 'cuppil' made up from 'siles', 'jest', 'bauk' and 'wee bauk'.

The term *cuppill* is defined in *DOST* as 'a pair of sloping rafters or one of these; (2) Used as a standard length (twelve feet) in a building; (3) Attrib with bigging, feit, room, treis'. A more accurate definition for a single side of a 'cuppill' would be 'cuppill-blade' or 'sile'. *Sile* appears to be more common in south-western Scotland and is defined in *SND* as 'A roof rafter or couple, usually one of a pair'. Jamieson contradicts the idea of the 'siles' being linked with 'jest and bauk' and states: 'Two transverse beams go from one sile-blade to the other to prevent the sides from being pressed down (out) by the superincumbent load, which would soon make the walls 'skail', that is, jut outwards. The operation of joining the beams together, which is a work of considerable nicety, is called 'knittin' the siles' (Jamieson [1825] in *SND* s.v. Sile. n.3). *SND* also gives the terms *cyle-blade* and *syle-cap* for the main tie and upper collar respectively. This takes the place of the 'jest' and 'bauk' mentioned previously.

The term *jest(e* is defined as 'a joist, a large timber beam' in *DOST*. An alternative spelling, *ge(i)st*, has the definition 'one of the beams supporting a bridge', again in the etymology and with a meaning that occurs in Old French. These forms are all spellings of the same word and no difference of meaning is implied by a different meaning in the etymology. The system is confusing to the user of *DOST* not familiar with this way of splitting up entries. More work is needed to establish a more exact definition for the period as well as the approximate time of the change of meaning to current usage. Its relationship to 'bauk' and 'wee-bauk' has already been discussed.

The structure running the length of the building is made up of 'ruf-tre' and 'pans' (Figs 13.12 and 13.13). The *ruf-tre* is defined as 'A horizontal pole running along and supporting the ridge of a roof; the main beam of a roof' (*DOST*). An alternative name was a *first* (*DOST* n.3). A *pan* is defined as 'n.2 One of a number of horizontal timbers lying along the length of the side of a house above the side-walls, fixed at right angles to the couples or principal rafters and supporting the cabers or common rafters, a purlin'. The records of the Burgh of Stirling show that this form of construction was also found in the Scottish burghs (*Stirling Burgh Records*: 1. 52). A report of 1548 reads: 'In gret tymmer, sic as cylle, pan and first and in kaboris, wattills and stray . . .' (*DOST*). A 'pan-ruiff' is one

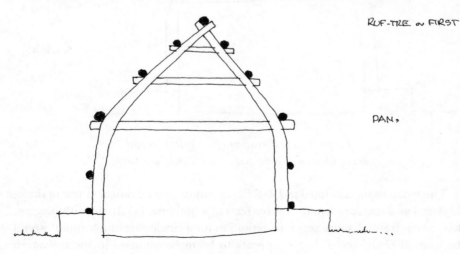

Figure 13.12 Cross-section through 'cuppil' structure showing the position of lateral timbers.

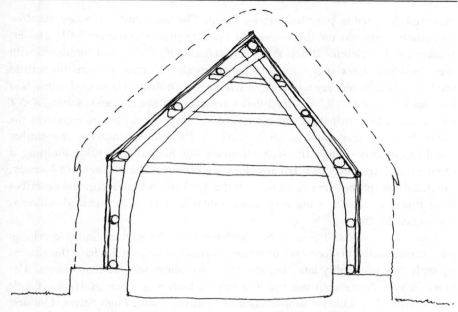

*Figure 13.13 Cross-section through 'cuppil' structure
showing position of cabers or wattlework.*

where the purlins span from gable to gable. It is interesting to note that the author
of the last quotation understood the difference between timber and wood. He
refers to great timber such as sile, pan and first and other wood such as cabers and
wattles. The 'stray' refers to the straw of the thatch.

This type of house also existed in the Scottish burghs. A report on a house at
Cadmuir, Peebles, in 1653 reads:

> The treasurer to pay . . . twentie-two pundes fur building ane hous at
> Trove boughtes upon Caidmure, of thrittie foot length within the walls
> and fifteine or fourteine foot of breadth, and for levelling the ground,
> theiking thereof, setting on doores and windows: the treasurer to advert
> they make sufficient work: the toune onlie supplying tymber and
> divoitt.

The contractual price for cutting divots was set on the 25 April 1653 thus: '. . .
twelve schillings Scottes without ane drink and viij s with ane drink is sufficient
for the casting of each thousand divoittes . . .' (*Peebles Burgh Records* 1910: 9).

The larger, multi-storey, timber-framed houses are much more difficult to
interpret since the only survivals are now enclosed in masonry. We know from a
number of sources that these buildings comprised a simple timber frame with
little or no cross bracing, often with jettied upper floors, the timber frames of the
walls having a wattle and daub infill, vertically boarded external finish and

plastered, boarded or panelled interior finish. The open timber floors were often decoratively painted on the underside (Walker and McGregor 2001; Davies, Walker and Pendlebury 2002). What is missing is any oral record connected with these buildings since they tended to be superseded by masonry structures from the late sixteenth century onwards. *A Glossary of Building Terms used in England from the Conquest to c. 1550* (Gee 1984) was consulted and checked against *DOST* for parallels, but with little success regarding timberwork. If one considers the urban building traditions of most northern European countries, the timber dwellings usually occupy the street frontage but behind the visible building is often a stone structure. In Germany these are known as the *steinwerk*; in Norway, the translation of the Norwegian name is the 'fire safe', which accurately describes their function, that is a place to move valuables into if the main dwelling is threatened by fire.

These structures still exist in Scotland but now the original timber dwellings have been encased in stonework or rebuilt as stone structures. Perhaps the clearest example is a reasonably late one, and therefore more hall-like than others. The house is now demolished but the 'fire safe' is known as Abertarf House, Castle Street, Inverness. Other examples include Gardyne Land, High Street, Dundee; the Bishop's House, Anstruther Fisheries Museum, Anstruther, Fife; St John's, South Street, St Andrews; John Knox's House, High Street, Edinburgh. Unfortunately we do not know the Scottish name for this class of structure. One in the High Street, Montrose, Angus, is known as the 'counting house', but if the German approach were taken they would simply be called the 'stanewark', something that would be generally accepted by a group of researchers with a long-standing belief in a stone building tradition. Bill Jack, Architect, St Andrews, recognised these early masonry features and assumed that these were the original dwellings and that the foreland and backland were built up at a later date.

There appear to be two generally recognised roof types: those with 'siles' carrying the weight of the roof into or through the walls and the 'sett on rufe' (*DOST set*, ppl. adj. 16(2) 1680) where the roof sits on the walls (Fig. 13.14), but not necessarily on a wallplate, as is normal in England. There is no distinction between the lean-to or monopitched roof and the standard pitched roof, only between 'platforme-rufs', that is, flat roofs, and the rest. Platform roofs are always associated with a lead covering.

A quotation in *DOST* relevant to both the platform roof and the roof timbers reads 'The spares wrocht in garronis and rabbis to the plateforme and ledyn ruyff' (*platform(e* n.1.1a 1531) and is typical of the type of description that causes confusion. Is this describing a roof or is it describing the process of breaking down the spars into ribs and garrons to be used as elements in a roof? The definitions in *DOST* have to be general enough to cover all the quotations and are often based on assumptions from the surviving linguistic evidence. The spars referred to above may be the complete supporting structure made up of two types of timber, that is, the garrons and ribs. This poses the question: is the garron larger than the

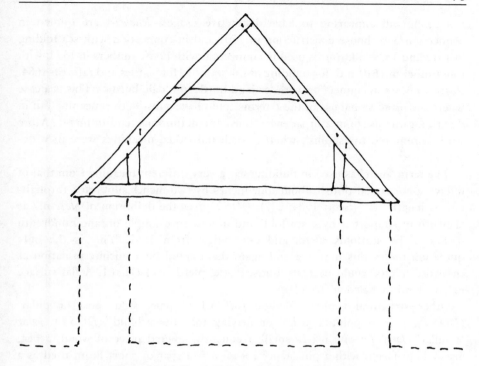

Figure 13.14 Section through typical 'sett-on' roof.

rib or vice versa? Elsewhere in *DOST* the *garron-nail* is described as 'A large nail or spike for use with garrons'. Does this imply that the 'garron' is the larger timber or could a garron be a timber nail? This hypothesis appears to be confirmed by the quotation 'For fyftie single garrons to nail downe dealles quhich were blawing up in the tree brigs 8. 4d' (1638–9 *Peebles Gleanings* 244 at *DOST tre* n.13a.). The quotation is incomplete since there is no mention of sarking, planks or flooring to support the lead sheets. The spars in this case might be worked into garrons and ribs, that is, two elements in a more complex timber structure to support the lead roof-covering.

There is a clear definition for the term *rib*: 'a horizontal timber or cross member forming part of a roof or supporting a floor' (*DOST* and see Fig. 13.13).

The term also refers to a piece of timber used in the framework of a partition wall (*DOST*). It is therefore possible to equate a 'rib' with a modern 'rafter', 'joist' or 'standard', but the role of the 'garroun' is still obscure. In modern usage the term 'spar' can refer to either 'a twenty-four inch piece of split hazel or willow used in thatching' or 'a common rafter'. A cross-spar is also known as a 'bougar' (*DOST*) or 'bougar staike' in the *Melrose Regality Records* (II, 413) of 1675.

A number of variants of the word 'rafter' appear in *DOST* under separate entries. These include *Rachtir*, *Raft* and *Raftre*, all defined as 'a plank, beam of wood', but all appearing to have distinctive usages. *Rachtirs* are quoted in connection with house construction in 1501 and in connection with scaffolding in 1513 and 1529–30. *Raft* is used in connection with house timbers in 1574, with roof timber in 1610 and 'for building of the wall . . . for wattles and rafts' in 1684. *Raftre* appears in connection with 'estland burd' and 'dale burdis'. This is a case where the professional use of these terms could have a distinctive meaning but in describing the usage in a broader lay sense the definitions tend to merge. More work is required to establish whether such individual meanings were in widespread use.

The term 'plate' as used in building has a very different meaning from that of today: 'a horizontal timber about four inches by two inches supported throughout its length . . .' (Scott 1964: 237). *DOST* gives the definition of *plate* n.7 as 'a platform supported by a scaffold' and quotes an example of 'ane hundredth dallies to be scaffolds pletts and ane staige' from 1661. This is the only quotation under this meaning and again there could be a misinterpretation as the word 'pletts' could be *plat* '(dims. Platie, plettie, -y) III n.1. A flat surface of any kind: a balcony' (*SND*).

Other structural timbers include *pall* n.1 'a pole, stout post or pillar' (*DOST*); *pale* 'a pointed stake for driving into the ground' (*DOST*); *pelar* 'a pillar' (*DOST*); *pin* 'n.1. a small, frequently tapered piece of wood, a peg, also v.1. to fasten with a pin or peg'; *nedil* n.5 'a spar or short beam used as a brace or short transverse prop in a scaffolding or to support the walls of a shaft' (*DOST*); and *corbel(l* n.2 'A thick wooden beam suitable for making corbels' (*DOST* and see Fig. 13.15).

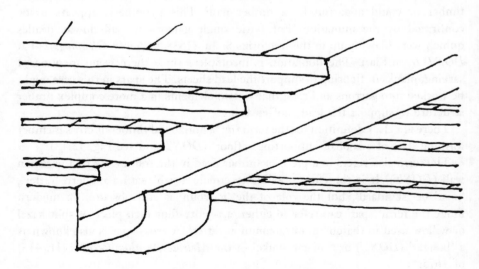

Figure 13.15 Sketch of underside of intermediate floor or loft showing corbel, 'jest' and 'ribbs'.

The verbal noun *sarking* provides another instance: 1. 'The furnishing of (a building or the roof of a building) with sarking as in 2 below. 2. Rough boarding, plain edged or rebated, nailed on top of rafters and to which slates are nailed' (*DOST*). Again there is a prejudice towards the current usage since most of the early surviving examples are pegged rather than nailed. The verb *sark* is defined as 'to cover the rafters of a roof with wood' (*DOST*) but since this is close boarded and the rafters are often otherwise unconnected it assumes the function of a wind brace to prevent the roof from racking, that is, sideways movement. *Tre* and *double-tre* are also purchased for roofing. These may be used as a major element of the structure or may be converted to smaller structural timbers (*DOST*). The house-wrights and other timber workers used a *caboodle*, 'a small wooden shed or cabin where they ate their carried meals' (*SND*).

The range of terms that have failed to appear is for the types of joint used by the wrights. The anglified French terms used in English carpentry do not appear in the Scottish dictionaries, but the evidence that the joints were in use is there in both the archaeology and in fragments of the re-used timber. Goodburn (personal communication) suggested 'taploch' and 'tappget' as possible cognates of terms in northern European Germanic languages but the only entry in *DOST* was *taploch* n. also *tauploch* and *tawploch*, 'A giddy foolish girl'. Since timber joints often have male and female parts this could be a coarse sexual innuendo. *DOST* also gives the term *tapon* n. also *tawpon*, *talpo(u)n*, *tap(p)oon*, *tawpen* as 'a peg'. Pegs are used in many of the joints either to prevent the joint from opening or to pull the joint tight in construction. The information may be found in some form of specification or early treatise on construction rather than the more general source books used by the dictionaries.

Three terms that were known to the author but did not occur in the quoted passages in the dictionaries were: *dwang* n.3 'A transverse piece of wood or strut inserted between joints or posts to strengthen them' (*SND*); *mitch*, n. 'The crutch or rest in which the top of the mast rests when lowered' (*SND*); *stang* n.1 'A pole, a wooden bar or rod in general. 2. A shaft or draught pole of a cart' (*SND*).

TIMBER FINISHES

There is also a large number of terms relating to internal arrangements formed in timber, timber grounds and timber finishes. Internal arrangements in timber include *loft* n.4 '(1) the upstairs part of a building. The upper storey of a two storey building. (2) An attic made by flooring the joists under the roof of a building or suspended on joists over a large room. (3) Any upper room in a building. (4) A joisted boarded ceiling or upper floor', also '(6) A loft or gallery in a church'. *Loft* also occurs as a verb meaning 'to ceil (a building or room) with the boarding which constituted a loft (n.4); to insert one or more upper floors into a building; to floor (an attic or upper room)'. *Lofting* is defined as 'the boarding constituting the ceiling of the room and the flooring of the room above = loft n.4d; 2(a) An upper floor or storey of a building; one of several floors or storeys of a building; 3 vbl.n. Furnishing with a floor or boarded ceiling' (*DOST*). *Parpal(l* 'a partition-wall' and *parpan* n.2 'A thin wall' (*DOST*), also entered under 'partitioun', could be made up of timber or wood as is shown in the following: 'Fyive daillis with xiii broken pieces of fir burdis tane of ane parpall vall' (1593) and 'For twa parpall walls of wattillis solit' (1597) (*DOST*).

A *pannel(l* n.2 is 'A wooden panel; a (? rectangular) piece of wood fitting into a larger wooden framework; 4(a) A pre-fabricated section of wooden walling making up part of the external wall of a house or part of a sea-wall or bulwork' (*DOST*). A *halland* or *hallen* is '(1) A partition door or screen in a room; (2) A covering screen erected above a shop door (*DOST*). A lath is . . . used in a building especially as ground work or sarking for a roof'. Later this is modified to the current usage of the split timber used as a ground for plaster on a partition, outside wall or ceiling. *Fluring* (flooring) is either the laying of a floor or the material of a floor (*DOST*), for example '. . . threttie daille to be fluiring to the hall' (1630). Fluring is not necessarily timber as the following citation shows 'leaving room for the flewering either with deallis or peament ston' (*DOST* 1699).

Internal finishes are reasonably straightforward. The term *bred*, meaning a board, plank or wooden tablet, could also mean a 'window shutter', as in the following entry in the 1517 *Treasurer's Accounts* (V, 119, s.v. *DOST* bred n.1) 'To vj wrychtis . . . reparland the gret hall with windows and breddis'; also 'the wyndowis to be made and braddit' (1448). The normal expression for a board is *burd* (*DOST*). *Brod* is used for a piece of timber or a tablet, often painted and decorated with a coat of arms. *Wanscot* is a good quality imported oak board (*DOST*), apparently used for the panelling of chambers. Modern English usage suggests that this stops at dado or chair-back height (Scott 1964: 351) but Scots usage seems to imply that it covered the whole wall in what modern usage terms panelling.

CONCLUSION

This is a preliminary study and requires a great deal more work. It is important to remember that a dictionary records the common usage of a term, which is not always technologically the same as the usage of a term within a specific subject area. To obtain a clearer definition of any term it is important to use passages written by those professionally involved in the trade or activity and treat with caution those produced by casual, and occasionally official, observers who are recording in layman's terms. This is similar to the way in which literary-based researchers are often cautious about the use of illustrations because of the distortions that can take place under artistic licence. Fortunately, 'artistic licence' is usually easier to identify than 'literary licence', which is often adopted to produce a more acceptable account and avoid the accusation of being 'pedantic'.

One of the major problems in the use of the historical dictionaries is the potential for words to change meaning over a period of time. To take a recent example, the 'breeze block' was produced in the 1930s as a lightweight insulation block made from the 'breeze' or fly ash from steam boilers. These were used as a stop-gap building block during the building materials shortage in the 1940s and 1950s. A combination of the inferior nature of these blocks and the change from coal-fired boilers put them out of production by the end of the 1950s but the name 'breeze block' was adopted by the pseudo-technologists who used it erroneously to describe the vastly superior 'concrete block'. Fifty years on the original material is long since forgotten but the term 'breeze block' persists and is now being accepted in the building industry.

Historical dictionaries are a useful tool in understanding past methods of construction but it is important to recognise that they provide only one small part of the story. Their material must now be studied together with other documentary evidence such as the vast amount of material which has come into the public domain through the setting up of the National Register of Archives. This is still not always readily available through the NRA catalogues since much of the building material is still listed under miscellaneous estate documents. Archaeological reports, drawings, etchings, paintings and photographs, not only from Scotland but from our medieval trading partners, also have to be considered. The data should also be thoroughly cross-referenced with other dictionary entries and the results tested against the information from other disciplines, particularly archaeology. We may then be able to fill the void that exists in our understanding of the development of Scottish building construction. Despite these provisos, the Scottish dictionaries provide the researcher with an immediate entry into almost all aspects of Scottish building construction and a valuable source of references which often extend far beyond those cited in the dictionaries themselves.

It is now seventy years since the publication of the first volume of *DOST* and since that time both *DOST* and *SND* have provided an increasingly valuable source for researchers in a number of disciplines. The completion of *DOST* is being marked by this publication, but should not this publication also herald the commencement of a new revised edition, or perhaps a series of thematic dictionaries, combining and updating the contents of both *DOST* and *SND*? The achievement so far is spectacular but it is also obvious that the work is far from complete.

ACKNOWLEDGEMENTS

The author wishes to thank: Marace Dareau and Dr Maggie Scott, *SLD*; Damien Goodburn, Museum of London; and Dr Tim Holden, Headland Archaeology, for their helpful comments on the text; also Audrey Bruce, University of Dundee, for preparing the typescript.

CHAPTER 14

DOST and LAOS:
a Caledonian Symbiosis?

Keith Williamson, University of Edinburgh

INTRODUCTION

The completion of the *Dictionary of the Older Scottish Tongue* is a significant milestone in the study of Scots. Reaching it after such a long journey is well worth celebration. But the study of Older Scots, as with any language and the cultures which it encodes, is a journey without a foreseeable final destination. There is always much new to learn and new places to go, while previously visited places and legs of the journey demand revisiting with an eye to fresh discoveries or new perspectives.

In this paper I consider the relationship between dictionaries and linguistic atlases, particularly in a historical context.[1] The lexicographical focus will, of course, be *DOST*. However, my perspective is that of a historical dialectologist whose subject of study is also Older Scots. The 'LAOS' of the title is the Linguistic Atlas of Older Scots. It is one of two historical linguistic atlases currently in preparation at the Institute for Historical Dialectology, University of Edinburgh. The other is A Linguistic Atlas of Early Middle English (LAEME).[2] So that my perspective on *DOST* is evident, I will first describe the aims, objectives and methodologies of LAOS, which are also *mutatis mutandis* those of LAEME. These will be compared to the aims, objectives and methodologies of the historical lexicographer. Further, I will suggest ways in which historical lexicographer and dialectologist can inform each other. While Older Scots is the setting for this discussion, reference will be made to other languages.

A LINGUISTIC ATLAS OF OLDER SCOTS

The first volume of *DOST* was published in 1931 and the dictionary was completed in 2002. A proposal for such a dictionary as *DOST* goes back at least to 1919 when Sir William Craigie presented his paper 'New dictionary schemes' to the Philological Society (*DOST* XII: ix; Craigie 1931; Aitken 1987). LAOS has a rather shorter history. It began as a project in its own right in the early 1990s (Williamson 1992–3). Its roots, however, go back to *A Linguistic Atlas of Late Mediaeval English, 1350–1450* (McIntosh, Samuels and Benskin 1986 = *LALME*). This was one of the projects initiated by Angus McIntosh following his appointment to the Forbes Chair of English Language and Linguistics at Edinburgh in 1948. What began in the early 1950s as the Middle English Dialect Project resulted in *LALME*'s publication in 1986. LAOS and LAEME can be viewed as the daughter projects of *LALME*. LAEME covers a period immediately before that of *LALME*, 1150 to 1300 – it is a prequel. LAOS overlaps in period with *LALME*, but takes as its material the written muniments of the Anglic language of late medieval and renaissance Scotland. There is some rather sparse coverage of Scots in *LALME*, but only of the area south of the Forth–Clyde. The material was included essentially as a token comparator for the Northern material in *LALME*.

That Older Scots could – and should – be the subject of a separate linguistic atlas was recognised by Angus McIntosh in a paper where he outlined the possibilities and problems of undertaking such a task (McIntosh 1978). In 1971, A. J. Aitken, in his revisionist paper on the orthography of Middle Scots texts, had already suggested that application of the methodology of the Middle English Dialect Project might profitably be applied to the orthography of Older Scots (Aitken 1971: 186). And in a survey of language study on Older Scots in 1991, he commented:

> For truly complete histories of Older Scots spelling and morphology, we would be well served if we also possessed a copious scattering of 'linguistic profiles' of chronologically, regionally and stylistically identified texts, holographs if possible, like those provided so far mainly for Middle English by the *Linguistic Atlas of Late Middle* [sic] *English* (*LALME*). (Aitken 1991: 30)

The methodology of the Middle English Dialect Project / *LALME* essentially entailed applying the methodology of modern language dialect surveys to texts of the late medieval period. That is, a questionnaire was compiled which contained a series of linguistic items that might be expected to exhibit formal variation. In a modern survey the informants are live speakers whose provenance is readily established. They can be carefully selected as representative of their speech community for the kind of factors that the linguistic surveyor is interested in. The linguistic witnesses of the medieval period are written texts. A medieval text is an accidental survival into our age and its provenance is of variable determination, if determinable at all. Nevertheless, certain types of text can be localised on the evidence of non-linguistic associations. These are the charters and local records – the council and court minutes of towns and other legally constituted entities.[3] The term we use for them is 'local documents'. The value of such texts is that they are dated and (from a dialectological point of view) they may offer *prima facie* evidence of their provenance.[4] A large quantity of such material written in the vernacular survives from the late medieval period in both England and Scotland. Indeed, by far the bulk of surviving Older Scots texts is of this kind. In the sixteenth and seventeenth centuries, localisable material is augmented by private writings, such as correspondence (Meurman–Solin 2001b, 2004b forthcoming). In the making of *LALME* it was possible to create a basic distribution of local documents on the map of England. Their linguistic forms were recorded under a set of items on the questionnaire. The items covered lexis (e.g. 'she', 'much', 'love'), and morphology (e.g. noun plural, third person singular present tense), derivational suffixes (e.g. '-er', '-ship'). The assemblage of forms recorded on the questionnaire for a text made up its *linguistic profile*. The collected forms under each item could then be compared, sets of features identified and plotted on maps. A set of diatopically diagnostic features was established, that is features whose distribution showed coherent geographical patterning. A feature might have a fairly wide distribution, for example 'h-' spellings for 'them' – *ham*, *hem*, *heom*, etc., which covers Southern England and Midlands, south of a line running from Lancashire to The Wash (*LALME* I: 314, Dotmap 40); or it may be more local, for example spellings of SHALL and SHOULD with initial 'x-' – *xal*, *xul*, *xuld*, *xulden*, etc., predominantly Norfolk, (*LALME* I: 342, Dotmap 149). The documents provided a matrix of *anchor* texts. Into this matrix could then be interpolated texts whose provenance was unknown, primarily literary texts. The linguistic assemblages of these texts were also recorded using the same questionnaire. Using a method called the *fit-technique* these texts could be localised by determining the areas where the forms recorded in their assemblages did *not* fit. These areas were then eliminated from further consideration in the fitting. The aim is to narrow down incrementally the area of possible provenance to a small area which can then be studied in more detail at a microdialectological level and a place for localisation can then be selected. The viability of the fit-technique had been tested with materials collected for the Linguistic Survey of Scotland (Scots Section). With this data the experimenter could verify the results of a fit against the known provenance of the informant.

LALME proved that this methodology could provide an important dialectological conspectus of a set of medieval text languages (Fleischman 2000: 34). LAOS and LAEME, while drawing on this basic methodology, have moved it on. Instead of using a questionnaire to collect a limited set of items, complete texts are now being transcribed and stored on computer. The databases for our atlases are computerised text corpora. The texts are transcribed diplomatically, that is we record and distinguish parts of words containing abbreviation and suspension marks in the manuscripts, non-roman letters (yogh 'ȝ', thorn 'þ', eth 'ð', wynn 'ƿ', insular g 'ᵹ'), punctuation and line ends. The aim is to preserve as far as possible the linguistic objects of the text. Only carefully conserved texts can safely be used for full linguistic description and analysis (for detailed arguments for this approach see Fleischman 2000; Laing 2001: 88–9; Lass 2004). Each word and morpheme in the texts is then lexico-grammatically tagged using an interactive computer program. Tags comprise a lexical and/or grammatical element. The lexical element (lexel) glosses the text word and the grammatical element (grammel) records its grammatical function at the point in the text where it occurs. The following samples are extracted from ECOS (Edinburgh Corpus of Older Scots) text # 99 NLS Ch[arter] B 1923 (Oliphant of Gask), 1469 June 18. (For explanations of the format and tagging see Williamson 1992–3.)

Basic Tagged Format of a Portion of Running Text

$til/im + C_TILL
$ride/vi_RIDE
$&/cj_&
$til/im + C_TILL
$gan/vi_GANE
$with/pr_WY^T
$/T_YE
$say/aj_SAIDE
$lord/n_LORDE
$as/av > = _ALSs
$oft/av_OFT
$as/cj < = _AS
$/P13NM_HE
$be/vfut13 < P + _BE + IS $/vfut13 < P + _ + IS
$charge/vpp_CHARG + IT $/vpp_ + IT
$against/pr_AGANIS
$all/aj_ALL
$man/n_MAn
$live/vpsp_LUF + ANDE $/vpsp_ + ANDE
$except/vpsp-pr_EXCEP + ANDE $/vpsp-pr_ + ANDE
$/P21G_OURe
$sovereign/aj_*SOUerANE
{\}
$lord/n_LORDE
$/T_YE
$king/n_KING

From the tagged texts we can create a Text Dictionary.

Part of a Text Dictionary

$june/n jU[]I 1
$keep/vpp KIPYT 1
$king/n KING 1
$lady/n LADY 1
$lady/npl LADEIS 1
$land/npl LANDIS 1
$leal/av LELELY 1
$lift/vpp <= +LUFTYT 1
$live/vpsp LUFANDE 1
$lord/n LORDE 7 LLORDE 1 LORD 1
$lord/nG LORDis 1
$lord/n {tl} LORDE 1
$make/vpp MAID 1
$man/n MAN 1 MAn 1
$manner/n MANer 1
$mighty/aj METHI 1
$money/n MONE 1
$more/aj MARe 1
$mother/n MODYR 1
$next/av NEXT 1
$notary/n NOTAR 1
$oath/n AITH~ 1
$of/pr OF 17

A Text Dictionary is equivalent to a *LALME* linguistic profile, but it provides a full profile of a text's language rather than being limited to a set of preselected items, and it provides precise frequency counts of the number of occurrences of a tagged form. Both the tagged text and the text dictionary provide input for linguistic analysis.

The tags partly serve the same function as a questionnaire item: they are a superordinate category that permits comparison of sets of varied forms within and between texts. However, their functionality is rather greater than the question-naire items. Because complete texts are recorded and tagged, there is the possibility of description and analysis at higher levels of unit than the word and morpheme: collocations, phrases, clauses, sentences. The tags allow the possibility of discovering the linguistic relationships of the texts from 'bottom up', rather than imposing structures on them from 'top down'. To aid with this the tags can be subject to further revision or elaboration with a view to investigating particular research questions (Meurman-Solin 2004a). The corpora for the linguistic atlases therefore have considerable potential as data sources.

The tagged texts for LAOS make up the Edinburgh Corpus of Older Scots

(ECOS). LAOS is being undertaken in phases. Phase 1, in progress, covers the period from 1380 to 1500. On completion of this part, the aim is to move on to the sixteenth and seventeenth centuries. The same transcription and tagging methodology is being used by Anneli Meurman-Solin of the University of Helsinki's Collegium for Advanced Studies for her corpora of Older Scots texts, the Corpus of Scottish Correspondence and the Corpus of Scottish Women's Writing (Meurman-Solin 2001a, 2001b, 2004b). The texts in these Helsinki corpora are mainly from the sixteenth and seventeenth centuries. The Edinburgh and Helsinki corpora are the subject of collaboration between Anneli Meurman-Solin and myself as part of the University of Helsinki English Department's VAR-IENG project.

HISTORICAL DICTIONARIES AND HISTORICAL LINGUISTIC ATLASES

The historical dictionary is a stock tool for the historian and literary scholar as well as the historical linguist. The past stages of English and Scots are particularly well-served: the *Oxford English Dictionary*, the *Middle English Dictionary*, the *Dictionary of Old English* (incomplete), the *Scottish National Dictionary* and, of course, the *Dictionary of the Older Scottish Tongue* are wonderfully rich resources. As well as on the bookshelf, we can have them on the computer desktop, online or on CD-ROM, with all the additional functionality this can offer.

The historical linguistic atlas is a less familiar concept. It requires a different methodology that involves detailed recording and analysis of original sources. Undoubtedly compilation of such a work has been made much more feasible in this age when there is ready access to computers. The importance of computers as a tool for the manipulation and analysis of linguistic data for *LALME* had been recognised by McIntosh and his colleagues at an early stage. The *LALME* questionnaire materials had been completed using paper and pencil on forms, but the data were transferred to computer disk. They were edited and produced mainly using the Edinburgh University Computing Services mainframe computers during the 1970s and early 1980s. Final typesetting was done on the Oxford University Computing Services Lasercomp, transferring precoded files to it from the Edinburgh mainframe. Although LAOS and LAEME began with questionnaires following the *LALME* method, this was soon abandoned and – initial transcriptions apart – the projects are fully computerised. Also, where the fit-technique was carried out with tracing paper and pencil in the days of *LALME*, it can now be done using a computer program. (On how the technique can be applied using *LALME*, see Benskin 1991; on the methodology underlying the computerised version, Williamson 2000, and on applications of it, Laing and Williamson 2004.) The dialectology of Old French (using a rather different methodology from *LALME*) was also tackled with the aid of computers. An atlas based on charter material (Dees, van Reenen and de Vries 1980) served to provide a basic matrix of localised texts and the information from this was used to create an atlas for literary texts (Dees, Dekker, Hubber and van Reenen-Stein 1987). Dees and his colleagues developed a statistical method for localising their texts.

Historical dictionaries and historical linguistic atlases share as their focus texts and the language of the texts. Their perspectives on the texts, however, are rather different and they have different aims and objectives. The material used for *DOST* is described in *DOST* XII, pp. clxiii–clxxiv ('The *DOST* Corpus') and pp. cxcii–ccxxxvii ('Revised Register of Titles'). While there are quite a number of references to manuscript sources in the Register of Titles, most of the sources cited are printed editions of texts. Such editions vary in the extent to which they preserve the linguistic objects of their manuscript texts. The diplomatic edition of a single manuscript text is very much the exception in the present time. In fact, so far as the Edinburgh atlases are concerned, only the original manuscript or a good facsimile of it (where access to the original is not possible) is acceptable as source for the corpus texts. We are crucially interested in the formal variation in the shape of the text words. Also, we are able to apply a consistent set of conventions to representation of the text in our corpora. Printed editions offer too much editorial variance and where texts have been 'homogenised' (e.g. abbreviations expanded and not distinguished, capital letters modernised, editorial punctuation added, perceived 'errors' 'corrected', words from 'better' texts substituted) they distort the language of the text and destroy linguistic information. While lexicographers of a medieval text language are less concerned with the linguistic details of form, since the interest is in the meaning and use of words, they will still want to record the variant spellings of words, as *DOST* does. For the compilers of *DOST* and the *Middle English Dictionary* the kind of text corpora I am championing were simply not available. To do their job they had to use the best material that was accessible, mostly editions. Even if reshaped by an editor a text word is recognisable and its meaning and grammatical form may be discerned perfectly adequately. Indeed, in various entries the reader is warned of problems. In the 'Guide to the Structure of Entries' (*DOST* XII: clxxxiv) a general health-warning is given: 'Readers should bear in mind that the original manuscript sources displayed many individual features, and that many printed editions are not completely diplomatic. Expansion of abbreviations, in particular, often involves the editor's personal preferences'. The problems of editorialised sources aside, *DOST* provides a huge amount of linguistic information – semantic, syntactic and stylistic – about Older Scots.

DOST AND LAOS

In this section I record some of my transactions with, and indeed debt to, *DOST* and its editors.

LAOS as a relative newcomer in the field of Older Scots scholarship inevitably already owes a significant debt to *DOST*. It is a *sine qua non* for anyone working with Older Scots texts. In transcribing texts I have frequently been able to use *DOST* to resolve or confirm manuscript readings of words new to me: has the word I have transcribed been recorded in the same or similar form in *DOST*? If so, what meaning(s) does it have? Are the meanings compatible with the word's semantic-syntactic context in the manuscript text?

Let me give an example of how *DOST* has been helpful in resolving such issues. In one of the set of 'protocol books' of the Edinburgh notary James Young (Edinburgh, National Archives of Scotland, B 22/22/3) an entry concerning the sasine of a tenement (fol. 46v–fol. 47r) contains the following piece of text (fol. 46v):

It is apu*n*ctit & acordit betuex Andro / nicolsone' ye sone' & air*e* to vmquhill Iohne' nicolson vy*er*wais / Callit <u>Iustar</u> on' ye ta p*a*rt & cristiane' his modir ye spous / to vmquhill ye said Iohne' oñ ye toy*er* p*a*rt[5]

The editor of the Scottish Record Society edition of Young's protocol books reads the word I have underlined as < inster > and suggests the meaning 'inkster', but no such word appears in either *DOST* or *MED*. The word is recorded in *OED*, s.v. *inkster*, but not until 1860 in the sense of 'A scribbler, inferior writer' and as a nonce word at that. The manuscript *figurae* of the *litterae* 'u' and 'n' in late medieval Scottish texts are often difficult, if not impossible, to distinguish. Another reading of this word in the manuscript is < iustar >.[6] Consulting *DOST* III, we find *juster*, n. 'One whose function was to keep or make "just" weights, coins, etc. (from *just* v.2)'. A verb s.v. *just* v.2 is also cited with the meaning 'To see that a weight or measure or anything which has to be exact in measurement, is "just" or accurate; to correct or bring to the standard size or weight; to standardise, "true"'. *DOST* supplies a plausible meaning for the manuscript word and thereby offers support for the reading. In the text it can be taken as the transfer of a person's occupation to an alternative name for the person. A close interest in the form of the text word and consultation of *DOST* offer a solution. If < Iuster > is the correct reading of the manuscript form with the sense of *juster* n., then it also offers earlier evidence for the word than is recorded in *DOST*. The earliest citation given for *just*, n. is 1602. The earliest cited form of the verb is 1558. If my interpretation of this text word is correct, James Young's protocol book seems to offer a much earlier instance of 'juster', in a text of 1489.

The protocol books of James Young were used as a source for *DOST*, but the 'Register of Titles' shows that the text used was the Scottish Record Society edition. It is interesting nevertheless that 'inster' does not appear in the dictionary. As the edition does not have 'iuster' the absence of the protocol book as a possible citation is explainable. It is also true that the use of the word in the text, whether read as < Inster > or < Iuster >, does not appear in a context that reveals its meaning.

Another feature of *DOST* that has been of enormous help to LAOS is the 'Register of Titles'. Mostly I have relied on the older list in volume 3 (H–L), but since 2002 we have had the revised final Register. The Register has pointed to potential source texts for LAOS. Even if the source is a printed edition, it is consulted and information about the manuscript sources can be discovered and followed up. Bibliographical details of textual editions are also recorded in the Index of Sources for the atlas, which records information about the manuscript source. An example of the information in a record in the ECOS Index of Sources is:

0469 [*ECOS text reference number*
Hull, University of Hull, Brynmor Jones Library DDEV/80/63
(Maxwell–Herries Papers)
   [*repository location and press mark*
4910215 [*date code, used for sorting*
302 565 [*OS National Grid code*
Tr < f; c–e; Tg [*transcribed from facsimile; corrected and edited; lexico-grammatically tagged*
DMF/maxwellch63.tag. [*name of ECOS file containing the tagged text*
1490/91 Feb 15 [*date of text*
Bond of manrent: (i) Sir alex < *ande* > r stewart and alex < *ande* > r, his son and apparent heir to (ii) Johñ, Lord Maxwell, for 7 years, in return for the marriage of Sir Alexander's daughter agnes to (ii); the king and Pat < *r* > ik, earl of Bothwell excepted. [*description of content*
Ed. Fraser, < *Book of Carlaverock* > II, no. 59, p. 448. Noticed in Wormald 1985: Appendix A 'Maxwell 3'. [*bibliographical information*
Sealed at carlau < er > ok (DMF, Caerlaverock Ca.) Witnesses named: Sir petir stewart, chaplain; Johñ M^{c}dowell; Johñ of crawfurde.
[*associations with places and peoples* DMF, Caerlaverock. [*county and name of place to which text has been localised*

The help has not been entirely one-way, although the predominant flow of the traffic has been to my benefit. Recourse to the manuscript source may be the only way to resolve a lexicographical problem. In the latter stages of *DOST*'s production I was working with the microfilms of the *Ayr Burgh Court Book* and *Wigtown Burgh Court Book*. Although the editors had transcriptions of these texts, they would occasionally ask me to check readings in the dictionary slips or transcripts that puzzled them or about which they were doubtful. I hope that my pronouncements on troublesome forms aided the cause: e.g. in the *Ayr Burgh Court Book*: < wrandand >, a form of 'warrant'; transcript < vanes in ysagis of courtes >, actually < vitnes In vysag*e* of courte >; < wys > (possibly, but not determinably, a 'spiral staircase'); in the *Wigtown Burgh Court Book*: < der >, actually 'dearer' = more expensive; < waid land >, 'land that has been put in pledge'; < ved sawis > ?'with sayings, gainsayings'; transcr. < in volunte >, actually Latin < in vo*luntate* > 'in the will'; < ʒowñ > 'oven'.

It has occasionally happened that, in tagging the texts for LAOS, I have found myself coming to a different interpretation of the sense of a word than *DOST* proposes. *DOST* s.v. *dede, deid*, n.2 'death' has as one of its illustrative quotations 1(c): Nother . . . harme, skaith, deide, . . . nor disherysing; 1482 *Reg. Morton* II. 246. Reg. Mort. II is *'Registrum Honoris de Morton*. Thomson, T., Macdonald, A. and Innes, C. (ed.); B[annatyne]C[lub], 2 vols., Edinburgh, 1853' (*DOST* XII, 'Revised Register of Titles': ccxxviii). The manuscript source is National Library of Scotland, MS 73, item 4, 10 May 1482. However, the issue here is not one of a manuscript reading, but of interpretation of the word underlined, < deide >. The text is a bond of manrent by (i) James gyfferde of the *schere*fhall to (ii) James, earl of Morton, lord of Dalkeith, for life, because (ii) had given to (i) 'in my grete necessite & myster*e*' a sum of money. Here is more of the passage in which the word occurs, taken from the ECOS text:

> I sall gefe to hyme' ye best consele I cane' gef he ony ask*is* at/me &
> conseill ye consell he schawis to me & yat I sall noy*er* wite here nor see
> harme' skaitht deide disworschip nor*e* disherys'ing'/tyll hyme' bot I sall
> mak hyme' tymouß warnyng' yarof & late It & defend It at my power*e*

The underlined passage may be translated: 'I shall neither know, hear nor see harm, scathe, deide, lack of respect nor deprivation of property [done] to him but I shall give him timeous warning thereof and prevent it and protect it at my power'. When tagging this I was unsure about how to gloss < deide > in this passage. On consulting *DOST* I found the quotation from this text noted above. But the sense of 'death' did not seem to me to fit in with the overall tenor of the passage, with the things that are to be warned of by James gyfferde – things that others might do to James, earl of Morton. It can hardly be the case that the earl is killed, although < deide > here might mean forewarning him of intentions to kill him, but *death* is not the exclusive preserve of human agency anyway. However, s.v. *dede, deid*. n.1 is given the sense (d) 'A wrong or criminal act; an act of violence'. I suggest that the sense of 'wrong-doing' or 'violent deed' could as well, if not better, fit the overall tenor and import of the passage than 'death'. In other bonds of manrent and maintenance I have not (so far) come across the specific mention of *death* as one the events from which the obligant is to protect his lord. (See Wormald 1985: ch. 6 for a detailed discussion of the content of bonds of manrent and maintenance.) I have preferred to gloss this occurrence of < deide > as 'deed' rather than 'death'.

In compiling and tagging ECOS, I have also come across lexical items that I have been unable to locate in *DOST*, e.g. 'skevyne':

at ye said/Iohñ stewart sal warrand his barge to ye said marc fra al
beyme brewis yᵗ is/beymyt vp ye schippis bothowme vnd*er* skevyne
Seele & notar*e* Signe (ECOS # 1762 Aberdeen Council Register: p346,
13 Feb 1458/59)

'That the said John Stewart shall warrant his barge to the said Marc
from all bruising to the beam which is beamed up the ship's bottom
under *skevyne*'s seal and notary's sign.'

This word is recorded in *OED* s.v. *skevin* 'A steward of a guild' and *MED* s.v.
skevein 'A guild officer next in rank below an alderman, a steward'.

The following extract is from ECOS # 836 (NAS, GD 172/144) 1449,
concerning the bounds and freedoms of the burgh of Culross:

deponand c*er*tane taky*n*is of pr*o*fe as taky*n*/of barkyt leddyr makand
prepediciouñ in tapping' of wy*n* & oy*er* marchandye3

'deponing certain tokens of proof [such] as token⁷ of barked leather,
making prepediciouñ in tapping [i.e. drawing off and selling small
quantites of] wine and other merchandise'

A possible source for < prepediciouñ > is medieval Latin *prepeditīo*, cf. Classical
Latin *praepedīo* 'to shackle, hobble; hinder, obstruct, impede', n. *praepetītio*,
-iōnis. The phrase < makand prepediciouñ > could be interpreted as '[the power
of] preventing or obstructing'.

The last example is from the Dunfermline Council Minutes (ECOS # 1849
NAS, B 20/10/1, 1494/95 Feb 25, p. 58):

Ye quhilk day Ioh*n* wemyß & wil3*em* Iakson c*om*perit in iug*is*me*n*t &
put yai*m* till añ knawleg*e* of añ worthi assyß for strublance/ilkane of
yai*m* of vthir*e* ye assiß suorne in iug*is*me*n*t herand ye weyemant of baith
ye p*ar*tis

'[On] which day John Wemyss and William Jackson appeared in
judgement and submitted themselves to a worthy assize for assault, each
one of the other; the assize sworn, hearing in judgement the weyemant
of both the parties . . .'

DOST appears not to record (in the published dictionary) < weyemant > . It does
have *waymentyng* vbl n. 'lamentation, wailing' (*DOST* XII). In the above extract,
the sense seems to be '[legal] (com)plaint'.

CHRONOLOGY AND PROVENANCE IN *DOST*

SND frequently provides indications of the provenance of words and phrases. Since it deals with Modern Scots (post-1700), there is much more information available, especially for the late nineteenth and the twentieth centuries. The *SND*-derived component in *The Concise Scots Dictionary* (*CSD*) also carries such information. Change of meaning and form in orthography and pronunciation through time is also recorded in these dictionaries. *CSD*, drawing on both *SND* and *DOST*, is able to offer a broad conspectus of change in many words from the early part of the Older Scots period to the present. While *DOST* is able to present material in its entries chronologically, indications of provenance of words and their variant forms are not usually explicitly given, simply because they were not easily determinable. That said, in the 'Guide to the Structure of *DOST* Entries' it is stated that 'Quotations have been selected to illustrate the use of a word with regard to its semantic, syntactic and geographical context' (*DOST* XII: clxxxiv).

Provenance

The sources of the illustrative quotations can sometimes give an impressionistic indication of the provenance of words or forms and occasionally these are explicitly noted. Below are some examples of words which are noticed as having varying degrees of local provenance. For more see *DOST* XII ('History of Scots': cxxviii) and Aitken 1971.

In *DOST* III, 'Additions and Corrections', p. 970, *helter* (n.2) is recorded as a special legal use in Ayr and Prestwick in the fifteenth century of *helter* n.1 'halter' with the meaning 'possession of an animal or article by one person which is formally challenged by another'. *DOST* III s.v. *lukismes, -mas, louksmes, luxmes*, n. 'The festival of St. Luke, 18th Oct.' has a note: 'Chiefly or only used in south-western and southern Scotland, where it was a customary date for the payment of debts and other dues . . . In Rutherglen, the date of one of the annual fairs . . .'. *Milve*, n. 'mill' is given as 'Sc. var. of MILN, chiefly south-western, also once in Inverness' (*DOST* IV). *Onstead, -steid*, n. 'Only in south Scotl. In the mod. dial. chiefly south Sc. and north. Eng. = A steading, farmstead, piece of ground with dwelling and outhouses built upon it'.

Less rarely the provenance of a phonological variant is noted. *DOST* II 'Additions and Corrections' records *fair* for 'where' 'with north-eastern *f* for *quh*' (1580), with a cross-reference to *folp* 'var. of QUHELP n. (whelp)' (1604), and in *DOST* VI, s.v. *quhare, quhair*, C1(*d*) 'for', in a quotation from the Aberdeen Burgh Records (1539). In *DOST* VII, (*refe*), *reif* n.2 is 'Var. of RUF(E n.1' 'roof' (1510, 1542, 1639), suggesting the unrounding of Middle Scots /y:/. The modern Scots reflex in the North-east is /i/ and this would be a plausible interpretation for the 1542 'rief' (Aberdeen) and 1639 (Cawdor) attestations. However, the 1510 attestation from the *Rentale Dunkeldense* is less certain and would require further investigation: does the text in the *Rentale* have local associations with Dunkeld? Is it a copy of a text from the North-east, or from elsewhere? If it is not north-eastern in origin can the spelling of the vowel in < reif > be interpreted as /e:/?[8] Or did MSc /y:/ → /i:/ (> ModSc /i/) have a wider provenance in the sixteenth century?

Spelling variants in *DOST* may permit inference about the phonology of a word and its provenance. An interesting example of a comment on the distribution of a phonological form occurs under *mak, make,* v.1.

> The pres. t. form with the lengthened vowel appears as *make, maik, mea(c)k*. The greater prevalence of the type with the unlengthened vowel is, however, indicated by the more frequent occurrence of the spellings *mak, mack, makk* . . .
> The spellings *maik, mea(c)k,* appear to be common only in texts localised to Fife and the south, ? especially the south-east, which agrees with the modern regional distribution of the form with the original lengthened vowel.

(For further comment on this example, see below.)

The variant spellings themselves in the context of the illustrative quotations may provide hints about their provenance, and may, as in the case of *mak(e,* be connected to modern distributions, although this is not explicitly noted. For example, < tre > and < tra > are given as variants for 'three' (*DOST* X, s.v. *thre, thrie,* etc.). < tre > is cited in two quotations from the Wigtown Burgh Court Book (A. *adj.* 1.b.) 'Ane schip of salt . . . contenand tre hundyr bollis' (1512) and 'The vrangus haldyne fra hym of tre schore of laid of pettis' (1525). The *Linguistic Atlas of Scotland* volume 3 records /tr-/ as the initial consonant cluster in *throat, thread, three, through* in 27.3 Kirkcowan, 27.6 Port Logan, 27.7 Monreith, 27.8 Whithorn. Also, in 27.4 Stoneykirk, although these words have /θr -/, this cluster is also recorded in *tread,* which could be interpreted as a hypercorrect form. This is a very nice connection between Older Scots evidence and modern dialectal forms. However, it seems also to be the case that Older Scots spellings in *thr-* are not exclusive to Wigtownshire. For example, *DOST* records the following forms for 'through' (*DOST* X: < troithe > Inverurie Court Book 1608; < trocht > Inverness Records 1561; < trocht > Wemyss charter (1389); < Trocht > Inverness Records 1571; < trocht > Inverness Sheriff Court 1558; < Trouch > Kirkcudbright Burgh Records 1577–8. One should also note < trh- > spellings, e.g. < trhow > Dumfries Council Minutes 1655.[9]

It must be borne in mind that even where certain dialectal features were present in the Older Scots period, we cannot suppose that their geographical distributions were the same. Dialect features may have occurred in the Older Scots period which no longer exist. Also, features of speech may only be reflected sporadically in the written record, while other regionalisms may in fact be purely orthographic. Such issues are, of course, kept very much in mind in the work on LAOS.[10]

Chronology

DOST made use of a large number of local documents. Their datability makes them especially useful for tracking the uses and changes in sense and forms of words through time. Other kinds of texts may be datable within greater or lesser ranges from other criteria, e.g. handwriting, indications of ownership and internal references to people and events.

Recording of changes in sense, use and developments into different parts of speech was a key objective of *DOST*. For example, *senatour* extends its sense from historical reference ('1. a member of a senate. a. A member of the senate of ancient Rome, b. A member of a senate or similar body in other ancient states') to take on also a specific Scottish legal reference, a 'Senator of the College of Justice, a judge of the Court of Session'. *Oratio(u)ne* has an earlier sense of 'act of praying, prayer'; in the later sixteenth century we find it with the sense of 'a formal or set speech or discourse in more or less elevated or dignified language'.

In dealing with a medieval vernacular language, the accidental survival of its muniments inevitably results in unevenness of coverage. Even allowing for that, one may find curious lacunae in the time-line of a word. An interesting example is *knave, knaifschip* (also s.v. *knaschip*) 1 (b) 'Chiefly, a small quantity of corn or meal in addition to the multure, levied on each lot of corn ground at a mill, as payment for the miller's servants'. The earliest recorded occurrence is in the *Scone Gloss* (c. 1360) in the form < cnaueschipe >, where it glosses the Latin phrase < Jure Seruien*tis* > 'servant's right'. Of the quotations in *DOST* for 'knaveschip' all but one (1476 *Peebles Burgh Records*) are from sixteenth- and seventeenth-century texts; the variant 'knaschip' is illustrated only post-1500. *DOST* notes regarding sense b: 'After *c* 1550, found commonly in grants or leases of lands, as one of the customary emoluments of a mill'. The first sense, (a), under *knaifschip* is 'The office of an under-miller or miller's assistant or the perquisites of this'. The 'under-miller' or 'miller's assistant' is also termed 'milnknave' or just 'knave'. In *DOST* IV, s.v. *miln-, milneknave* an early citation c. 1380 is given from *Liber Dryburgh*, but the other citations are all much later, the earliest being 1582. One citation, though, is from *Regiam Majestatem* (actually Skene's edition) of which, however, there exist fifteenth-century manuscripts with Scots versions of the text. The term *bannok* n., in the sense of 'A quantity of meal sufficient for a bannok, due to the servant of a mill from those using it' (*DOST* I, s.v. *bannok* n.2), shows a similar pattern of dates. In a number of the *DOST* quotations *bannok* is linked with *knaveschip*. Illustrative quotations in *DOST* entries are intended to be representative, not exhaustive, but the patterning for the above terms seems to indicate a curious paucity of evidence before 1500 in vernacular charters and local records where there is reference to mills and multures.

FUTURE PROSPECTS FOR THE LEXICOGRAPHY OF OLDER SCOTS – A HISTORICAL DIALECTOLOGICAL VIEW

I want to suggest in this section how ECOS–LAOS and the Helsinki corpus projects might usefully inform future lexicographical work in Older Scots. What shape that work might take I cannot say – a revision of *DOST*, a 'Concise *DOST*', a full Historical Dictionary of the Scots Language (i.e. a merging of the materials in *DOST* and *SND*). The online *DSL* gives some idea of the value of having ready access to information about Scots of all periods in one package.

A dictionary of Older Scots that was able to give reasonably good indications of the provenance and/or date of some words and their forms would clearly be an advance. Even where texts are dated in *DOST*, the use of printed editions as the immediate source of information may cause problems. For example, under the entry for *mark, merk* n.2 'unit of weight', 'money of account' there is a note: 'In the earlier instances the form *merk* normally represents only an editorial expansion of the abbreviated m*ark* (taken as m*erk*). Ascertained instances of *merk* have not been found before the late 16th c.' In fact, out of 272 texts in ECOS at the time of writing in which a form of 'mark' occurs, there are 300 tokens with < ar > spellings, 246 with < er > (i.e. abbreviated) and 8 instances of < er > spellings. The < merk(–) > forms occur in 4 texts dated respectively 1393 (1 occurrence), 1477 (1), 1497 (4), 1500 (2).[11] The ECOS texts are able to give information about the dates of < er > spellings to provide explicit evidence of earlier occurrence. As the corpus grows and in further phases of the project more occurrences of < er > forms in the late fifteenth century and the sixteenth century may emerge.

The ECOS data can be used to compare the occurrence of words through time. An interesting case is the temporal distribution of 'betwix' and 'between' functioning as prepositions. Table 14.1 shows the mean relative proportions of occurrence of the two lexical items in the ECOS corpus. Figure 14.1 displays the mean relative proportions in a graph.

Table 14.1 Mean relative proportions of occurrence of 'between' and 'betwix' in the ECOS corpus through time.

		1380–1409	1410–1439	1440–1469	1470–1499
Mean relative proportions	between	0.401	0.202	0.164	0.019
	betwVx	0.599	0.798	0.836	0.978
Number of tokens	between	24	12	38	7
	betwVx	29	84	181	353

It is evident that 'between' seems to suffer a dramatic decline in use in the ECOS texts through the period up to 1500. *DOST* cites few instances s.v. *betwene*, prep. in texts datable after 1500. Further investigation of sixteenth- and seventeenth-century texts might reveal more about its later use: is it restricted stylistically or geographically? Does it occur later in anglicising contexts?

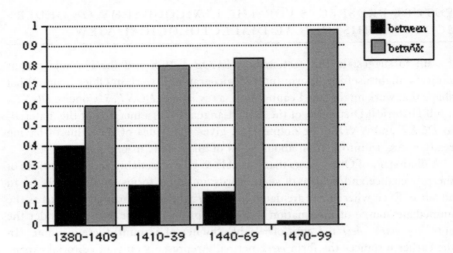

*Figure 14.1 Distribution in the period 1380 to 1500 of 'betwix, betwex' prep. and
'between' prep. The scale on the y-axis indicates the mean relative proportion of
occurrence of each lexical type in each of the four periods.*

Consider the comment on the provenance of forms of *mak(e, maik* cited above.
Now, this is just the kind of question that LAOS is concerned with. Figure 14.2
shows the distribution of long-vowel spellings of 'make' in ECOS texts for the
period 1380 to 1500. The distribution agrees largely with the impressionistic one
offered in *DOST* (see above). It is also interesting to compare this with the
distribution of the modern reflexes of the vowel in the data collected for the
Linguistic Survey of Scotland's phonological questionnaire, published in the
Linguistic Atlas of Scotland, volume 3 (word map 108, p. 340). There the /e/-type
reflex, indicating a long vowel source, is shown in East Lothian, Berwickshire,
Roxburghshire, Dumfriesshire, Kirkcudbright, Wigtownshire and South Ayrshire, with one instance in Clackmannanshire. This kind of reflex occurs also in
Nairn, Easter Ross, East Sutherland and Caithness, and there are also instances in
Orkney and one in Shetland. Elsewhere the /a ~ ɑ/-type reflex is recorded,
implying a short vowel as source. The outliers in the LAOS map also show some
hints of the wider modern distribution. The significance of such maps for future
lexicographical work on Older Scots will be obvious.

In the course of making *LALME* and LAEME, it has been possible to
investigate various problems with literary texts, from the single-word crux, to
matters concerned with textual transmission and scribal origins. For example, see
the collections of papers in Laing 1989 and in Samuels and Smith 1988; also
Laing 1998, 1999; Laing and McIntosh 1995. Laing 2001 is a specific lexicographically focused study which deals with the relationship of manuscript
readings and entries in the *Middle English Dictionary*. The paper draws on work
on LAEME to resolve four cruces in Early Middle English texts.

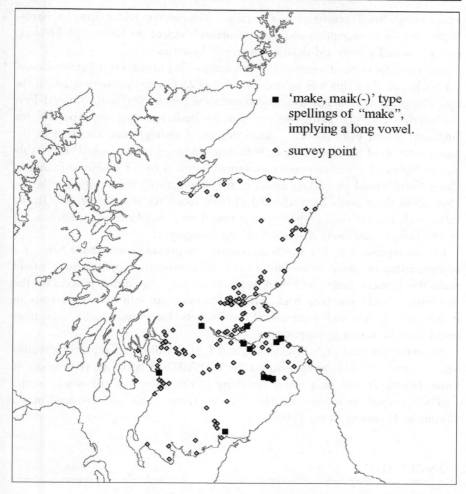

'make, maik(-)' type spellings of "make", implying a long vowel.

◇ survey point

Figure 14.2 Distribution of < make, maik(−) > spellings of 'make' in localised ECOS texts, 1380–1500.

With literary texts there is the issue of manuscript copying to take into account. What is the linguistic character of the copy? Has it been copied *literatim*, in which case the language of its exemplar may belong to an earlier period and/or different provenance from those of the copyist; was the exemplar then the product of more than one hand, possibly with different linguistic habits? Or has the language of the exemplar been 'translated' into the preferred linguistic forms of the copyist? Does the language lie somewhere in between these two practices? Is the text a *Mischsprache*? – that is, is it a *literatim* or partially-*literatim* copy in a single hand from an exemplar written by more than one scribe with different linguistic assemblages (see Benskin and Laing 1981 on the principles of dealing with scribal translations and *Mischsprachen*, and Laing and Williamson 2004 forthcoming for a case study). Such investigation of literary texts written in Older Scots has hardly begun and the transcription and tagging methodology of the Edinburgh-Helsinki projects would greatly aid detailed linguistic investigation.

One basic function of a corpus for lexicographical purposes is the generation of concordances. And this was indeed done for *DOST* with the compilation of the Older Scottish Textual Archive, now transferred (since 1984) to the Oxford Text Archive (*DOST* XII: xxii). One problem for basic text corpora, especially for languages which exhibit even a small degree of orthographic variation in the representation of 'the same word', is finding tokens of the key word. Inevitably output has to be edited to remove unwanted items. A rather problematic case in Older Scots would be finding forms of the verb *ge(i)f-*, *ge(i)v,gif-*, etc. 'give'. How could these easily be distinguished from forms for *ge(i)f-*, etc. 'if'? In the Edinburgh and Helsinki corpora we get round such problems by concordancing on the tags, which easily disambiguate the homonyms.

Concordancing with key words in context can provide ready-made 'slips' for editing, either on paper or on-line. Lexico-grammatically tagged corpora would make this process easier. And there is no reason why the editing process for the dictionary should not feed back into the corpora. An editor may develop an insight into the use and grammatical distribution of a word, which information could then be added to corpus tags.

An important part of both LAEME and LAOS will be a Corpus of Etymologies. At present this is being compiled for LAEME by Roger Lass (University of Cape Town). It will be a major rewriting of the history of the words in the LAEME corpus, to account for their various forms. This will also feed into a Corpus of Etymologies for LAOS.

CONCLUSION

I hope that I have demonstrated in this paper through the comparison of *DOST* and LAOS that historical dictionaries and linguistic atlases have a lot of common interests. A leitmotiv in Modern Scots and its literature has been the *Caledonian antisyzygy*, an obsession with wrestling with opposites and contradictions. In the different Older Scots world we – whether lexicographers, historical linguists, historical dialectologists, literary scholars – might rather take as the leitmotiv for our work the idea of *symbiosis*.

NOTES

1. It was Margaret Mackay who suggested the topic of this paper and I would like to thank her and Christian Kay for the opportunity to put on record my indebtedness to *DOST* and its editors in the work I describe here. I am also very grateful to Anneli

Meurman-Solin, Roger Lass, Margaret Laing and Sandy Fenton for their helpful comments and, of course, corrections.

2. A Linguistic Atlas of Early Middle English (LAEME), Margaret Laing, Roger Lass and Keith Williamson; A Linguistic Atlas of Older Scots (LAOS), Keith Williamson and Anneli Meurman-Solin. I gratefully acknowledge that these projects at Edinburgh are currently being supported (2003–2006) by a Research Grant from the UK Arts and Humanities Research Board.

3. In Scotland these would include sheriffdoms, regalities and, for the later period, presbyteries and kirk sessions.

4. There are of course procedures for, and caveats to be observed in, their use in making an atlas: on local documents for *LALME* see Benskin 1977 and *LALME* II: 40–50, esp. 40–7); for their use in LAOS, see Williamson 2001.

5. This piece of text in its untagged format in the ECOS corpus has the following form: jT IS APUnCT + IT & ACORD + IT BETUEX "*ANDRO/NICOLSONE "YE SONE" & AIRe TO VMQUHILL 'jOHNE" = NICOLSON VYerWAIS {\} *CALL + IT 'jUSTAR ON" @YE-TA ParT & 'CRISTIANE" HIS MODIR YE SPOUS {\} TO VMQUHILL YE SAID 'jOHNE" ON~ @YE-TOYer ParT Examples taken from ECOS texts are reformatted to a more familiar shape.

6. The importance of not normalising capitals is supported here. In the SRS edition the word is given as 'inster'. If we were to infer from this that the manuscript form could be read as having three initial minims, we would also have to consider as readings < nister >, < uister > (< m > before < ster > is unlikely except as an error). In fact, < uister > could be interpreted as a form of 'vesitour': *DOST* XII, s.v. *vesitour*, 1. 'An inspector or examiner a. of ecclesiastical matters, esp. with regard to organisation and church government, esp. in the post-Reformation period . . .'; 2 (a) 'In the burghs: A superintendent or inspector of the craft guilds . . . b. An inspector of places with regard to states of repair, etc. c. An inspector or supervisor in other contexts'. 'u' as a spelling for word-initial [v] does occur in Older Scots texts, much less commonly than 'v' or 'w', but it is possible. At present ECOS contains transcriptions of James Young's protocol books from January 1485/86 until September 1495 and there is only one occurrence of < u > for word-initial /v/, < uertu > for 'virtue' in NAS B 22/22/6 (fol. 30r), in an entry dated 1494 June 4. And there is no instance of the word 'vesitour'. As well as an untypical spelling for Young we would also have to hypothesise a form with loss of the second syllable. A reading as < uister > seems much less plausible.

7. I read this as 'token' (cp. < takynis >), although a case could be made for *taking* vbl n in the sense of 'confiscation of goods as a penalty' (*DOST* X s.v. *taking* vbl n. 5; s.v. *tak* v. 1, 10) or 'the exaction of (prices, interest, etc.)' (*DOST* X s.v. *taking* vbl n. 6; s.v. *tak* v. 11). But note < makand > pres. part. in the next phrase which parallels < takyn > in the construction following < as >; later in this text we find as the pres. part. < takand >. But variation in orthographic representation of verb morphology in the same text is not unusual.

8. The quotation cited is '[For repair of their] domus et reif', so it is a use of a vernacular word in a Latin text.

9. Cf. also in ECOS: TRUCH *through* prep (# 481 NAS GD3/1/3645, unlocalised) 1389; TRYS *thrice* adverb (# 1507 Peebles Court Book) 1456; +TRE *three* (# 1525 Peebles Court Book) 1457; TRHE *three* (# 109 NLS Ch[arter] B 1933 (Oliphant of Gask)) 1484; TRHOW *through* prep (# 578 Ayr Burgh Court Book) 1438. < trh >, if we suppose that it represents for the writer something other than [tr-], could reflect something like [tr̩] or [t ɹ]. Cf. realisations in Modern Scots varieties where historical

initial /θr/ can be realised as [r̠] or [ɹ], with loss of the initial consonant entirely: in the *Linguistic Atlas of Scotland*, vol. 3, note Midlothian: 21.1 Newhaven [ɹ-] *three*, 21.2 Stow [r̠-] *three*; East Lothian: 22.2 Elphinstone [ɹ-] *throat, thread, three, through*, 22.4 Oldhamstocks [r̠-] *three, through*; Berwickshire; 23.2 Cockburn [r̠-] *thread, three, through*, 23.4 Ladykirk [r̠-] *through*, 23.6 Earlston [ɹ-] *thread, through*, 23.7 Mertoun [r̠-] *three*; Roxburghshire: 24.1 Roxburgh [ɹ-] *thread*, 24.3 Eckford [ɹ-] *throat, thread, three, through*, 24.5 Oxnam [ɹ-] *thread, three, through*, 24.6 Hounam [r̠-] *throat, thread, three, through*, 24.7 Edgerston [r̠-] *thread*; 25.1 Dumfriesshire: [r̠-] *throat, thread, three, through*.

10. For an important discussion of spelling variation in Middle Scots, see Aitken 1971: esp. 190–5 and Aitken 2002, where the relationship between the Linguistic Survey of Scotland phonological data and Older Scots sound changes is discussed at various points.

11. ECOS texts: # 166 = National Library of Scotland, MS 72, fol. 19v, 29 May 1393 (SLK 'Edybredschelis', nr. Selkirk); # 196 = National Library of Scotland, CH 17098, 26 July 1477 (EDB, Edinburgh); # 775 = National Archives of Scotland GD 220/2/1/99, 1496/97 January 30 (RNF, 'Lyle'); # 418 = National Archives of Scotland, GD 86/43 Fraser Charters, 1499/1500 March 12 (DMB, Dunbarton).

CHAPTER 15

Envoi

William Gillies, University of Edinburgh

The completion of the *Dictionary of the Older Scottish Tongue* is an occasion for rejoicing for many categories of student. As the essayists in this volume show, it is an indispensable portal through which students of older Scottish literature must pass. It is our key to the usage of Barbour and Blind Harry and Gavin Douglas, Henryson and Dunbar and Lindsay and many more. Equally, it is an invaluable aid to anyone who wishes to work with Scottish records, or Scots Law, or Scottish architecture or medicine or sport – indeed, with any aspect of our cultural history. *DOST* is a treasure trove for students of the Scots language itself, in the historic background to the modern dialects, or in the long-standing relationship between literary Scots and literary English. In this last context, we may also view *DOST* as taking its place beside other great specialist dictionaries of varieties of English language. One thinks especially of *DOST*'s sister publication, the *Middle English Dictionary* recently completed at Ann Arbor, Michigan.

Last, but not least, we may add to the list of those whose lives are enhanced by the completion of *DOST* the wider public of Scotland, who may not consult *DOST* very often, but who can now grow accustomed to the fact that it is at last available in its entirety. And, as we shall explain in a moment, *DOST* is now available in a readily accessible on-line form that may well lead to greater popular exploitation than its mighty volumes traditionally enjoyed. Nor is *DOST* without an important emblematic value: it is a matter of palpable national pride for the Scottish public that this resource has been stabilised at last. Possessing *DOST*, together with the *Scottish National Dictionary* for post-Union usage, brings Scotland finally into line with the majority of European countries which have a vernacular literary history and historical records worth talking about.

To some people the completion of *DOST* is not only a source of joy but also of relief. This must include, in the first place, the Universities of Aberdeen, Dundee, Edinburgh, Glasgow, St Andrews and Stirling, which continued to support this project through times that were not financially propitious for the university sector, when projects involving long-term commitments of the sort engendered by *DOST* had dwindled almost to vanishing point. It may not be out of place to salute the efforts of Dr Martin Lowe, Secretary to the University of Edinburgh in the 1990s, for rallying his fellow Secretaries in the cause of *DOST* during those years of recurrent funding crises. At the same time a debt of gratitude is owed to Professor Sandy Fenton, Chairman of the Friends of *DOST*, who was able to attract continuing subventions from central sources, whose symbolic value in cementing the precarious funding package together was at least as great as their monetary worth as invested in editorial staff to speed the dictionary to completion.

The lexicographers themselves also felt relief, as well as joy, at the completion of *DOST*. As Marace Dareau's paper explains, they had risen to the challenge of producing the latter sections of *DOST* 'better and faster', where the weight of traditional wisdom on the subject would have tended strongly to conjoin 'better' with 'slower' and 'faster' with 'worse'. This was actually a triumph, a privilege to witness and help happen; and we should salute unequivocally the achievement of the heroes and (more numerously) the heroines who came up with the requisite quality of originality (e.g. in breaking with existing norms and wisdom), analytical thinking (e.g. to solve the 'faster and better' problem), judgement (e.g. in matching tasks to the capabilities of available individuals) and professionalism (e.g. in determination to put the needs of *DOST* ahead of personal considerations). The requirement that each editor should edit for six years continuously 'against the clock' was a taxing and potentially stressful assignment. Its successful completion, with a minimum of fuss and flap, is an achievement worthy of our admiration as well as our gratitude.

Of course, the lexicographer's work is never finally completed. Even in *DOST*'s medieval Scots territory new texts turn up from time to time (e.g. notarial documents in family papers or in the offices of traditional country lawyers), and these may offer new words or forms or meanings. Again, the progress of scholarship in Middle Scots literature means that editors of texts are able to propose enhanced readings and interpretations which add to the range of meanings attested for a given word, and hence need to be recorded in *DOST*. Indeed, it has to be remembered that *all* big dictionaries undergo constitutional changes over the years. Although it escaped from the drastic threat it once faced, of having its latter sections demoted to the status of a 'Scottish Supplement to *OED*', *DOST* was indubitably growing more portly when the middle letters of the alphabet were being edited; and it then grew leaner (though not less semantically comprehensive) for the remaining letters. Finally, the experience of editing words from later sections of the alphabet can suggest improvements to definitions or entry structures for words in already published parts of a dictionary. For all these reasons, as *DOST* was being wound up, there were already piles of slips (or their electronic equivalent) mounting up, containing material needed for the revision of the earlier parts of the alphabet. The first fascicles of the revised edition of *Geiriadur Prifysgol Cymru*, the Welsh equivalent of *DOST* and *SND*, have now started to appear, and they show us clearly, if we needed reminding, just how much the experience of 'doing' the whole alphabet enables one easily to improve the product which was the result of one's very best efforts at the outset of a major dictionary.

In other ways too, the completion of *DOST* brings highly desirable additional work into the realm of what is possible. The electronic basis of the later parts, together with great improvements in scanning technology, have already enabled *DOST* to be put on-line. Moreover, having these precious materials on-line makes feasible a vast range of smaller, more specialised projects: studies of the vocabulary of hunting or diseases or childhood or sailing, or of the usage of individual authors or periods or localities or literary genres. Some of the contributions to the present volume provide eloquent 'trailers' to what could be done in this respect. It is to be hoped that a relatively quiet period in the study of Scots as a language will be terminated by the massive boost which such electronic resources as these can provide.

That is why we must welcome and support and encourage the work of the new Scottish Language Dictionaries Ltd (SLD), which has inherited some staff from *SND* and *DOST*, and also goodwill from the Scottish National Dictionary Association (1929–2002) and from the Scottish universities which supported *DOST* from 1931 till 2002. For SLD was founded with the express aim of carrying out precisely the sorts of linguistically and lexicographically based research projects and enterprises I have just mentioned, and of retaining the hard-won and precious nucleus of expertise and training capacity which we now have in Scotland for these sorts of work.

I have already referred to the digitisation and data-capture project which, with funding from the Arts and Humanities Research Board, has put *DOST* on-line. In fact, it has also done the same, and with the same technology and protocols, for the *SND* (or 'Dictionary of the Younger Scottish Tongue', as one might call it in the present context). Hopefully, the grant from the AHRB's Resource Enhancement Scheme which enabled this major first step to take place will be matched by funding to secure an even more desirable prize. For the recently completed piece of work has been seen all along as a move towards the provision of a comprehensive, integrated Dictionary of the Scottish Language.

In other words, we have now moved relatively painlessly to a position where we can contemplate the editorial work needed to meld the two dictionaries into a single, fully compatible, fully searchable on-line resource for Scots. The academic, educational and social benefits of this resource need no further emphasis from me.

It should be recorded here how much we owe to the Scottish Arts Council, and especially to its Literature Department, for its strongly committed and supportive role in the conception, gestation and birth of SLD. It is, of course, entirely appropriate that 'the word' should be recognised as a vital component in the nation's cultural make-up, underpinning the efforts of poets, playwrights and novelists; it has been refreshing to work with Literature staff and committee members who have grasped this truth from the outset. It will be important to ensure that, whatever future reconfiguration may await the SAC, this commitment to the word retains its key position in the thinking of the architects of future cultural provision.

The dreams of those involved in these recent developments go beyond the mere bringing into being of SLD. This is actually seen as a minimum requirement. For as Alasdair MacDonald and Marace Dareau have indicated in this volume, the 'whither now?' discussions which the *DOST* team helped to generate in the late 1990s blew up quite spontaneously into a quite remarkable display of support for a more permanent and central institution which those involved have come to call 'The Institute for the Languages of Scotland'. A series of widely advertised meetings held under the auspices of the Royal Society of Edinburgh revealed a breadth of interest going far beyond academe and including writers and journalists, teachers of literature and drama in school and community contexts, arts administrators, broadcasters, language theorists and activists and community leaders for linguistically defined minorities.

It was quickly pointed out that many other countries have such institutes, though their composition varies quite widely, from academies which guard the purity and correct forms of a nation's language, through to repositories of the linguistic riches of dialects, place names and folklore. The form of institution which people would find most appropriate and acceptable in Scotland has duly been explored in depth with the help of a research grant from the Carnegie Trust; and the results have been placed before the Scottish Executive. The concept is one that is hard to deny, when one considers the linguistic wealth contained in Scotland's past and present, and the existence of such monumental resources as *DOST* and the archive that lies behind it. It is earnestly to be hoped that this opportunity is recognised and grasped before it is too late.

Whatever has been achieved now comes as a result of the vision and determination of William Craigie almost ninety years ago, at a time when the nation as a whole was attempting to move forward from the trauma of the First World War. In terms of getting academic enterprises off the ground, Craigie, as *DOST*'s 'onlie begetter', lived in a very simple world. When he contemplated dedicating the rest of his working career to the creation of *DOST*, he exercised choice of a sort that is meaningless to today's scholars, with their manifold teaching and administrative commitments and productivity hurdles. He could not have foreseen the gradual expansion of *DOST* in its middle years under Aitken and Stevenson, in which it seems to have tended to become a surrogate thesaurus of Scots usage or a cultural encyclopaedia of medieval Scotland; nor yet the more ascetically structural version of historical description implemented by Dareau,

Pike and Watson in *DOST*'s final phase. Whatever he might have thought of these varying interpretations of what is needful for a 'dictionary according to historic principles', he would, I am sure, have been marvellously pleased with the final outcome. After many days, and not a few buffets and vicissitudes, the great barque that is *DOST* has finally, majestically, sailed into port.

The Editors of *DOST*

M. G. Dareau and K. L. Pike

WILLIAM ALEXANDER CRAIGIE

Sir William Alexander Craigie (1867–1957) was born in Dundee, the youngest son of James Craigie, a jobbing gardener, and Christina Gow. As a child he learned some Gaelic from his maternal grandfather. He attended the West End Academy in Dundee, where he gained a knowledge of phonetics from the headmaster, and graduated from St Andrew's University with honours in Classics and Philosophy in 1888. He had also learned French and German and had begun studying Danish and Icelandic. He then went to Balliol College, Oxford, where he gained firsts in Mods and Greats and continued his interest in the Scandinavian languages. From 1893 to 1897 he was assistant to the Professor of Latin at St Andrews. In June 1897 he joined the staff of the *New (Oxford) English Dictionary* and in 1901 was appointed co-editor with James Murray and Henry Bradley. He worked on *OED* until its completion in 1933, producing the letters N, Q, R, U, V, Si–Sq and Wo–Wy and about half of the Supplement. In 1907 Craigie's suggestion that Scottish words, legends and traditions be collected led to the formation of the Scottish Dialects Committee, which in turn led to the compiling of the *Scottish National Dictionary*. In 1905, as well as continuing his work on *OED*, Craigie was appointed Taylorian Lecturer in the Scandinavian languages at Oxford and in 1915 was elected to the newly restored Rawlinson and Bosworth chair of Anglo-Saxon. Apart from *OED*, *DOST*, and the *Dictionary of American English (DAE)*, begun when he was in Chicago, Craigie produced a supplement to Vigfusson's *Icelandic Dictionary* (1957), *Specimens of Icelandic Rímur* (1952), and many other publications. Craigie was Editor responsible for the letters A–G in *DOST*.

ADAM JACK AITKEN

Professor Adam Jack Aitken (1921–98) was born in Bonnyrigg, a mining village to the south of Edinburgh. He attended Lasswade Secondary School, Midlothian,

Sir William A. Craigie and Jessie K. Craigie, 1936.
All photographs used with the kind permission of Scottish Language Dictionaries.

and began his undergraduate career at Edinburgh University in 1939. War service in the Royal Artillery from 1941–5 interrupted his studies and he graduated with first class honours in English Language and Literature in 1947. In 1948 he became Assistant Lecturer in English Language at Edinburgh, and from 1948 to 1964 Research Fellow at the Universities of Glasgow, Aberdeen and Edinburgh. From 1948 to 1979 he combined work on *DOST* with teaching in the University of Edinburgh, and during the 1960s and 1970s developed a wide-ranging series of courses in Scots language and literature. During his editorship of *DOST*, in collaboration with Paul Bratley and Neil Hamilton-Smith, he established the *Older Scottish Textual Archive*, an electronic database of the key Older Scottish texts. In 1983 he was awarded a D.Litt. by Edinburgh University for his work on *DOST* and other publications, and in 1985, in recognition of his outstanding academic achievements, the same university appointed him Honorary Professor. Aitken worked on G under the supervision of Craigie. He was Editor responsible for H–O and part of P and was revising editor of Pa and parts of Pe and Q in collaboration with Stevenson. He also edited part of S.

JAMES ALEXANDER COOPER STEVENSON

Dr James Alexander Cooper Stevenson (1917–92) was born and grew up in Edinburgh, attending George Watson's College and Edinburgh University,

J. A. C. Stevenson (left), A. J. Aitken (centre)
and H. D. Watson (right), early 1980s.

where, as one of the first graduates of the new Honours English Language school, he took a first class honours degree. After war service with the Eighth Army in the Western Desert he lectured in English at the University of Alexandria. In 1949 he completed a Ph.D. at the University of Edinburgh on the influence of Hobbes, Locke and Berkeley on the English and Scottish aestheticians of the eighteenth century. He held teaching appointments at the Lahore Government College in Pakistan and at a number of secondary schools in Scotland including his *alma mater*, George Watson's, concluding his teaching career as Head of English at St Andrew's RC High School in Kirkcaldy. In 1966 he took an editorial post on *DOST* and continued his career in lexicography until his retirement in 1985. He co-edited (with Matthew McDiarmid) an edition of the Edinburgh MS of Barbour's *Brus* for the Scottish Text Society, acted as a consultant to the *Australian National Dictionary* and in 1989 co-produced (with Iseabail Macleod) *Scoor-Oot*, a delightful small dictionary of current Scots. Stevenson worked on M and O under the supervision of Aitken and was Joint-Editor responsible with Aitken for P. He was Editor responsible for R, editing and revising it in collaboration with Dareau, and Sc–, Sch–, and Sk–.

MARGARET GRACE DAREAU

Margaret Grace Dareau (1944–) was born and grew up in Dumfriesshire, attending Annan Academy and Edinburgh University. She graduated with first class honours in English Language and Literature in 1966 and worked briefly with Professor Angus McIntosh on Middle English historical dialectology before gaining a Kennedy Scholarship to the Massachusetts Institute of Technology. In 1969 she took a post as Junior Assistant Editor on *DOST*, continuing her career there until 1973 when her first child was born. She returned in 1976 for three years and again in 1984, remaining until the conclusion of the dictionary in 2001. In the interim period (1979–84) she worked as an editor on the *Concise Scots Dictionary*, and in the early 1990s as Glossary Editor for the *Encyclopedia of Language and Linguistics*. In 2001 she transferred to the staff of the Scottish National Dictionary Association and since 2002 has been Editorial Director of Scottish Language Dictionaries. Dareau worked on N, O, R and S under the supervision of Aitken and was revising editor of R in collaboration with Stevenson. She was Senior Editor (1988) responsible for revising S excluding Sc–, Sch–, and Sk–, then Editorial Director (1997) responsible for S–Z.

HARRY DUFF WATSON

Harry Duff Watson (1946–) grew up in the East Neuk of Fife, attending Waid Academy, Anstruther, and Edinburgh University. He graduated in 1968 with an M.A. Honours in English Language and Literature. He worked briefly in Fife County Library headquarters in Kirkcaldy before enrolling at Moray House College of Education in 1969 to train as a secondary school teacher of English. After Moray House he worked as a language teacher for the Folk University in Sweden. Subsequent teaching posts took him to Germany and to various further education institutions in Scotland and England. In 1979 he joined *DOST* as Junior Assistant Editor, becoming Editor-in-chief in 1985, Director and Senior Editor in 1988, and Administrative Director in 1997. In 1980 he obtained a University of London B.A. in Scandinavian Studies. Literary translation from the Scandinavian languages has been a long-term interest. He has also published regularly in the field of local history. Watson worked on S–U and Y–Z.

KATHRYN LORNA PIKE

Kathryn Lorna Pike (1956–) was born and brought up in Fort William, Inverness-shire. She attended Lochaber High School and Edinburgh University, graduating with upper second class honours in English Language and Linguistics in 1978. She began her career in lexicography as an Editor on the *Concise Scots*

Dictionary from 1979 to 1983. She then joined the staff of *DOST* as an Editorial Assistant, becoming an Editor in 1987 and remaining a full-time member of staff until the end of the project. From 1989 until 2001 she served as Secretary of the Scottish Text Society. Since the completion of *DOST*, she has worked as part-time Research Officer for the Feasibility Study for an Institute for the Languages of Scotland and part-time Senior Editor with the Scottish National Dictionary Association. Until October 2004, she was part-time Project Co-ordinator for Faclair na Gàidhlig and part-time Senior Editor with Scottish Language Dictionaries. She is now full-time with Faclair na Gàidhlig. Pike worked on *DOST* S–Z.

Dareau, Pike and Watson made up the editorial team which brought *DOST* to completion in 2001. The final parts of the dictionary were published by Oxford University Press in 2002.

Margaret Grace Dareau and Kathryn Lorna Pike.

Contributors to this volume

PRISCILLA BAWCUTT

Priscilla Bawcutt is an Honorary Professor in the School of English, University of Liverpool. She has written many articles on the language and literature of medieval and early modern Scotland, and critical books on Gavin Douglas and William Dunbar. Her most recent publication is a two-volume edition of the works of William Dunbar for the Association of Scottish Literary Studies.

M. G. DAREAU

Margaret Grace (Marace) Dareau is Editorial Director of Scottish Language Dictionaries. She was Senior Editor, then Editorial Director of the *Dictionary of the Older Scottish Tongue* (*DOST*) from 1987 to 2001. She was an editor of the *Concise Scots Dictionary* and is the author of the Glossary of the *Encyclopedia of Language and Linguistics*.

JANE E. A. DAWSON

Dr Jane Dawson is the John Laing Senior Lecturer in the History and Theology of the Reformation in the School of Divinity, University of Edinburgh. She has edited the *Campbell Letters, 1559–1583* for the Scottish History Society and has recently published a monograph on *The Politics of Religion in the age of Mary, Queen of Scots: the fifth earl of Argyll and the struggle for Britain and Ireland*, and is currently completing the 1488–1587 volume in the *New Edinburgh History of Scotland*.

ALEXANDER FENTON

Professor Emeritus Alexander (Sandy) Fenton is Director of the European Ethnological Research Centre, Edinburgh, and was Secretary to the Friends of the Dictionary of the Older Scottish Tongue. He is the author of *Scottish Country Life, The Northern Isles: Orkney and Shetland, The Shape of the Past, The Rural Architecture of Scotland* (with B. Walker) and other books, as well as numerous articles, many of which deal with the relationships between words and things. His book of short stories, *Craiters*, is a representation of the dialect of Auchterless, Aberdeenshire, as spoken in the mid-twentieth century.

A. D. M. FORTE

Angelo Forte is Professor of Commercial Law at the University of Aberdeen. He has written widely on contemporary commercial law and on commercial legal history. He is a member of the European Project Group for the Restatement of Insurance Law and a past-president of the Scottish Legal History Group and the Scottish Society for Northern Studies.

WILLIAM GILLIES

William Gillies is Professor of Celtic at the University of Edinburgh. He has published widely on linguistic and literary topics in the field of Gaelic and Celtic Studies. He is General Editor of *Survey of the Gaelic Dialects of Scotland* and was Manager of the *DOST* project from 1994 till its completion in 2001.

CHRISTIAN J. KAY

Christian Kay is Professor of English Language at the University of Glasgow and Convener of Scottish Language Dictionaries Ltd, which has taken on responsibility for the future development of *DOST* and *SND*. She is joint author of *A Thesaurus of Old English* and a director of the Historical Thesaurus of English and SCOTS corpus projects at Glasgow.

ALASDAIR A. MACDONALD

Alasdair MacDonald is Professor of English Language and Literature of the Middle Ages, University of Groningen. He is the author of articles on Older Scots literature and has co-edited several books, including *The Renaissance in*

Scotland: Studies in Literature, Religion, History and Culture offered to John Durkan (1994); *A Palace in the Wild: Essays on Vernacular Culture and Humanism in Late-Medieval and Renaissance Scotland* (2000); *Rhetoric, Royalty, and Reality: Essays on the Literary Culture of Medieval and Early Modern Scotland* (forthcoming, 2005).

MARGARET A. MACKAY

Dr Margaret A. Mackay is Director of the School of Scottish Studies Archives and Senior Lecturer in Scottish Ethnology at the University of Edinburgh. She is a graduate of the University of Toronto and the University of Edinburgh, where she carried out research under the supervision of Professor A. J. Aitken, Editor of *DOST*.

ISEABAIL MACLEOD

Iseabail Macleod is Editorial Consultant to Scottish Language Dictionaries Ltd. She has been joint editor of several of their dictionaries and has a special interest in the language of food and drink. She was joint editor with Caroline Macafee of *The Nuttis Schell: Essays on the Scots Language* (1988). In 1986 she edited *Mrs McLintock's Receipts for Cookery and Pastry-Work*, Scotland's earliest published cookery book; other publications include *The Pocket Guide to Scottish Words* (1986) and the *Edinburgh Pocket Guide* (1996).

DONALD E. MEEK

Donald Meek is Professor of Scottish and Gaelic Studies at the University of Edinburgh, and was formerly Professor of Celtic at the University of Aberdeen (1993–2001). His academic interests extend from the Middle Ages (the Book of the Dean of Lismore) to the present day, covering Ossianic ballads, early and modern Gaelic prose, nineteenth-century politics and poetry, religious life in the Highlands and Islands since 1700, and the history of Celtic Studies. His published work includes editions of medieval Gaelic poetry and nineteenth-century Gaelic verse. He is Convener of the Strategy Committee of Faclair na Gàidhlig.

W. F. H. NICOLAISEN

W. F. H. (Bill) Nicolaisen earned his doctorate in Comparative Linguistics at the University of Tübingen and the degree of M.Litt. in Celtic Studies at Glasgow. He was Head of the Scottish Place-Name Survey in the School of Scottish Studies of the University of Edinburgh from 1956 to 1969 before joining the Department of English at the State University of New York at Binghamton, from which he retired as Distinguished Professor of English and Folklore in 1992. He is currently an Honorary Professor of English at the University of Aberdeen. He has published widely in name studies and folk-narrative research.

PAUL SCHAFFNER

Paul Schaffner did his postgraduate work at Cambridge and Cornell, spent eight years as a lexicographer for the *Middle English Dictionary*, and managed the production of the electronic version of the *MED* and associated resources on behalf of the University of Michigan Library. As the librarian in charge of the Library's electronic text unit, he currently directs the publication of some 3,500 early English and Scottish books every year in electronic form.

W. D. H. SELLAR

David Sellar is an Honorary Fellow of the Faculty of Law of the University of Edinburgh, where he has taught for a number of years. He has published widely on law, legal history and family history. He is currently Bute Pursuivant of Arms.

A. D. C. SIMPSON

Dr Allen Simpson is a postdoctoral Fellow in Scottish History in the School of History and Classics at Edinburgh University, and a Research Fellow in the History of Science Research Unit at the National Museums of Scotland (NMS). He was previously Senior Principal Curator in the History of Science Section at NMS, where his main curatorial and research interests were in the teaching and patronage of science and in precision devices. He is a member of the Scientific Instrument Commission of the International Union for the History and Philosophy of Science and is co-author of *Weights and Measures in Scotland: a European Perspective*.

BRUCE WALKER

Dr Bruce Walker was formerly on the staff of the University of Dundee and Historic Scotland. He is the author of *Farm Buildings in the Grampian Region: The Rural Architecture of Scotland* (with A. Fenton); *Exploring Scotland's Heritage: Perthshire, Fife and Angus* (with G. Ritchie); *Thatch and Thatching in Scotland*,

The Hebridean Blackhouse, and *Earth Structures and Construction in Scotland* (with C. McGregor and G. Stark).

KEITH WILLIAMSON

Dr Keith Williamson is an AHRB-funded Research Fellow in the Institute for Historical Dialectology, University of Edinburgh. He is compiling the first phase of A Linguistic Atlas of Older Scots and has published articles on spatio-temporal variation in Older Scots and on theory and methodology for historical dialectology.

Bibliography

Dictionaries are listed by title and editions by editor. See also 'References and Sources' in Chapter 8.

ACRS, see Henryson, Edward.

Aitken, A. J. (1971), 'Variation and variety in written Middle Scots', in A. J. Aitken, Angus McIntosh and Hermann Pálsson (eds), *Edinburgh Studies in English and Scots*, London: Longman, pp. 177–209.

Aitken, A. J. (1977), 'Textual problems and the dictionary of the older Scottish tongue', in P. G. J. van Sterkenburg (ed.), *Lexicologie, een Bundel Opstellen voor F. de Tollenaere*, Groningen: Walters-Noordhof, pp. 13–15.

Aitken, A. J. (1981), '*DOST*: how we make it and what's in it', in Roderick J. Lyall and Felicity Riddy (eds), *Proceedings of the Third International Conference on Scottish Language and Literature (Medieval and Renaissance)*, Stirling and Glasgow: University of Glasgow, pp. 33–51.

Aitken, A. J. (1983), 'The language of Older Scots poetry', in J. Derrick McClure (ed.), *Scotland and the Lowland Tongue: Studies in the Language and Literature of Lowland Scotland, in Honour of David D. Murison*, Aberdeen: Aberdeen University Press, pp. 18–49.

Aitken, A. J. (1987), 'The period dictionaries', in Robert Burchfield (ed.), *Studies in Lexicography*, Oxford: Clarendon Press, pp. 84–116.

Aitken, A. J. (1991), 'Progress in Older Scots philology', *Studies in Scottish Literature*, 26, pp. 19–37.

Aitken, A. J. (2002), *The Older Scots Vowels: A History of the Stressed Vowels of Older Scots from the Beginnings to the Eighteenth Century*, ed. Caroline Macafee, Edinburgh: Scottish Text Society.

Amours F. J. (ed.) (1897), *Scottish Alliterative Poems in Riming Stanzas*, vol. 2, Edinburgh: Scottish Text Society.

Ancient Laws and Customs of the Burghs of Scotland. Vol. I. A.D. 1124–1424, [Ancient Laws] (1868), Edinburgh: Scottish Burgh Records Society.

APS, see Thomson, Thomas.

Asher, R. E., Benbow, T., Macafee, C., and Skretkowicz, V. (1994), 'Report of the Review of the Dictionary of the Older Scottish Tongue', *DOST* Archive, University of Edinburgh.

Balfour, James, see McNeill, P. G. B.

Barrow, G. W. S. (1988), *Robert Bruce*, 3rd edn, Edinburgh: Edinburgh University Press.

Bawcutt, Priscilla (1976), *Gavin Douglas: A Critical Study*, Edinburgh: Edinburgh University Press.

Bawcutt, Priscilla (1992), *Dunbar the Makar*, Oxford: Oxford University Press.

Bawcutt, Priscilla (1996), 'An early Scottish debate-poem on women', *Scottish Literary Journal*, 23:2, pp. 35–42.

Bawcutt, Priscilla (ed.) (1998), *The Poems of William Dunbar*, 2 vols, Glasgow: Association for Scottish Literary Studies.

Bawcutt, Priscilla (ed.) [1967] (2003), *The Shorter Poems of Gavin Douglas*, Edinburgh: Scottish Text Society.

Bell, G. J. (1858), *Commentaries on the Laws of Scotland*, 6th edn, Edinburgh.

Bell, G. J. (1893), *Principles of the Law of Scotland*, 10th edn, Edinburgh.

Benskin, Michael (1977), 'Local archives and Middle English dialects', *Journal of the Society of Archivists*, 5: 8, pp. 500–14.

Benskin, Michael (1980), 'An analytical technique for computational placing of Middle English dialect material on a map', Edinburgh: Middle English Dialect Project Working Paper [unpublished MS].

Benskin, Michael (1991), 'The "fit"-technique explained', in Felicity Riddy (ed.), *Regionalism in Late Medieval Manuscripts and Texts*, Cambridge: D. S. Brewer, pp. 9–26.

Benskin, Michael, and Laing, Margaret (1981), 'Translations and Mischsprachen in Middle English manuscripts', in Michael Benskin, and M. L. Samuels (eds), *So meny people longages and tonges: Philological essays in Scots and mediaeval English presented to Angus McIntosh*, Edinburgh: Benskin and Samuels, pp. 55–106.

Beveridge, E. (ed.) (1924), *Fergusson's Scottish Proverbs*, Edinburgh: Scottish Text Society.

Bossy, J. (1973), 'Blood and baptism: kinship, community and Christianity in western Europe from the fourteenth to the seventeenth centuries', in D. Baker (ed.), *Sanctity and Secularity: The Church and the World*, Oxford: Blackwell for the Ecclesiastical History Society, pp. 129–43.

Bossy, J. (1977), 'Holiness and Society', *Past and Present*, 75, pp. 119–37.

Bossy, J. (1984a), 'Godparenthood: the fortunes of a social institution in early modern Christianity', in K. von Greyerz (ed.), *Religion and Society in Early Modern Europe 1500–1800*, London: Allen and Unwin, pp. 194–201.

Bossy J. (1984b), *Christianity in the West*, Oxford: Oxford University Press.

Boulton, E. H. B., and Jay, B. Alwyn (1945), *Building Timbers Dealing with softwoods and hardwoods with notes on selection, marketing, seasoning, preservation and use*, London: George Newnes.

Brown, K. (1986), *Bloodfeud in Scotland, 1573–1625: Violence, Justice and Politics in an early modern society*, Edinburgh: John Donald.

Brown, R. Allen, Colvin, H. M., and Taylor, A. J. (1963), *The History of the King's Works: The Middle Ages*, London: HMSO.

Buchanan, George (1829), *Table for converting the Weights and Measures hitherto in Use in Great Britain . . .*, Edinburgh: D. Lizars.

Burrell, Lawrence (1961), 'The Standards of Scotland', *The Monthly Review: The Journal of the Institute of Weights and Measures Administration*, 69, pp. 49–62.

Burt, Edmund (1754), *Letters from a Gentleman in the North of Scotland*, London.

Burton, J. Hill et al. (eds) (1877–1970), *Register of the Privy Council of Scotland* [RPCS], 3 series, 36 vols, Edinburgh: H. M. General Register House.

Burwash, D. (1947), *English Merchant Shipping 1460–1540*, Toronto: University of Toronto Press.

Callender-Wade, T. (ed.) (1937), *Acta Curiae Admirallatus Scotiae (1557–1562)*, Edinburgh: Stair Society.

Cameron, Jamie (1998), *James V: The Personal Rule, 1528–1542*, East Linton: Tuckwell Press.

Campbell, D., and Paton, H. (eds) (1913–22), *The Clan Campbell*, 8 vols, Edinburgh.

Cartwright, J. (ed.) (1986–90), *The Buik of King Alexander the Conquerour*, 2 vols, Edinburgh: Scottish Text Society.

Chance, Jane (ed.) (1999), *The Assembly of Gods*, Kalamazoo, MI: Consortium for the Teaching of the Middle Ages.

Clive, E. (2000), 'Interpretation', in K. Reid and R. Zimmermann (eds), *A History of Private Law in Scotland*, Oxford: Oxford University Press, 2 vols, pp. 47–71.

Cochran-Patrick, R. W. (1876), *Records of the Coinage of Scotland*, 2 vols, Edinburgh: Edmonston and Douglas.

Cody, E. G. (ed.) [1596] (1885–95), *The Historie of Scotland written first in Latin by . . . Jhone Leslie . . . and translated in Scottish by Father James Dalrymple*, 2 vols, Edinburgh: Scottish Text Society.

Coldwell D. F. C. (ed.) (1957–64), *Virgil's Aeneid Translated by Gavin Douglas*, 4 vols, Edinburgh: Scottish Text Society.

Concise Scots Dictionary [CSD] (1985), ed. Mairi Robinson, Aberdeen: Aberdeen University Press.

Connor, R. D., and Simpson, A. D. C. (2004), *Weights and Measures in Scotland: A European Perspective*, ed. A. D. Morrison-Low, Edinburgh: National Museums of Scotland and Tuckwell Press.

Cooper, Lord (ed.) (1946), *Register of Brieves*, Edinburgh: Stair Society.

Coopland G. W. (1949), *The Tree of Battles/Honoré Bonet: An English Version, with Introduction*, Liverpool: Liverpool University Press.

Coster, W. (2002), *Baptism and Spiritual Kinship in Early Modern England*, Aldershot: Ashgate.

Craigie, W. A. (1893), 'Barbour and blind Harry as literature', *Scottish Review*, 22, pp. 173–201.

Craigie, W. A. (1898), 'Rolland's Court of Venus', *Modern Quarterly of Language and Literature*, 1, pp. 9–16.

Craigie, W. A. (ed.) (1923), *The Asloan Manuscript: A Miscellany in Prose and Verse*, vol. 1, 2nd series 14, Edinburgh: Scottish Text Society.

Craigie, W. A. (1931), 'New dictionary schemes', *Transactions of the Philological Society*, 1925–30, pp. 6–9.

Craigie, W. A. (1942), 'The Scottish alliterative poems', *Proceedings of the British Academy*, 28, pp. 217–36.

Crawford, Donald (ed.) (1900), *Journals of Sir John Lauder Lord Fountainhall, with his observations on public affairs and other memoranda 1665–1676*, Edinburgh: Scottish History Society.

Crockett, T. (ed.) (1913), *The Poems of John Stewart of Baldynneis*, Edinburgh: Scottish Text Society.

Dallas of St Martin, George (1697), *System of Styles as now Practicable within the Kingdom of Scotland: And Reduced to a clear Method not heretofore*, Edinburgh.

Dareau, Marace (2002a), 'Dictionary of the Older Scottish Tongue: an A-Z of its history and nature', *Review of Scottish Culture*, 15, pp. 77–87.

Dareau, Marace (2002b), '*DOST*: its history and completion', *Dictionaries: Journal of the Dictionary Society of America*, 23, pp. 208–31.

Dareau, M. G., Pike K. L., and Watson, H. D. (1994), 'Response of Editors to the *Review of DOST*, *DOST* Archive, University of Edinburgh.

Davies, I., Walker, B., and Pendlebury, J. (2002), *Timber Cladding in Scotland*, Edinburgh: Scottish Executive.

Dawson, J. (ed.) (1997), *Campbell Letters 1559–83*, Edinburgh: Scottish History Society, 5th series.

Dawson, J. (2002), *The Politics of Religion in the age of Mary, Queen of Scots: The Fifth Earl of Argyll and the Struggle for Britain and Ireland*, Cambridge: Cambridge University Press.

Dawson, Jane E. A. (2002–3), ' "There is nothing like a good gossip": baptism, kinship and alliance in early modern Scotland', *Review of Scottish Culture*, 15, pp. 88–95; reprinted in this volume pp. 38–47.

Dees, Anthonij, Dekker, Marcel, Hubber, Ono, and van Reenen-Stein, Karen (1987), *Atlas des formes linguistiques des textes littéraires de l'ancien français*, Tübingen: Niemeyer.

Dees, Anthonij, van Reenen, Pieter Th., and de Vries, J. A. (1980) *Atlas des formes et des constructions françaises du 13ᵉ siècle*, Tübingen: Niemeyer.

Dictionary of Old English [*DOE*] (1988–), eds A. C. Amos, S. Butler, A. Cameron, and A. diP. Healey, Toronto: University of Toronto.

Dictionary of the Older Scottish Tongue [*DOST*] (1931–2002), eds W. A. Craigie, A. J. Aitken, J. A. C. Stevenson, H. D. Watson, and M. G. Dareau, 62 fascicles in 12 vols, Chicago: Chicago University Press (1931–77); Aberdeen: Aberdeen University Press (1983–91); Oxford: Oxford University Press (1994–2002).

Dictionary of the Scots Language [*DSL*], www.dsl.ac.uk/dsl/

Dingwall, Helen M. (1994), *Late 18th-century Edinburgh: A Demographic Study*, Aldershot: Scolar Press.

Dodgshon, R. A. (1981), *Land and Society in Early Scotland*, Oxford: Oxford University Press.

Donaldson, Gordon (ed.) (1952), *Protocol Book of James Young, 1485–1515*, Edinburgh: Scottish Record Society, 74.

Dossena, Marina, and Lass, Roger (eds) (2004), *Methods and Data in English Historical Dialectology*, Bern: Peter Lang.

Duncan, A. A. M. (1975), *Scotland: The Making of a Kingdom*, Edinburgh: Oliver and Boyd.

Duncan, A. A. M. (ed.) (1976), *Formulary E: Scottish Letters and Brieves, 1286–1424*, University of Glasgow, Scottish History Department Occasional Papers.

Duncan, A. A. M. (ed.) (1997), with translation and notes, *John Barbour: The Bruce*, Edinburgh: Canongate.

Dunlop, Annie I. (1950), *The Life and Times of James Kennedy, Bishop of St Andrews*, Edinburgh: Oliver and Boyd.

ERBE, see next.

Extracts from the Records of the Burgh of Edinburgh AD 1403–1528 [*ERBE*] (1869, 1871, 1875, 1882), Edinburgh: Scottish Burgh Records Society.

Fenton, A. (1987), *Scottish Country Life: Our Rural Past*, Edinburgh: John Donald.

Fitzsimmons, Fiona (2001), 'Fosterage and gossiprid in late medieval Ireland: some new evidence', in P. Duffy, D. Edwards, and E. Fitzpatrick (eds), *Gaelic Ireland c1250–c1650: Land, Lordship and Settlement*, Dublin: Four Courts, pp. 138–49.

Fleischman, Suzanne (2000), 'Methodologies and ideologies in Historical Linguistics: on working with older languages', in Susan C. Herring, Pieter van Reenen, and Lene Schøsler (eds), *Textual Parameters in Older Languages*, Current Issues in Linguistic Theory, 195, Amsterdam and Philadelphia: John Benjamins, pp. 33–58.

Fleming, D. H. (ed.) (1889–90), *Register of the Ministers, Elders and Deacons of the Christian Congregation of St Andrews*, 2 vols, Scottish History Society (= Register of St Andrews Kirk Session [*RSTAKS*]).

Forte, A. D. M. (1987), 'Marine Insurance and Risk Distribution in Scotland before 1800', *Law and History Review*, 5, pp. 393–412.

Forte, A. D. M. (1998a), ' "Kenning be Kenning and Course be Course": maritime jurimetrics in Scotland and Northern Europe 1400–1600', *Edinburgh Law Review*, 2, pp. 56–89.

Forte, A. D. M. (1998b), 'The identification of fifteenth-century ship types in Scottish legal records', *Mariner's Mirror*, 84, pp. 3–12.

Forte, A. D. M. (2000), 'Insurance', in K. Reid and R. Zimmermann (eds), *A History of Private Law in Scotland*, 2 vols, Oxford: Oxford University Press, vol. 2, pp. 333–68.

Fox, Adam (2000), *Oral and Literate Culture in England 1500–1700*, Oxford: Oxford University Press.

Fox, Denton (ed.) (1981), *The Poems of Robert Henryson*, Oxford: Oxford University Press.

Friel, I. (1995), *The Good Ship: Ships, Shipbuilding and Technology in England 1200–1520*, London: British Museum Press.

Furnivall, F. J. and Locock, K. B. (eds) (1899–1904), *John Lydgate, The Pilgrimage of the Life of Man*, London: Early English Text Society, ES, 77, 83 and 92.

Gardiner, R. (ed.) (1994), *Cogs, Caravels and Galleons*, London: Conway Maritime Press.

Gee, Eric (1984), *A Glossary of Building Terms used in England from the Conquest to c. 1550*, Frome: Frome Historical Research Group.

Gemmill, Elizabeth, and Mayhew, Nicholas (eds) (1995), *Changing Values in Medieval Scotland: A Study of Prices, Money, and Weights and Measures*, Cambridge: Cambridge University Press.

Gibson, A. J. S., and Smout, T. C. (1995), *Prices, Food and Wages in Scotland 1550–1780*, Cambridge: Cambridge University Press.

Glenn, Jonathan A. (ed.) (1943), *Gilbert of the Haye's Prose Manuscript (A.D. 1456)*, Vol. 2 (*The Buke of Knychthede and the Buke of the Governaunce of Princis*), Edinburgh and London: Scottish Text Society.

Grabiner, Judith (1996), 'A mathematician amongst the molasses barrels: Maclaurin's unpublished Memoir on volumes', *Proceedings of the Edinburgh Mathematical Society*, 39, pp. 193–240.

Gregor, W. (ed.) (1884), *John Rolland, The Court of Venus*, Edinburgh: Scottish Text Society.

Haliburton, S., and Hepburn, T. (1761), *Memories of a Magopico*.

Hallen, Cornelius A. W., (ed.) (1894), *The Account Book of Sir John Foulis of Ravelstoun 1571–1707*, Edinburgh: Scottish History Society.

Hamer, D. (ed.) (1931–6), *The Works of Sir David Lindsay of the Mount*, 4 vols, Edinburgh: Scottish Text Society.

Hamilton-Grierson, P. J. (ed.) (1920–6), *Habakkuk Bisset's Rolment of Courtis*, 3 vols, Edinburgh: Scottish Text Society.

Hanham, Alison (1971), 'A medieval Scots merchant's handbook', *Scottish Historical Review*, 5, pp. 107–20.

Henryson, Edward (ed.) (1566), *Actis and Constitutionis of the Realm of Scotland maid halden be . . . Kingis James the First, Secund, Thrid, Feird, Fyth and in time of Marie now Quene of Scottis . . . [ACRS]*, Edinburgh: Robert Lekpreuik.

Hillerbrand, H. J. (ed.) (1996), *The Oxford Encyclopaedia of the Reformation*, 4 vols, Oxford, vol. 2.

Hollenbach, M. W. (2003), 'Synderesis', in *New Catholic Encyclopedia*, Detroit: Thomson/Gale, vol. 13, pp. 679–81.

Huntar, A. (1624), *A Treatise of Weights, Mets and Measures of Scotland*, Edinburgh.

Imrie, John, and Dunbar, John G. (1982), *Accounts of the Masters of Works for building and repairing Royal Palaces and Castles*, Vol. 2, 1616–49, Edinburgh: HMSO.

Innes, C. (ed.) (1855), *Black Book of Taymouth*, Edinburgh: Bannatyne Club.

Innes, C. (ed.) (1859), *Book of the Thanes of Cawdor*, Edinburgh: Spalding Club.

Innes, C. (ed.) (1867), *Ledger of Andrew Halyburton, Conservator of the Privileges of the Scotch Nation in the Netherlands, 1492–1503, together with the Book of Customs and Valuation of Merchandises in Scotland, 1612*, Edinburgh: HM General Register House.

Irving, D. (ed.) (1830), *Clariodus: A Metrical Romance*, Edinburgh: Maitland Club.

Jamieson, John (1879), *An Etymological Dictionary of the Scottish Language*, 5 vols, Paisley: Alexander Gardner.

Kay, Billy, and Maclean, Cailean (1985), *Knee Deep in Claret: A Celebration of Wine in Scotland*, Edinburgh: Mainstream Publishing.

KLNM see next.

Kulturhistorisk Leksikon for nordisk middelalder [*KLNM*] (1956–78), Oslo: Gyldendal Nordisk Forlag.

LAEME, see McIntosh et al. 1986.

Laidlaw J. C. (ed.) (1974), *The Poetical Works of Alain Chartier*, Cambridge: Cambridge University Press.

Laing, D. (ed.) (1871), *The Poetical Works of Sir David Lindsay*, 2 vols, Edinburgh.

Laing, Margaret (ed.) (1989), *Middle English Dialectology: Essays on Some Principles and Problems*, Aberdeen: Aberdeen University Press.

Laing, Margaret (1998), 'Raising a stink in the *Owl and the Nightingale*: a new reading at line 115', *Notes and Queries*, 243, pp. 276–84.

Laing, Margaret (1999), 'Confusion *wrs* confounded: litteral substitution sets in early Middle English writing systems', *Neuphilologische Mitteilungen*, 100, pp. 251–70.

Laing, Margaret (2001), 'Words reread: Middle English writing systems and the dictionary', *Linguistica e Filologia*, 13, pp. 87–129.

Laing, Margaret, and McIntosh, Angus (1995), 'Cambridge, Trinity College, MS 335: its texts and their transmission', in Richard Beadle and A. J. Piper (eds), *New Science out of Old Books*, Aldershot: Scolar Press, pp. 14–47.

Laing, Margaret, and Williamson, Keith (2004), 'The archaeology of Middle English texts', in Christian J. Kay and Jeremy J. Smith (eds), *Categorization in the History of English*, Amsterdam and Philadelphia, John Benjamins, pp. 85–145.

Lass, Roger (2004), 'Ut custodiant litteras: editions, corpora and witnesshood', in Dossena and Lass 2004.

Linguistic Survey of Scotland [*LSS*] (1951), Edinburgh: University of Edinburgh.

Lyall, R. J. (ed.) (1989), *Ane Satyre of the Thrie Estaitis | Sir David Lindsay of the Mount*, Edinburgh: Canongate Press.

Lyall, R. J. (2001), 'The stylistic relationship between Dunbar and Douglas', in Sally Mapstone (ed.), *William Dunbar, the 'Nobill Poyet': Essays in Honour of Priscilla Bawcutt*, East Linton: Tuckwell Press, pp. 69–84.

Lynch, Joseph H. (1986), *Godparents and kinship in early medieval Europe*, Princeton, N.J.: Princeton University Press.

Lynch, M. (1990), 'Queen Mary's Triumph: the baptismal celebrations at Stirling in December 1566', *Scottish Historical Review*, 69, pp. 1–21.

Macadam, J. H. (1903), *The Baxter Books of St Andrews: A Record of Three Centuries*, Leith: Scottish Association of Master Bakers.

Macafee, Caroline, and Macleod, Iseabail (eds) (1987), *The Nuttis Schell: Essays on the Scots Language*, Aberdeen: Aberdeen University Press.

McClure, J. Derrick (1986), 'A comparison of the Bannatyne MS and the Quarto texts of Lyndsay's *Ane Satyre of the thrie Estaitis*', in Dietrich Strauss and H. W. Drescher (eds), *Scottish Language and Literature, Medieval and Renaissance*, Scottish Studies, 4, Frankfurt: Peter Lang, pp. 409–22.

Macfarlane, Walter, see Mitchell, Arthur.

McGladdery, Christine (1990), *James II*, Edinburgh: John Donald.

McIntosh, Angus (1978), 'The dialectology of mediaeval Scots: some possible approaches to its study', *Scottish Literary Journal, Supplement*, 6, pp. 38–44. Reprinted in Laing (1989), pp. 81–5.

McIntosh, Angus, Samuels, M. L., and Benskin, Michael (1986), *A Linguistic Atlas of Late Mediaeval English, 1350–1450 (LAEME)*, 4 vols, Aberdeen: Aberdeen University Press / Edinburgh: Mercat Press.

Mackay, Margaret A. (2003), '"Mony notabill narratioun": Scots language research, a resource for the study of folklore, literature and history', *Scottish Language*, 22, pp. 3–15.

Mackay-Mackenzie, W. (1934), 'Clay castle building in Scotland', *Proceedings of the Society of Antiquaries of Scotland*, 68, pp. 117–27.

Mackenzie, G. S. (1809), *Treatise on the Diseases and Management of Sheep*, Inverness.

McNeill, P. G. B. (ed.) [c. 1580] (1962–3), *The Practicks of Sir James Balfour of Pittendreich*, 2 vols, Edinburgh: Stair Society.

MacQueen, Hector L. (1991), 'The laws of Galloway: a preliminary study', in Richard D. Oram and G. P. Stell (eds), *Galloway: Land and Lordship*, Edinburgh: Scottish Society for Northern Studies, pp. 131–43.

Maher, G. (1996), 'Statutory interpretation: the Wilsonian analysis', in H. L. MacQueen (ed.), *Scots Law into the 21st Century: Essays in Honour of W. A. Wilson*, Edinburgh: W. Green / Sweet & Maxwell, pp. 103–12.

Marshall, Rosalind K. [1973] (2000), *The Days of Duchess Anne*, East Linton: Tuckwell Press.

Marwick, J. D. (ed.) (1871), *Charters and Other Documents Relating to the City of Edinburgh 1143–1540*, Edinburgh: Scottish Burgh Records Society.

Marwick, J. D. (1890), *Index to Extracts from the Records of the Convention of the Royal Burghs of Scotland with a Glossary of Peculiar Words*, Edinburgh: Scottish Burgh Records Society.

Meston, M. C., and Forte, A. D. M. (eds) (2000), *The Aberdeen Stylebook 1722*, Edinburgh: Stair Society.

Meurman-Solin, Anneli (2001a), 'Structured text corpora in the study of language variation and change', *Literary and Linguistic Computing*, 16: 1, pp. 5–27.

Meurman-Solin, Anneli (2001b), 'Women as informants in the reconstruction of geographically and socioculturally conditioned language variation and change in sixteenth- and seventeenth-century Scots', *Scottish Language*, 20, pp. 20–46.

Meurman-Solin, Anneli (2004a), 'Towards a variationist typology of clausal connectives. Methodological considerations based on the Corpus of Scottish Correspondence', in Dossena and Lass 2004.

Meurman-Solin, Anneli (forthcoming 2004b), 'The manuscript-based diachronic Corpus of Scottish Correspondence', in *Models and Methods in the Handling of Unconventional Digital Corpora, vol. 2, Diachronic Corpora*, eds J. Beal, K. Corrigan and H. Moisl, London: Palgrave-MacMillan.

Middle English Dictionary [MED] (1956–2001), eds H. Kurath, S. M. Kuhn, and R. Lewis, Ann Arbor: University of Michigan; republished electronically as part of the *Middle English Compendium*, ed. F. McSparran et al. (1999–) at http://ets.umdl.umich.edu/m/mec

Migne, J. P. (1884), *Patrologiae Cursus Completus, series latina*, vol. 25, Paris.

Mitchell, Arthur (ed.) (1907), *Geographical Collections relating to Scotland made by Walter Macfarlane*, Vol. 2, Edinburgh: Scottish History Society.

Mitchell, G. (1994), *Medieval Ships and Shipping*, Leicester: Leicester University Press.

Munro, Robert (1882), *Ancient Scottish Lake-Dwellings or Crannogs*, Edinburgh: David Douglas.

Newton, Michael (2000), *A Handbook of the Scottish Gaelic World*, Dublin: Four Courts.

Nicholson, Ranald (1974), *Scotland: The Later Middle Ages*, Edinburgh: Oliver and Boyd.

Nicolaisen, W. F. H. (1969), 'Scottish place names: 31. Falkirk', *Scottish Studies*, 13, pp. 47–58.

Nicolaisen, W. F. H. (1980), 'Onomastic dialects', *American Speech*, 55, pp. 36–45.

Nicolaisen, W. F. H. (1984), 'Maps of space – maps of time', *Names*, 32, pp. 358–66.

Nicolaisen, W. F. H. (1989), 'The spelling of Scottish place names as a linguistic resource: Stirling vs. Dunfermline', in J. Lachlan Mackenzie and Richard Todd (eds), *In Other Words*, Dordrecht: Fortis, pp. 301–14.

Nicolaisen, W. F. H. (1991), 'Place name maps: how reliable are they?', *Namn och Bygd*, 79, pp. 43–50.

Nicolaisen, W. F. H. (1993), 'Scottish place names as evidence for language change', *Names*, 41, pp. 306–13.

Nicolaisen, W. F. H. (1996), 'Language contact and onomastics', in Hans Goebl, Peter H. Nelde, Zdenek Stary, and Wolfgang Woelck (eds), *Contact Linguistics: An International Handbook of Contemporary Research*, vol. 1, Berlin and New York: Walter de Gruyter, pp. 549–54.

Nicolaisen, W. F. H. (1999), 'The earliest English place names in North East Scotland', *Northern Scotland*, 18, pp. 67–82.

Nicolaisen, W. F. H. (2001), *Scottish Place Names: Their Study and Significance*, revised edn, Edinburgh: John Donald.

Nys, Ernest (1883), *L'Arbre des Batailles*, Bruxelles and Leipzig: Librairie Européene C. Muquardt.

Oxford English Dictionary [OED] (1888–1928), eds James A. H. Murray, H. Bradley, William A. Craigie, and C. T. Onions, Oxford: Oxford University Press.

Paterson, A. A., and Bates, T. StJ. N. (2003), *The Legal System of Scotland*, 3rd edn, Edinburgh: W. Green / Sweet and Maxwell.

Paterson, James (ed.) (1849), *The Poems of the Sempills of Beltrees*, Edinburgh: Thomas George Stevenson.

Paton, Henry M. (1957), *Accounts of the Masters of Works for building and repairing Royal Palaces and Castles Vol I: 1529–1615*, Edinburgh: HMSO.

Paul, J. Balfour (ed.) (1904–14), *Scots Peerage*, 9 vols, Edinburgh: David Douglas.

Pitcairn, R. (1833), *Criminal Trials in Scotland from 1488 to 1624*, 3 vols, Edinburgh: Bannatyne and Maitland Clubs.

Plummer, C. (1896), *Venerabilis Baedae Opera Historica*, 2 vols, Oxford: Clarendon Press.

Prestwich, Michael (1997), *Edward I*, 2nd edn, New Haven and London: Yale University Press.

PRS see Robertson, W.

Pryde, Glen L. (1996), *Dictionary of Scottish Building*, Edinburgh: Rutland Press and Historic Scotland in association with Scottish National Dictionary Association.

Purdie, Rhiannon (2002), '*Clariodus* and the ambitions of courtly romance in later medieval Scotland', *Forum for Modern Language Studies*, 38, pp. 450–61.

Rademaker, Abraham (1725), *Kabinet van Nederlandsche Outheden en Gezichten*, Amsterdam.

Report on the Laing Manuscripts preserved in the University of Edinburgh (1914), vol. 1, London: Historical Manuscripts Commission (HMSO).

Ritchie, W. Tod (ed.) (1928–34), *The Bannatyne Manuscript*, 4 vols, Edinburgh: Scottish Text Society.

Robertson, Joseph, and Grub, George (eds) (1843–69), *Collections for a History of the Shires of Aberdeen and Banff*, Aberdeen: Spalding Club.

Robertson, Una A. (1987), 'A taste of Hopetoun: food and drink in a Scottish household, 1754–55', *Food and Foodways*, 2, pp. 61–3.

Robertson, W. (ed.) (1804), *Parliamentary Records of Scotland in the General Register House, Edinburgh [PRS]*, vol. 1, Edinburgh: Record Commission.

Rodger, A. (1993), 'Stealing Fish', in R. F. Hunter (ed.), *Justice and Crime: Essays in Honour of the Right Honourable Lord Emslie*, Edinburgh: T & T Clark, pp. 1–14.

Rohmer, J. (1903–50), 'Syndérèse', in *Dictionnaire de théologie catholique*, vol. 14, 2, Paris, cols. 2992–6.

RPCS, see Burton, J.

RSTAKS [Register of St Andrews Kirk Session], see Fleming.

Samuels, M. L., and Smith, J. (eds) (1988), *The English of Chaucer and his Contemporaries*, Aberdeen: Aberdeen University Press.

Scott, John S. (1964), *A Dictionary of Building*, Harmondsworth: Penguin.

Scottish National Dictionary [SND] (1929–76), eds W. Grant and D. Murison, 10 vols, Edinburgh: Scottish National Dictionary Association.

Scott-Moncrieff, Robert (ed.) (1911), *The Household Book of Lady Grisell Baillie*, Edinburgh: Scottish History Society.

Sellar, W. D. H. (1978–80), 'Marriage, divorce and concubinage in Gaelic Scotland', *Transactions of the Gaelic Society of Inverness*, 51, pp. 464–93.

Sellar, W. D. H. (1991), 'Forethocht felony and malice aforethought', in *Legal History in the Making*, eds W. M. Gordon and T. D. Fergus, London and Rio Grande: Hambledon Press, pp. 43–59.

Sellar, W. D. H. (1995), 'Marriage, divorce and the forbidden degrees: canon law and Scots law', in W. M. Osborough (ed.), *Explorations in Law and History: Irish Legal History Society Discourses, 1988–1994*, Dublin, pp. 59–82.

Shire, H., and Fenton, A. (1955), 'The sweepings of Parnassus', *Aberdeen University Review*, 36, pp. 43–54.

Simpson, A. D. C. (1992), 'Grain packing in early standard capacity measures: evidence from the Scottish dry capacity standards', *Annals of Science*, 49, pp. 337–50.

Skene, Sir John (1597), *De Verborum Significatione*, Edinburgh: Robert Waldegrave, King's Printer.

Smout, T. C. (1963), *Scottish Trade on the Eve of Union 1660–1707*, Edinburgh, London: Oliver and Boyd.

Stair, see Walker, D. M. (1981).

Stevenson, J. H. (ed.) (1901), (Sir Gilbert of the Haye) *The Buke of the Lawe of Arms or Buke of Batailles*, Edinburgh: Scottish Text Society.

Stewart, W. J. (1995), *Scottish Contemporary Judicial Dictionary of Words and Phrases*, Edinburgh: W. Green / Sweet and Maxwell.

Stones, E. L. G. [1965] (1970), *Anglo-Scottish Relations 1174–1328: Some Selected Documents*, re-issue, Oxford: Clarendon Press.

Taylor, Louise B. (ed.) (1972), *Aberdeen Shore Work Accounts 1596–1670*, Aberdeen: Aberdeen University Press.

Thomson T. (ed.) (1827), *James Melville of Halhill, Memoirs of His Own Life*, Edinburgh: Bannatyne Club.

Thomson, T. (ed.) [1572–5] (1833), *A Diurnal of remarkable occurrents, that have passed within the country of Scotland since the death of King James the Fourth, till the year 1575*, Edinburgh: BC.

Thomson, T. (ed.) (1839–45), *The Booke of the Universall Kirke of Scotland: Acts and Proceedings of the General Assembly of the Kirk of Scotland*, 3 vols, Edinburgh: Bannatyne Club.

Thomson, Thomas, and Innes, Cosmo (eds) (1814–75), *Acts of the Parliaments of Scotland 1124–1707 [APS]*, 13 vols, Edinburgh: Record Commission.

Todd, Margo (2002), *The Culture of Early Modern Scottish Protestantism*, New Haven, CT: Yale University Press.

Turnbull, W. B. (ed.) (1858), *William Stewart, The Buik of the Croniclis of Scotland*, 3 vols, Rolls Series, no. 6, London: Longman.

Unger, R. W. (1980), *The Ship in the Medieval Economy 600–1600*, London, Montreal: Croom Helm, McGill-Queen's University Press.

Unger, R. W. (1994), 'The fluit: specialist cargo vessels 1500 to 1650', in R. Gardiner (ed.), *Cogs, Caravels and Galleons*, London: Conway Maritime Press.

van Heijnsbergen, T. (1994), 'The interaction between literature and history in Queen Mary's Edinburgh: the Bannatyne Manuscript and its prosopographical context', in A. A. MacDonald, M. Lynch, and I. B. Cowan (eds), *The Renaissance in Scotland: Studies in Literature, Religion, History and Culture offered to John Durkan*, Leiden: E. J. Brill, pp. 183–225.

van Niekerk, J. P. (1999), *The Development of Principles of Insurance Law in the Netherlands from 1500–1800*, Cape Town: Juta; Johannesburg: Wetton.

Viollet-le-Duc, E. (1854–61), *Dictionnaire Raisonné de L'Architecture Française du XIe au XVIe siècle*, Paris.

Walker, Bruce (2001), 'The use of "skaile" in medieval and post-medieval Scotland', *Antiquity*, 75, pp. 163–171.

Walker, Bruce, and McGregor, Christopher (1996), *The Hebridean Blackhouse: A Guide to Materials, Construction and Maintenance*, Edinburgh: Historic Scotland.

Walker, Bruce, and McGregor, Christopher (2001), 'Traditions in timber', in *Designing with Timber*, Edinburgh: Forestry Commission, pp. 10–17.

Walker, Bruce, McGregor, Christopher, and Stark, Gregor (1996a), *Thatch and Thatching Techniques: A Guide to Conserving Scottish Thatching Techniques*, Edinburgh: Historic Scotland.

Walker, Bruce, McGregor, Christopher, and Stark, Gregor (1996b), *Earth Structures and Construction in Scotland: A Guide to the Recognition and Conservation of Earth Technology in Scottish Buildings*, Edinburgh: Historic Scotland.

Walker, Bruce, McGregor, Christopher, and Stark, Gregor (forthcoming), *Scottish Turf Construction*, Edinburgh: Historic Scotland.

Walker, D. M. (ed.) (1981), *James Dalrymple, Viscount Stair, The Institutions of the Law of Scotland* (1693 edn), Edinburgh, Glasgow: University Presses.

Walker, D. M. (2001), *The Scottish Legal System: An Introduction to the Study of Scots Law*, 8th edn, Edinburgh: W. Green / Sweet and Maxwell.

Walker, Ralph S. (ed.) (1948), *James Beattie's Day-Book 1773–1798*, Aberdeen: Third Spalding Club.

Watson G. (ed.) (1890), *Bell's Dictionary and Digest of the Law of Scotland*, 7th edn, Edinburgh.

White, Kenneth D. (1970), *Roman Farming*, London: Thames and Hudson.

White, Kenneth D. (1975), *Farm Equipment of the Roman World*, Cambridge: Cambridge University Press.

White, R. M., and Willock, I. D. (2003), *The Scottish Legal System*, 3rd edn, Edinburgh: LexisNexis.

Whiting, B. J. (1949–51), 'Proverbs and proverbial sayings from Scottish writings before 1600', *Mediaeval Studies*, 11, pp. 123–205; 13, pp. 87–164.

Whiting, B. J., with H. W. Whiting (1968), *Proverbs, Sentences and Proverbial Phrases from English Writings mainly before 1500*, Cambridge, MA: Harvard University Press.

Whyte, Ian D. (1995), *Scotland Before the Industrial Revolution: An Economic and Social History c. 1050–c. 1750*, Harlow: Longman.

Williamson, Keith (1992–3), 'A computer-aided method for making a linguistic atlas of Older Scots', *Scottish Language*, 11/12, pp. 138–73.

Williamson, Keith (2000), 'Changing spaces: linguistic relationships and the dialect continuum', in Irma Taavitsainen, Terttu Nevalainen, Päivi Pahta, and Matti Rissanen (eds), *Placing Middle English in Context*, Topics in English Linguistics, 35, Berlin: Mouton de Gruyter, pp. 141–79.

Williamson, Keith (2001), 'Spatio-temporal aspects of Older Scots texts', *Scottish Language*, 20, pp. 1–19.

Wilson, C. Anne [1973] (1976), *Food and Drink in Britain*, Harmondsworth: Penguin Books.

Wilson, W. A. (1984), *Introductory Essays on Scots Law*, 2nd edn, Edinburgh: W. Green and Son Ltd.

Wormald, J. (1980), 'Bloodfeud, kindred and government', *Past and Present*, 87, pp. 54–97.

Wormald, J. (1985), *Lords and Men in Scotland: Bonds of Manrent 1442–1603*, Edinburgh: John Donald.

Young, Alan (1997), *Robert the Bruce's Rivals: the Comyns, 1212–1314*, East Linton: Tuckwell Press.

Index